The Gilbert and Sullivan Lexicon

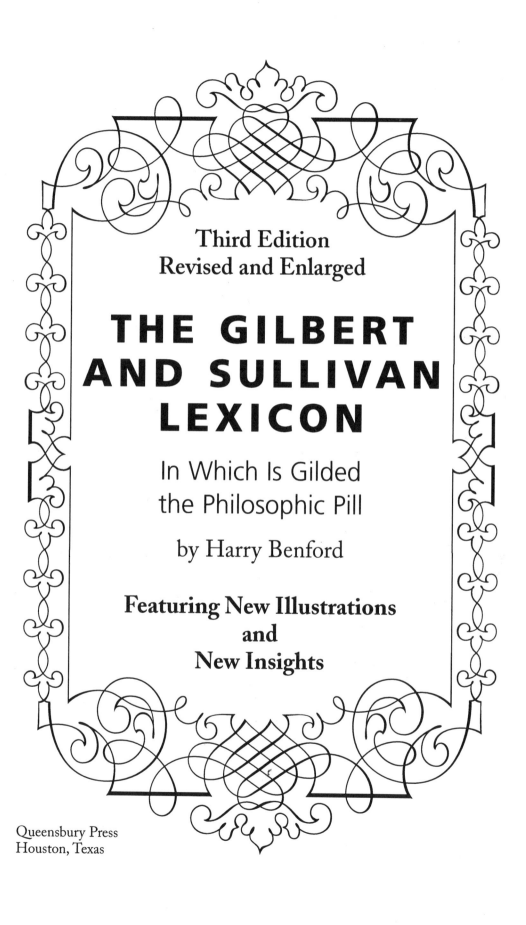

Third Edition
Revised and Enlarged

THE GILBERT AND SULLIVAN LEXICON

In Which Is Gilded
the Philosophic Pill

by Harry Benford

**Featuring New Illustrations
and
New Insights**

Queensbury Press
Houston, Texas

Published in 1999 by Queensbury Press
13507 Queensbury Lane
Houston TX 77079-6017

Ann Arbor, Michigan 48105

Third Edition

Library of Congress Cataloging-in-Publication Data
ISBN 0-9667916-1-4 (hardcover : alk. paper)

Benford, Harry.
      The Gilbert and Sullivan Lexicon in which is gilded the philosophic pill: featuring new illustra-
tions / [Harry Benford].-3rd ed., rev. and enl. p. 272 cm. 25.5
      Includes bibliographical references (p. 8) and index.
      1. Sullivan, Arthur, Sir, 1842-1900-Dictionaries Indexes. 2. Gilbert, W.S. (William Schwenck),
1836-1911-Dictionaries Indexes. I. Title. II. Title: Gilbert and Sullivan Lexicon. ML410.S95B44
1999
782.1'2'03—dc21

                                                                                          99-22606
                                                                                          CIP

Manufactured in the United States of America

To Betty Benford,
The maple syrup on
my pancake of life

HARRY BENFORD leads a double life. By day he is a semi-retired Professor of Naval Architecture and Marine Engineering at the University of Michigan. As the shades of night fall over Ann Arbor, however, a sinister transformation takes place. His teeth lengthen into fangs, his hair (what's left of it) bristles in all directions, his hands turn into paws (but not until after he has unbuttoned his spats), his eyebrows grow together over his nose, and he becomes a Gilbert & Sullivan fiend of the most rabid kind. Fortunately for their marriage, his wife, Betty, is equally afflicted and looks upon his eccentricities as being altogether normal. The history of this shared idiosyncrasy dates back to 1956 when Betty and Harry started serving as faculty advisors to The University of Michigan Gilbert and Sullivan Society. They are still associated with the Society and look back with satisfaction at having founded its friends' group,

FUMGASS, and having for thirteen years published its widely-read journal GASBAG (an acronymn for Gilbert & Sullivan Boys & Girls). They carry on a lively exchange of correspondence with G&S fans around the globe, and sometimes manage to travel abroad to make face-to-face contacts and attend productions of G&S shows.

Where it will all end is easily foretold. There will appear on the scene one day a corpulent contralto in gypsy dress, who will reveal that either Harry or Betty (she's not sure which), while still in infancy, was secretly betrothed to some prince or princess of Barataria, but was later kidnapped by the Beadle of Burlington and entrusted to an Arcadian shepherd, who . . . But, behold, we have said enough. Our allotment of words is completely exhausted. Besides, we're not about to give away the whole plot before the first act. Just, read on and you'll find all sorts of clues.

KENNETH SANDFORD

in his rôle as

LORD HIGH INSCRIBER of FOREWORDS

ABOUT KENNETH SANDFORD

Kenneth Sandford, who wrote the foreword, is arguably the greatest singer-actor ever to grace the D'Oyly Carte name. He has been associated with the works of Gilbert & Sullivan since 1957, when he joined the illustrious company. For more than forty years he has set a standard of performance that has proved inspirational to fellow-professionals and amateurs alike. Now 74 years of age, he still delights audiences with his lovely singing, and takes every opportunity to pass on to the next generation of Savoyards the benefits of his vast experience. He is a man of unfailing modesty, wit, and good humour. Happily, his legendary interpretations of the "Pooh-Bah" roles are, preserved for posterity courtesy of his many fine recordings. Kenneth Sandford's legacy will last well into the next millenium -- not bad for a north-country lad who had set out to be a painter!

Roberta Morrell

ABOUT GEOFFREY SHOVELTON

Geoffrey Shovelton, who designed the dust jacket cover and the frontispiece illustrations, has long had an interest in the Savoy operas. This interest was strengthened while he was a principal tenor with the D'Oyly Carte Opera Company. He still sings the Savoy operas but now as a freelance performer. He also performs a wide range of works from Viennese operetta to oratorio, while specializing in the Italian repertoire. Geoffrey teaches, lectures, and is in demand as an after-dinner speaker. Since 1995 he has accepted invitations to direct productions of Savoy operas. His wife, the American soprano Deborah Clague, joins him as assistant director and choreographer. Still, he finds time to be an active illustrator, calligrapher, and cartoonist, believing in the old adage that "a change is as good as a rest."

Foreword

What in the world is a Groom of the Back Stairs? or a Chancery Lane young man? or spleen and vapours? or Dithyrambic revels? or Time's teetotum? or *asinorum pons*? And how does one tuck in one's tuppenny? These are words or phrases that I have carefully mouthed hundreds of times in my forty-one-year professional career as a performer of the Savoy operas. I had at best only some vague idea of what they meant. And, to be frank, I seldom had the time to find out what Mr Gilbert really had in mind. Then, in 1978 Harry Benford published the first edition of this book and the full genius of Gilbert's creativity began to come to light. Harry brought out a second edition in 1991, which enlarged the scope of coverage. Now, in this third edition he has provided not only an even greater scope, but a significant increase in the depth of understanding. Each of these editions has given me a heightened appreciation of the G&S librettos and enhanced my pleasure in performing my parts

Gilbert's skill as a word-smith deserves much of the credit for the continuing popularity of the comic operas he and Sullivan brought forth. But Gilbert's genius is seldom fully appreciated because new nuances of meaning have crept into the language during the more-than-hundred years that have passed since he wrote the lines. Even when the operas were freshly minted, admirers in the United States and Canada continually ran across unfamiliar, unfathomable terms. Now, however, this book opens the door to a complete understanding of Gilbert's genius, hence an enhanced pleasure in the Savoy operas. You could even derive a new appreciation of Sullivan's musical genius in matching Gilbert's words.

I have made extensive use of the book and recommend it to all G&S admirers, whether in the audience, on the stage, or behind the scenes.

Kenneth Sandford

Preface to the Third Edition

Why this third edition? When I published the second edition I thought we had printed enough copies to satisfy the potential demand for at least a decade. The inventory dropped to zero in about four years, however, and the demand continued. Then, too, I began receiving suggestions for including additional terms (a surprising number of them!) and for correcting or at least clarifying the inevitable minority of ill-considered entries.

There are, as before, several terms in which Gilbert's meaning is obscure. Examples include *rig, grig, gondolet, Montero, barndoor owl, daphnephoric bound, catchy-catchies, Italian glance,* and *fleshly men of full habit*. We must also watch out for those few cases where Gilbert may have been careless — as when he says "first take off his boots with a boot tree," but illustrates it with a picture of a boot jack. Then, too, poetic license must be granted. In his children's version of *The Mikado* Gilbert cautions that "when people lapse into poetry you can never be quite sure what they mean."

I have once again attempted advice on how to pronounce some of the words, and again I recommend tailoring your pronunciation to suit your audience's ears. That, I am sure, is exactly what Sir William would urge.

The libretto for *The Zoo* is now readily available (from R. Clyde at 6 Whitelands Ave., Chorleywood, Rickmansworth, Herts WD3 5RD, England) so I have chosen to omit it from this edition.

In re-considering nearly every definition, my researches often led to new insights into Gilbert's ingenious lines. I like to think the shade of Sir William is perhaps looking down with satisfaction on the greater understanding now accorded his unique literary talents, and getting a chuckle out of our remaining perplexities.

I do hope all of you good readers will find this book pleasant reading and a reliable, easily understood guide to a deeper appreciation of the Savoy operas.

Let me close by quoting Samuel Johnson: "Every other author may aspire to praise; the lexicographer can only hope to escape reproach, and even this negative recompense has been yet granted to very few."

Harry Benford

Ann Arbor
1998

Acknowledgements

First Edition

I have relied heavily on the opinions of many of my friends who also happen to be Gilbert and Sullivan enthusiasts and scholars. Some have carefully reviewed and criticized all of my early-draft efforts. Those individuals merit special acknowledgement, including fanfare and laurel wreaths. Here they are, in alphabetical order: Tantantara!

George Applegate (now deceased)
H.D. Cameron
Terence Rees
Jane W. Stedman
John Stell (now deceased)
Michael Walters

I also want to recognize advice given in response to specific questions by the following fellow-enthusiasts (again, in alphabetical order): Michael Andrewes, Isaac Asimov (deceased), Earl F. Bargainnier, Betty Benford, Gloria Bennish (deceased), J. Stuart Bradshaw, Diana Burleigh, Warren Colson (deceased), Vivian Denison (deceased), James Drew, Aidan Evans (deceased), J.C.G. George, Andrew Goodman, Sara Kane, Wilfred Kaplan, Phyllis Karr, Daniel S. Knight, Ralph MacPhail, George McElroy, Gershom Morningstar, Ronald Orenstein, Christopher Orr, Elinor Parker, Patricia and Thomas Petiet, Beverley Pooley, Colin Prestige, Dorothy Raedler, Thomas G. Robinson, Vicki Rise, Jesse Shereff, Sir Alfred Sims (deceased), Constance Thompson, Blanca Torres, Albert Truelove (deceased), Richard Walker (deceased), Claude A. Walmisley, Em Ware, and Peter Zavon.

Second Edition

I want to pay particular tribute to these dozen acknowledged G&S scholars who kindly criticized both the first edition and, later, a "dress rehearsal" of this second edition. And I must confess that every one of them would be better qualified than I to write this book. In alphabetical order they are: Andrew Goodman, John Huston, William Hyder, Tony Joseph, Daniel Kravetz, Ralph MacPhail, Colin Prestige, Terence Rees, Marc Shepherd, Jane W. Stedman, David Stone, and Michael Walters.

To gain the reaction of more typical readers, I elicited suggestions from James and Mary Anne Wilkes, and John Cederquist, and his wife, Meg Kennedy-Shaw. Their suggestions have done much to improve the readability of this book.

My eagle-eyed wife, Betty, served the double function of full-time consultant and fastidious proof-reader.

Isaac Asimov (deceased) was kind enough to revise his original foreword to bring it up to date, and to give the latest score on the number of his publications. Geoffrey Shovelton has designed the front cover and prepared another of his clever cartoons as a frontispiece for *The Zoo*. I am grateful to both of those talented friends.

Five good friends submitted many detailed suggestions on how to improve the first edition. I am pleased to recognize the value of their contributions. They are; George Applegate (deceased), James Devlin, Aidan Evans (deceased), Phyllis Karr, and George McElroy.

Many other friends submitted less extensive suggestions. They can be sure their ideas were warmly received. Here they are: Gordon Barnett, Michael Bernitsas, Stuart Bradshaw, Gladys Breuer, John Caldwell, H.D. Cameron, Sarah Cole, Warren Colson (deceased), Ronald and Jean Fava, Silvano Gandusio, Charles Hayter, Arthur Jacobs (deceased), David E. Jones, Sylvan Kesilman, and Daniel S. Knight.

The list continues: Mitchell Krieger, Gershom Morningstar, Roberta Morrell, Roy Jay Nelson, Anastassios Perakis, Beverley Pooley, Ronald Orenstein, Rosemary Russell, Jesse Shereff, George Shirley, Edward Stasheff, Leslie and Joyce Thurston, Albert Truelove (deceased), William Venman, Jocelyn Wilkes, George Williams, and Fredric Woodbridge Wilson.

Toward the end of my lexicographic struggles, I enjoyed the privilege of spending an hour absorbing the advice of six professional Savoyards: Patricia Cope, Lorraine Daniels, Alistair Donkin, David Mackie, Kenneth Sandford, and Geoffrey Shovelton. They kindly explained the meanings of some twenty terms that had been causing me prolonged difficulty.

Finally, particular praise must be directed toward Paula Bousley, whose nimble fingers and even-more-nimble mind forged this opus into its final form.

Acknowledgements

Third Edition

While I was working on this third edition I was surprised by the number of kind-hearted volunteers who sent me suggestions for improvements, or found other ways to advance the project. Let me list their names: Forrest Alter, Janet Jeppson Asimov, John Atkinson, Anne S. Benninghoff, Lisa Berglund, Stuart Bradshaw, Diana Burleigh, Phillip Cameron, Marion Leeds Carroll, Kenton Chambers, William Chase, Andrew Crowther, William Dahms, Eleanor De Lorme, Stan DeOrsey, Timothy Devlin, and Howard Dicus.

There were yet more volunteers: Geoffrey Dixon, James Drew, David Duffey, Leta Hall, David Hawkins, George W. Hilton, Doreen Jensen, Hal Kanthor, David Mackie, Alexander MacPhail, William McCann, Derrick McClure, Paul McShane, Rica Mendes-Barry, Mark Mullinax, Ronald Orenstein, Eugene Ossa, Christopher Papa, and Peter Parker,

And the list goes on to Janet Pascal, Thomas Robinson, Jeff Satterfield, John Schultz, Meg Kennedy-Shaw, Thomas Shepard, Jesse Shereff, Jane W. Stedman, Selwyn Tillett, Julia Turnbull, William Venman, Christopher Wain, Fred Walker, Philip Walsh, Em Ware, Douglas Whaley, Derek E. Williams, F. W. Wilson, R. Clive Woods, and John B. and Ann Woodward.

A long-suffering crew helped settle the question of the meaning (if any) of "Lalabalele" and those other strong words uttered by Tarara, the Public Exploder in *Utopia Limited*: Patricia Belcher, Byron Bender, David Cookson, David Craven, Gavan Daws, Jeffrey G. Heath, Raymond C. Kelly, Peter Kline, Ernest Lee, Gene Leonardi, Jocelyn Linnekin, Daniel Lufkin, Pamella Miller, Judith R. Neale, Karen Peacock, Edward Six, Richard Rames, Theodore Rice, Arthur Robinson, Constance Thompson, Daniel Weaver, and Duane Wenzel.

A few exceptional individuals deserve special mention: Geoffrey Shovelton, obligingly created a new front cover and modified two of the chapter-head illustrations. Mary Bosdêt (deceased) submitted many excellent suggestions based on her extensive knowledge of British history. Daniel S. Knight freely provided expert guidance in many pertinent matters, particularly concerning British law and courts. Terence Rees was a continuing source of information and good-natured encouragement. Elinor S. Wright contributed several cogent points in the still simmering debate about the meaning of a daphnephoric bound.

I am indebted to Kenneth Sandford for contributing the perceptive Foreword, and to Roberta Morrell for writing Ken's brief biographical outline.

Several well-known G&S authorities were good enough to read and criticize drafts of nearly fifty radically changed definitions. These were: Silvio Aurora, John W. Barker, Ian Bradley, David Eden, Mitchell Scott Gillette, Andrew Goodman, William Hyder, Gareth Jacobs, Ralph MacPhail, Jr., Marc Shepherd, Elizabeth Thomson, and Michael P. Walters.

Three highly qualified critics kindly reviewed semi-final manuscripts and submitted valuable suggestions for enhancing the final product: Daniel Kravetz, David Stone, and Stephen Turnbull. Their carefully considered advice led to many vital improvements in the outcome of my labors.

As usual, my able and willing wife was always ready with suggestions when I found myself stuck on some grammatical point or recollection of some pertinent fact. More importantly, however, she was always the very model of patience in the face of the neglect inherent in the wife of a conscientious author.

As in the second edition, Paula Bousley played an important role in the design of this finished product.

I am sincerely grateful to all of the above; and as is customary in these matters, while expressing this public thank-you, I simultaneously declare that any and all mistakes within these covers are of my own creation and design.

Contents

Plates

W.S. Gilbert was a master of the English language. His verses flow in rhythmic cadences that smoothed Sullivan's task of generating suitable scores. Gilbert had an enormous vocabulary, and we have good reason to believe that he was in love with words. Above all, he had every right to be in love with his own words. He toiled over his librettos and he wanted his audiences to hear, to understand, and to laugh at what he had to say. That is why I am sure that Gilbert would approve of this book: a lexicon specifically tailored to help his admirers appreciate his skillful manipulation of the language.

Semanticists warn that a word is a poor substitute for a thought, especially as passing years, cultural differences, and geographic distances effect their "silent alchemy." As a result, and I may as well confess it here, there are probably at least a few booby traps I have missed altogether — words that have quite different meanings on the two sides of the Atlantic. I happened to discover enough to make me suspicious that there might be more. For example, until I undertook this task I had assumed that the lady from the provinces who dresses like a guy was one who wore men's clothing. I had pictured mustard and cress as a jar of mustard and a dish of watercress; and I always assumed that the coster who jumped on his mother was an accoster (i.e., a hold-up man). I know better now and so will you after you have gone through this book.

Although Gilbert generally aimed to amuse his listeners with easily caught wit, there are many cases where the humor is in the phonetics rather than in the meaning. In such instances, hanging too heavily on word definitions will simply obscure the thought. I try to warn you when that is the case. In other instances Gilbert exhibits a penchant for incongruous combinations: "semi-despondent fury" and "modified rapture" are two examples. Again, precise meanings are not called for and only tend to spoil the fun.

Several older Gilbert and Sullivan glossaries, dictionaries, and concordances were available during my studies, and I acknowledge my thorough browsings therein. I have, however, tried as much as possible to make this effort independent of those earlier works. Nearly all of them were aimed at English, rather than American, audiences. As a result,

the earlier publications frequently omitted terms that Americans need to have explained. Moreover, there are several cases where my research convinces me that the older publications contain mistakes.

One must admit, of course, that no amount of research can uncover all of Gilbert's meanings. Where multiple interpretations seem possible, I call them to your attention — and, where necessary to make a choice, I usually recall Occam's razor and go for the simple version. (Remember, Gilbert wanted you to catch on.) In a paper presented before the Popular Culture Association Meeting on April 23, 1976, Professor Earl F. Bargainnier made this pertinent observation:

> Gilbert was a popular writer, and he was never ashamed of that fact. He wanted to entertain his audiences, not to uplift them. In an interview in 1895, he said, "I am not ambitious to write up to epicurean tastes, but contented to write down to everybody's comprehension. For instance, when I am writing, I imagine it is for one particularly dull individual not quick to grasp an idea; so I make nothing long and explanatory, but short, sharp, and clear." (The internal quotation is from an article by Joseph Anderson in the January 18, 1895, issue of the *Boston Transcript*.)

As one who has had no little difficulty in dredging up some of Gilbert's meanings, I must comment that he may have overstated himself in claiming to write for "one particularly dull individual." Nevertheless, his claim is one to keep in mind whenever we may be tempted to read some obscure meaning into his words.

The terms in this lexicon are arranged in their written order. That is, the book contains one chapter for each opera, with those chapters placed in the sequence in which the operas were written, while the individual entries are listed in the order in which they first appear in the libretto. The only exceptions are Burnand and Sullivan's *Cox and Box*, and Stephenson and Sullivan's *The Zoo*, which tag along at the end as encore numbers. I believe the sequence I have used will make it easy for you to seek out any given term in the libretto and to make the context more evident, much as in a concordance. Having a distaste for footnotes and appendices, I have chosen to clutter my definitions

Introduction

with various elaborations. All references are collected in a single list at the end of the book, just before the index. The latter is included for those readers who may be curious about a term but have no idea where it may occur within the canon. Please note that the lexicon includes terms from the stage directions as well as from the lines themselves.

I believe I can justly claim that what follows is a scholarly exposition. My background studies have been exhaustive, I have subjected my manuscripts to the scrutiny of real experts in the Gilbert and Sullivan world, and I have carefully cited my many sources of information. The work is not pedantic, however, in that it avoids turgid prose. Indeed, like Bunthorne, I have endeavored to blend amusement with instruction. (And be warned, in some instances I have written with tongue in cheek.) As Jack Point so wisely said:

When they're offered to the world in merry
    guise,
Unpleasant truths are swallowed with a will—
For he who'd make his fellow-creatures wise
    Should always gild the philosophic pill!

The several published versions of the operas are not altogether uniform. My principal source was the Oxford University Press two-volume set called *The Savoy Operas* (1962 and 1963). I have, however, drawn on several other versions so as to include many verses or spoken lines that happen to be omitted in the Oxford set.

So here they are: some twenty six hundred words or phrases that should help you better understand and appreciate the unique and pleasurable genius of Sir William S. Gilbert, extraordinary gilder of the philosophic pill.

William Schwenck Gilbert

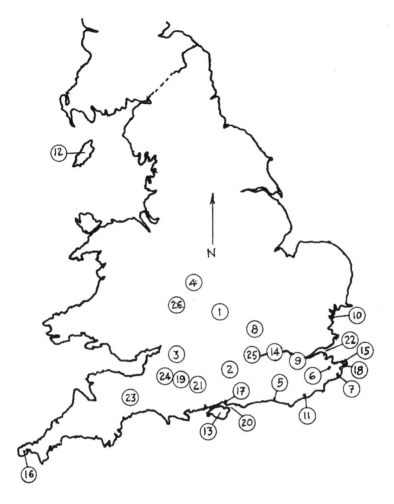

English Geographic Place Names Mentioned in the Lexicon

Note: London encompasses Barking, Camberwell, Clerkenwell, Greenwich, Hampton Court, Islington, Peckham, Richmond, and Tooting.

Key

1.	Banbury	14.	London
2.	Basingstoke	15.	Margate
3.	Bath	16.	Penzance
4.	Birmingham	17.	Portsmouth
5.	Brighton	18.	Ramsgate
6.	Canterbury	19.	Salisbury Plain
7.	Dover	20.	Spithead (strait)
8.	Dunstable	21.	Stonehenge
9.	Gravesend	22.	Thames River (mouth)
10.	Harwich	23.	Wellington
11.	Hastings	24.	Wells
12.	Isle of Man	25.	Windsor
13.	Isle of Wight	26.	Worcester

THESPIS

Chapter I   Thespis

Gilbert and Sullivan's first collaboration, *Thespis*, was written at the instigation of an imaginative London showman named John Hollingshead. Londoners in those days were fond of frothy theatrical shows that traditionally opened during the Christmas holidays and continued for several weeks thereafter. *Thespis* was commissioned as such a "Christmas operatic extravaganza," and ran for 63 performances following its opening on December 26, 1871. That was a long run for such a seasonal production, particularly when one considers that the show was slapped together in a hurry and was seriously under-rehearsed.

Sad to relate, nearly all of the music has been lost, although amateur operatic groups occasionally produce their own versions of the opera using Gilbert's words and Sullivan's music from other works or, perhaps, Sullivanesque music of their own composition.

The story concerns a troupe of actors who climb Mount Olympus on a picnic and discover the Roman gods, grown old and ineffectual. The actors agree to take over matters on Olympus while the gods go down to mingle with ordinary mortals to learn what they (the gods) can do to regain their old influence and prestige. Upon their return a year later the gods discover that the thespians, in their impractical way, have made a botch of things. They have, for example, given the Athenians a foggy Friday in November for six months—and now propose to make up for it with "a blazing Tuesday in July for the next twelve." Jupiter, in his wrath, sends the thespians back to earth and condemns them all to become "eminent tragedians, whom no one ever goes to see."

The libretto used for this chapter is that edited by Rees (252).

CHARACTERS AND SETTING

Jupiter: In Roman mythology, the king of the gods, equivalent to the Greek Zeus.

Apollo: Greek and Roman god of the sun. Also god of prophecy, song, music, manly youth, and beauty (75). Most of the stories about Apollo center on his lusty affairs with women of high or low degree.

Mars: Roman god of war, equivalent to the Greek Ares.

Diana: Roman goddess of the moon, equivalent to the Greek Artemis. A virgin, a huntress, and the twin sister of Apollo. Her private life was altogether in contrast to that of her twin.

Venus: Roman goddess of love and beauty, equivalent to the Greek Aphrodite.

Mercury: In Roman mythology the messenger of the gods, equivalent to the Greek Hermes. He was sometimes considered the patron of thieves, among his many duties.

Thespians: Actors and actresses. The word comes from the Athenian dramatist Thespis (sixth century B.C.), who is believed to have originated the tragic form of the drama.

Sparkeion and Nicemis: These are the young lovers and require no definitions; but

Chapter I

there is some debate about how their names should be pronounced. Most directors assume Gilbert was making puns, so Sparkeion should be pronounced SPARKee-un (something like Sparky one) and Nicemiss as NICE miss. Arthur Robinson (256) argues that the correct Greek pronunciations would be Spar-KEI-on and Ni-KAY-mis. He may be right, but I think we owe it to our audiences to go along with Gilbert's apparent intent and wink at the correct Greek pronunciations. As Shepherd (263) and Walters (302) point out, Englishmen in Gilbert's day almost always Anglicized foreign words. Younger readers should be made aware that "spark" once meant flirt.

[**Note:** Gilbert has given most of the actors artificial names appropriate to their roles, and they should be pronounced with that in mind. Stupidas, for example would be "Stupid Ass" and Tipseion "Tipsy One."]

ACT I

Respirator: A filter, or mask, worn over the face for warming or purifying the air breathed in.

Goloshes: What Americans call "galoshes": rubber overshoes. Not the dainty footwear one would expect to find on the feet of a goddess. See also Chapter XIV.

Smoking cap: A pill box shaped ornamental cap formerly worn at home by male smokers (75). They were Turkish in origin, and often came to Britain as souvenirs of eighteenth century grand tours to Vienna and Istanbul (43).

Blow me up: To scold me (229).

Life Pills: Rees (251) provides this definition: "Small, tasteless, and most probably useless placebos; they were sold for the treatment of vague disorders and were usually consumed by people who felt that it was a long time since they had taken any medicine."

Peruke [An invisible peruke]: A peruke is a wig. An invisible peruke is one so skillfully fitted that only your wigmaker knows.

Chignon [A full-bottomed chignon]: A hairpiece in the form of a rolled-up bun at the back of the neck. Very fashionable at that time.

Auricomous fluid {awe-RICK-oh-muss}: A hair dye that was advertised as producing "that rich golden colour so much admired in ladies and children." Auric pertains to gold, comous to hair.

Pearl-powder: Face powder. English ladies in the nineteenth century tried to remain pale because tanned skin was associated with a working-class existence. Recall, for example, Ralph Rakestraw's "honest brown right hand." In *Pride and Prejudice* (20) the snobbish Miss Bingley criticizes the heroine, Elizabeth Bennet, by remarking, "She has grown brown and coarse!" Pearly white or gray powder was most effective in covering any such signs of exposure to the sun (251). You will now understand why the Mikado's threat to darken ladies' faces with permanent walnut juice was so frightening.

Hare's foot: A powder puff shaped rather like a hare's foot (251). Stedman (274) mentions that originally they truly were made from hares' feet.

Commissionaire: The Corps of Commissionaires was organized in Victorian times to find jobs for former military men of good character. They had their own uniform and could be hired for light duty such as doorkeepers, hall porters, and messengers (162).

Beadle [parish beadle]: A minor parochial official, or other liveried flunky; sometimes a watchman. Often presented as personifying stupid officiousness (43).

Dustman: Garbage man or trash collector.

Christmas boxes [Your Christmas boxes ought to be something considerable]: Gifts of cash, food, or anything else given to servants, mail carriers, trash collectors, paper carriers, and the like, on Boxing Day (the first weekday after Christmas). In bygone days the gifts were collected in boxes, which explains the term (58, 107, 229, 245, 257).

Odes: Poems intended to be sung, or lyric poems of exalted tone.

Hymen: The Greek god of marriage.

Cupid: In Roman mythology the god of love, equivalent to the Greek Eros. He was supposedly the son of Mercury and Venus, but his mother's personal life was such that one could never be sure as to his sire. He is generally portrayed as a winged infant with bow and arrow, and is most in demand around Valentine's Day.

Celestial [I'm the celestial drudge]: Pertaining to the heavens.

Ranked [I'm ranked for it]: Mercury is implying that his services rank him at the bottom of the celestial hierarchy (11).

Noodles [Though noodles are baroned and earled]: Simpletons.

Baroned: Elevated to the rank of baron.

Earled: Elevated to the rank of earl. (You will find a summary of these noble ranks on page 85.)

Rate [though I rate at 'em]: Scold, censure, berate. In short, yell. See also Chapter XIV.

Nectar: The fabled drink of the gods, conferring immortality.

Rack [a terrible liquor to rack us]: In this case, to cause pain.

Bacchus {BACK-uss}: The god of wine. Bierce (39) defines him as "A convenient deity invented by the ancients as an excuse for getting drunk."

Minerva: Roman goddess of wisdom, equivalent to the Greek Athena.

Plate-powder: Polishing paste, for silverware, with chalk powder content. Mercury has made a verb of the expression, meaning to polish.

Jove [Jupiter, by Jove!]: Another name for Jupiter.

Votive offerings [sacrifices and votive offerings]: Offerings to the gods, given in keeping with vows.

Demented [he's quite demented]: Insane.

Tartarus {TAR-ter-uss} [Tartarus is the place]: In Greek mythology, the equivalent of hell.

Alpine Club: Upper middle-class Victorians were much enamored of the Swiss Alps, and mountain climbing was a popular sport. The Alpine Club was formed in London in 1857 for the express purpose of fostering this interest and is still extant.

"Cook's Excursion": A trip arranged by Cook's Travel Bureau, not an expedition of chefs. Thomas Cook and Son was the first modern travel agency and created the package holiday (142). In 1841 the company arranged what is believed to have been the first publicly advertised railway excursion in England (284).

En tête-à tête {on TET ah TET}: Literally: in head to head: a private conversation, often of a romantic nature.

Claret-cup [A piece of ice-for the claret-cup]: A drink consisting of claret (red Bordeaux wine), ice, carbonated water, lemon, sugar, and other flavorings (56). Samuel Johnson opined claret was so weak "that a man would drown in it before it made him drunk" (45).

Burrage [A bunch of burrage for the claret-cup]: The OED (140) defines *burrage* as an obsolete form of *borage*, which is a

Chapter I

genus of plants of the family Boraginacae: "Formerly much esteemed as a cordial, and is still largely used in making cool tankard, claret cup, etc." We understand it is also good in lemonade.

Convivial [you engaged me to play convivial parts]: Festive, merry, jovial and all those other adjectives applicable to a gathering of G&S admirers. Hyder (161) says "convivial parts" is probably a euphemism for "stage drunks."

Low Comedian: Low comedy is defined as depending "on physical action, broadly humorous or farcical situations, and often bawdy jokes" (250). You can take it from there.

Minion: An obsequious servant. In this case simply a contemptible person. See also Chapter XVI.

Odious: Repulsive.

A-hate [I a-hate you]: *Hate* used as a verb. (In melodramas the villain frequently interpolates meaningless syllables to emphasize his exaggerated oratory.)

Conundrum: A riddle, the answer to which involves a play on words. Particularly popular with third grade kids. See also Chapter XI.

Misanthropical [It's a misanthropical question]: Pertaining to one totally lacking faith in one's fellow man.

Diddlesex junction: From the context we may conclude that Thespis is talking about a railroad line. The "junction" in the name implies that it is a connector between two or more main lines. Turnbull (294) suggests that an 1871 audience would have recognized "North South East West Diddlesex junction" as "any" railway company. He adds that the "Diddle" might be taken to imply shady management.

Affable [For his affable ways and easy breeding]: Friendly, relaxed, and ready for any sort of social intercourse.

Fivers [He tipped the guards with brannew fivers]: Five-pound notes—about $25 in

those days. Turnbull (294) says this would be what a railway guard would earn for three or four days of work in the 1870s.

Compunction: Remorse.

Unction: The word has various meanings. Perhaps the best fitting definition deals with words that arouse deep religious devotion (75).

Stoker: The fireman in a steam locomotive.

Bath-buns {Bahth-buns} [rich Bath-buns for the outside porters]: Sugar-topped buns containing fruit, nuts, and raisins — usually split, and buttered. The name comes from their city of origin (142, 257).

Outside porters: Station baggage carriers.

Hunters [He'd mount the clerks on first-class hunters]: Horses used in fox hunting.

Roadside shunters: Rail yard employees who throw switches to divert trains from one set of tracks to another.

Tooting [He'd ask them down to his place in Tooting]: It was then a lower-middle class suburb in the southwest part of London (166, 245). It is now a London borough (142).

Siding [on lonely siding]: A railroad spur where rail cars can be temporarily idled.

Perth [If he wished to go to Perth or Stirling]: A city in Scotland, to say nothing of another in Australia. (But Gilbert meant the former.)

Stirling: Another city in Scotland.

Barking [At four a.m. in the wilds of Barking]: Then a working-class town about seven miles east and a little north of London; now a London suburb.

Peelers [with its rails and guards and peelers]: Policemen. The word goes back to the English statesman Sir Robert Peel (1788-1850), who established the metropolitan police force in England. He became Prime Minister in 1841 and served in that office for five years (105). Brewer (56) adds that the nickname "Bobby" was derived from Peel's first name.

Work'us [The shareholders are all in the work'us]: Workhouse, a place where poor people were lodged and given work. In the USA a workhouse is more likely a jail for petty criminals, and as Goodman (142) describes the old British workhouses, they weren't much better. Turnbull (294) sadly informs us that the old Savoyard Rutland Barrington ended his days in one.

Pipe-lights [And he sells pipe-lights in the Regent Circus]: Rees (251) defines these simply as matches. Perhaps they were an oversize variety especially suited to igniting stubborn pipes.

Regent Circus: This is the old name for what is now called Piccadilly Circus. It's not the kind of circus with lions and tigers; but it does have a statue surrounded by loafers, surrounded by vehicular traffic, surrounded by shoppers (and street vendors), surrounded by stores—all in a swirling pattern of concentric circles.

Flash paper [Throws flash paper]: Paper chemically treated so that contact with a piece of glowing string will cause a sudden little flash and puff of smoke (254). The consumed paper leaves no ash (245).

Danae {DANN-uh-ee} [those shocking affairs with Danae—and Leda—and Europa]: Princess of Argos. To protect her virginity, her father locked her in a bronze tower. Zeus (Jupiter), not one to overlook such a challenge, "transferred himself into a golden shower, and descended through the apertures of the roof into her embrace." The "issue" was Perseus. All this is from Lemprière's *Classical Dictionary* (187) — as is much of the rest that follows. Young women who are free with their favors may wish to file these unique explanations for future reference.

Leda {LEE-duh}: Queen of Sparta, who carried on with Zeus, who came calling in the form of a swan, or so she claimed. Their offspring were Pollux and Helen. Leda also produced two legitimate offspring: Castor and Clytemnestra (54, 187).

Europa: A Phoenician charmer who was abducted by Jupiter, who assumed the form of a bull (thus cowing her), "and swam with his prize to the island of Crete." The results of all this swimming, and so forth, were Minos, Sarpedon, and Rhadamanthus.

EUROPA & CHILD

Oi polloi: The common horde (Greek). Cameron (66) says the preferred spelling is "hoi polloi." To this Aurora (15) adds that the correct pronunciation also includes that initial h.

Thessalian {thuh-SAY-lee-an} [Thespis of Thessalian Theatres]: Pertaining to Thessaly, or Thessalia, the northeastern region of ancient Greece. I suppose Gilbert chose that location because it chimes in well with both "Thespis" and "Theatres." On the other hand there is a darker meaning to the word, namely treacherous (56). Stone (284) mentions that there really is a Thessalian Theatre.

Burlesque [we don't use you much out of burlesque]: A comic stage piece that derives its laughs from ridiculing or vulgarizing some serious subject. A travesty or parody.

Six-sheet poster: A large printed advertising poster assembled from six separate sheets.

Limelight [Limelight effects by the original Moon]: A strong theatrical spot light generated by projecting a mix-

LEDA & CHILD

Chapter I

ture of oxygen and hydrogen on a small piece of quicklime (calcium oxide). Invented by British army engineers in 1824, it was quickly adapted for magic lanterns (early form of slide projectors) and later for the stage (253).

Milo {MY-lo} [I appeared in a vision to Mr Milo]: The famous Venus de Milo statue in the Louvre derives its name from the island of Milo, or Melos, on which it was discovered in 1820. Venus here is clearly afflicted with Alzheimer's disease. Mr Milo, indeed!

Gauze [use a gauze next time]: A stage scrim: a thin semi-transparent screen filling the proscenium and partially or totally obscuring the stage, depending on the source of light. Gauzes may also be used to cover openings upstage.

Incog. [Why don't you all go down to Earth, incog.]: Short for incognito: in disguise, with hidden identity.

Deities [with all the other deities]: Gods.

"Clo" [I'll fill his place and wear his "clo"]: Clothes. Rag collectors in the streets used to call, "Any old clo?" (274).

Phoebus {FEE-bus} [Phoebus am I, with golden ray]: Another name for Apollo, particularly when in his role as sun god.

Calliope {kah-LIE-oh-pee}: One of the muses. She was the daughter of Jupiter and Mnemosyne, and her official duties required her to preside over eloquence and heroic poetry. Apollo was her half-brother and, if you'll recall, he too was supposed to preside over some of the arts. In their collaborative efforts with the Hellenic Arts Council they worked so intimately that they became the parents of Orpheus. You never can tell where committee work may lead.

ACT II

Symposia: Drinking parties.

Ambrosia: The food of the gods, which, like nectar, conferred immortality.

Inebriate: To intoxicate, make drunk.

Rosy [Olympian rosy]: Rosé or other wine (274).

Vulcan [Then why object to Vulcan?]: In Roman mythology the god of fire and metalworking.

Arcadee [Little maid of Arcadee]: Arcadia, the poetic land of rustic contentment in the Peloponnesus, which is a large peninsula in the southern part of Greece, and location of Sparta.

Tenpenny nail: A common nail. They are nearly three inches long and there are from 70 to 90 of them in a pound. The "penny" term dates back to fifteenth century England. Nail sizes then were designated by the retail price per hundred (229). The prices have changed, but the designation has not.

Squint [And Venus should not have a squint in her eyes]: Having eyes that point in different directions, perhaps cross-eyed (229).

Pluto: In Greek mythology, the god of the lower world, also known as Hades. He is also sometimes known as the giver of wealth, hence the term *plutocrat*.

Onus [On some it has come as a serious onus]: Burden or responsibility.

Life Office: Life insurance company.

In the court: Presumably the bankruptcy court.

Popping [Young ladies are popping all over the place]: Popping the question. Proposing marriage.

Artist who sugars the cake: The confectioner who decorates wedding cakes.

Dab [there isn't a dab in it]: Expert.

Quibble [quibble and shuffle and shirk]: Use sneaky, evasive arguments.

Shuffle: "To make use of false pretenses or unfair shifts" (115).

Shirk: To avoid doing what one should.

Downing Street: The British prime minister's residence has been at 10 Downing Street since 1735. The street, built in 1684, was named after its original developer, the speculative contractor Sir George Downing. After the "Glorious Revolution" of 1688 all those properties, which had been owned by the Earl of Lichfield, became forfeit to the crown. Number ten was included. Later, during the reign of George II, the house became vacant. The king offered it to his prime minister, Sir Robert Walpole. That gentleman replied that it should not be a personal gift but should be attached to the office of prime minister, and so it remains to this day (140).

Lemprière's Classical Dictionary: John Lemprière's definitive compendium of who's who on Olympus (187). The book, first published in 1788, was founded on Sabatier's *Dictionaire des Auteurs Classiques* (105).

Issa {ISS-uh} ["Apollo was several times married, among others to Issa, Bolina, Coronis, Chymene, Cyrene, Chione, Acacallis, and Calliope."]: Lemprière (187) tells us Issa was "a daughter of Macareus, the son of Lycaon. She was beloved by Apollo, who to obtain her confidence changed himself into a shepherd to whom she was attached."

Bolina {BO-line-ah or BO-lean-ah}: "A virgin of Achaja, who rejected the addresses of Apollo, and threw herself into the sea to avoid his importunities. The god made her immortal" (187).

Coronis {co-ROE-nis}: This mythological lady was loved by Apollo, who made her pregnant, but later killed her because she had an affair with Ischys the Thessalian.

According to some accounts, Diana killed her because of her infidelity to Apollo, and Mercury saved the child from her womb. The child was Aesculapius, whose name reappears in Chapter XVI.

Chymene {KY-men-ee}: Gilbert (or his printer) may have misspelled this. He presumably means *Clymene* {KLY-men-ee}, an oceanid (a sea nymph and inferior deity), "the mother of Phaeton by Apollo" (187).

Cyrene {sigh-REE-nee}: Daughter of Peneus. Apollo carried her off to Africa, where she produced Aristaeus as a souvenir of her travels. The ancient Greek state of Cyrenaica was named after her.

Chione {KY-oh-nee}: Daughter of Daedilion, panted after by both Apollo and Mercury. To obtain her unwitting favors, Mercury lulled her to sleep with his caduceus (that winged staff with entwining serpents). Apollo, disguised as an old woman, managed to share those favors as well. She says.

Acacallis {ah-cah-CAL-is}: A nymph, and yet another victim (whether willing or not) of Apollo's versatile courting techniques. She bore him two offspring: Philander (named in honor of his father?) and Phylacis. These children were exposed to the wild beasts of Crete, but a motherly goat nursed them and preserved their lives.

"Thing" [he goes out every evening with that "thing."]: A term applied to a person held in pity or contempt. In this case we may infer that Daphne was using it as a euphemism for a woman of easy virtue, which is a euphemism for a wayward woman, which is a euphemism for a slut. Oh, I could go on. The point is that proper Victorian ladies liked their words to be well insulated from anything sounding the least bit vulgar.

Espoused [I espoused him properlee]: Married.

Portal [He may take you to his portal]: The door of his house, meaning he may take you home as his bride.

Scurvy [Oh villain scurvy]: Low, vile, and contemptible.

Chapter I

Maxims [running over with celestial maxims]: Accepted principles or proverbs.

Gratis: Free. From the Latin *gratia*, a favor.

Tichborne trial {TITCH-born}: The longest trial in the history of English courts, at least until 1871. Concerned with sorting out the rightful heir to the Tichborne estates, the trial lasted 188 days. (*Trial by Jury* takes less than an hour.) Goodman (142) says both Gilbert and Sullivan attended the case as spectators.

Usual attributes [As Time, with the usual attributes]: Equipped with a big hour glass and scythe.

Sticks [That's where my experiment sticks]: Meets with insuperable difficulties.

Mytilene {mit-eh-LEEN-ee}: [the associated wine merchants of Mytilene]: Also known as Mitylene, also Lesbos. Historic island of the Aegean archipelago, famous for wine and dissolute manners. "An abode of pleasure and licentiousness" (187). Mitylene is now the principal city of the island of Lesbos (66).

Ginger beer [They only grow ginger beer]: A bubbly drink made by fermenting ginger, cream of tartar, sugar, etc. (75). Goodman (142) describes it as "a very fine soft drink." See similar terms in Chapters XIV and XVI.

Ceres {series}: The Roman goddess of agriculture, equivalent to the Greek Demeter.

Clearance [make a clearance]: Go away!.

Arrant [arrant folly]: Notorious, or thorough.

[**Note:** A comprehensive mastery of these terms will give you an automatic diploma in classical studies at any truly liberal arts college. Tell the admissions officer we said so.]

IF YOU DON'T GET THE **POINT** JUST HOLD AT ARM'S LENGTH

Chapter II Trial By Jury

The theatrical entrepreneur Richard D'Oyly Carte was convinced that English audiences would pay to attend respectable, well-written and well-produced musical entertainments. He was also convinced that he knew who among his contemporaries were most likely to write the works he envisaged. Although *Thespis* had been a modest success, Carte was sure the team could do even better. He knew that Gilbert was the nation's best-known wit and dramatist, and that Sullivan was England's preeminent composer. Given the right encouragement, surely they could work together to produce first-class musical theater. Carte succeeded in effecting this collaboration when he commissioned them to write *Trial by Jury*. Gilbert had at hand a libretto based on one of his earlier ballads (in the form of a brief operatic sketch) and Sullivan quickly set it to music. The mini-opera was intended to fill out a program built around Offenbach's *La Périchole*, and was first performed at the Royalty Theatre on March 25, 1875. Gilbert labeled it "A novel and entirely original dramatic cantata, in one act." *Trial* soon became more of an attraction than *La Périchole*, and Carte knew he had been right in assessing the worth of Gilbert and Sullivan as a team. This view was emphasized by a reviewer for the *Times*, who wrote that Sullivan's score fitted Gilbert's words as though words and music had proceeded from the same brain. This turned out to be an astute observation that was frequently applied to all the pair's joint operas (178, 275).

Trial by Jury ran for 131 consecutive performances, and still delights audiences everywhere. The plot is simplicity itself. The scene is a courtroom where a jilted bride is suing her former fiancé. After considerable argument — much of it carried off in mock Italian/Handelian operatic style — the judge determines to make everyone happy by marrying the plaintiff himself. Being himself a lawyer, Gilbert had no difficulty in poking this sort of fun at the British legal system. There are no spoken lines in the opera and the music sparkles from beginning to end.

CHARACTERS AND SETTING

Defendant: The person who stands accused.

Counsel [Counsel for the plaintiff]: This is the barrister who presents the accusations brought by the plaintiff against the defendant, who will plead his own case aided only by his guitar.

Plaintiff: Person who asks the court for a remedy against another person.

Usher: The doorkeeper and messenger in a court of law, also charged with maintaining dignity and decorum. Knight (178) observes that Gilbert has expanded the fellow's duties by having him swear the jury, a duty normally reserved for an associate.

Associate [A mime role listed among the *Dramatis Personae*]: Goodman (142) says "In this context it means the clerk of the court." Prestige (154) notes that, "he sits robed beneath the judge and acts as a sort of note taker." Stone (284) states that Gilbert himself played the role in at least six benefit performances. One such performance was on behalf of burlesque queen Nellie Farren (155).

Barristers: A barrister is a professional trial advocate who until 1990 had the exclusive right to plead cases in the higher courts (both civil and criminal) in England and Wales. A citizen who had need of legal help would approach a solicitor, a pre-trial attorney. If the situation involved a pleading before a higher court, the solicitor would turn the case over to a barrister who specialized in the kind of law involved. Otherwise the solicitor might handle the case without benefit of barrister. Each barrister belonged to one of four independent "Inns of Court," which had the sole right of licensing barristers to appear in the superior courts. What I describe above applies to the situation in Gilbert's day (143, 243, 309). Since January 1990, however, the division of advocacy work between solicitors and barristers has been largely removed, although all other divisions of work remain.

TEXT

Subpoena {suh-PEEN-ah} [Summoned by a stern subpoena]: A legal order to appear in court. Knight (178) points out that a defendant would be notified by a "writ," but

17

Chapter II

Gilbert needed a word to rhyme with Angelina.

Edwin ... Angelina [Edwin, sued by Angelina]: This was a traditional pairing of names of faithful lovers (302). They were linked by Oliver Goldsmith in a ballad, *The Hermit*, or *Edwin and Angelina*, written in 1764 (28). The names were also linked in a long series of articles in the then-current periodical *Fun* (284).

Fortissimo [Usher sings *fortissimo*]: Real loud, like an elephant with a bull horn.

Condole [Condole with her distress of mind]: To join in grief.

Court of the Exchequer: This was a court of common law established to deal with financial disputes between the crown and ordinary citizens. Burgess (60) says it was established by Henry II (who reigned from 1154 to 1189), whereas Knight (178) credits Henry I (who reigned from 1100 to 1135). It was merged with the Queen's Bench either in 1873 (60) or 1881 (178). Shipley (266) says the term relates to the checkered table and colored counters the king's counselors used to calculate national revenue. But, why would a breach of promise case be tried there? Knight (178) explains that such a breach would render the injured party unable to pay her taxes to the Crown. A nice example of a legal fiction.

Pecker [Be firm, my pecker]: We can thank Queen Victoria herself for help here. In a letter to one of her daughters, she wrote that, "Keep up your pecker" means, "Keep up your spirits, and don't be downhearted" (258). Despite the queen's implied approval of the expression, American directors may want to effect some discreet substitution. They might try this:

> **Edwin:** Is this the court of family cases? *(alarmed)* I see no smiles upon their faces!

Or, as suggested by Green (89): "It is, it is the Exchequer."

Evil star [Your evil star's in the ascendant]: Your astrological timing couldn't be worse.

Damages [dread our damages]: Compensation paid to an injured person.

Pleadings [On the merits of my pleadings]: The formal written arguments between the parties in a law suit or action (178).

Tink-a-Tank: Simulated sound of a guitar, or whatever instrument Edwin chooses to play. The OED (229), in its characteristic style, pins it down thus: "Tink: A representation of the abrupt sound made by striking resonant metal with something hard and light. Often reduplicated in imitation of the repetition of such a sound, also with such variations as tink-tank, tink-a-tink, etc." Kravetz (181) opines that tink-a-tank is too clumsy a sound for a guitar, more like a banjo. Green (145) would seem to agree. Knight, however, votes for a mandolin (178). One cannot be too meticulous in vital matters such as these.

Rover: An irresponsible fellow who toys with a young woman's affections.

Cad: A low, vulgar fellow (56).

Cloy [And love, unchanged will cloy]: Become too much, or too sweet, for pleasure. In his Bab Ballad, "Peter the Wag" (127), Gilbert uses it to describe a jam of people: "And flocking crowds completely cloyed the mazes of Soho."

OH, I WAS LIKE THAT WHEN A LAD

Reversed in banc [And never be reversed in banc]: A judgment overturned by a superior court employing a full bench of judges. In those days in England that was the only way of reversing a ruling.

Breach of Promise: Until 1970 in England breaking a marital engagement (normally by a man) was treated as a breach of legal contract and left the man vulnerable to legal action (24).

Called to the bar [When I, good friends, was called to the bar]: As explained under "Barristers" above, anyone aspiring to such a career must take training at one of London's four "Inns of Court." These are ancient institutions fulfilling the role of colleges of legal education for barristers and for maintaining professional standards. In addition to offices, apartments and a dining hall, each institution has a meeting hall, which originally featured a barrier or partition, "the bar," separating the candidates from the fully-qualified members. When the senior members were satisfied with a candidate's level of knowledge, that individual would be "called to the bar" to join the privileged members on the other side (54, 106, 178, 245). In short, "to be called to the bar" means to become accepted as a fully qualified barrister. *The bar*, incidentally, is also a collective term for the entire profession of barristers.

Impecunious [An impecunious party]: Short of money.

Swallow-tail coat: A coat the back of which is split in two halves that hang down about to the knees, while the front terminates at the waist. Goodman (142) says they are called "morning coats" and are still considered proper court dress for those upper-level barristers known as Queen's Counsel. On the other hand, for a newly qualified barrister, such attire might have seemed hopelessly old-fashioned (302), and perhaps that "beautiful blue" was too gaudy (257).

Brief [A brief which I bought of a booby]: The papers summarizing a court case, prepared by a solicitor for the benefit of a barrister. A brief summarizes the history of the case, the witnesses and what they will testify, and facts for cross examination (177).

Booby: Brewer (54) defines a booby as "A spiritless fool, who suffers himself to be imposed upon." A few have even been known to write lexicons.

Collar [A couple of shirts and a collar or two]: At the time the opera was written men's dress shirts were likely to have detachable collars, which were held in place by two little rivets ("collar buttons") front and back. This allowed the easily soiled collars to be laundered more often than the rest of the shirt.

Westminster Hall: A part of the Palace of Westminster adjacent to the Houses of Parliament. It was used as the High Court of Justice from 1755 to 1883 (60) or 1884 (142).

Semi-despondent fury [I danced a dance like a semi-despondent fury]: In classical mythology, furies were female divinities who punished crimes at the instigation of the victims (250). The term "semi-despondent fury" should not be taken literally. It is, rather, an example of Gilbert's fondness for wringing humor from the shotgun wedding of incongruous words.

Third-class journeys: The cheapest form of public transport on British railroads (178).

Pluck [You shall reap the reward of your pluck, my boy, at the Bailey and Middlesex Sessions]: Courage or spirit. Bosdêt (43) observes that "pluck" is a generic term for the liver and lungs of animals, which Americans might call "guts," which is also a slang term for bravery.

Bailey: Brewer (54) explains that this refers "to the Central Criminal Court of the City of London … situated in the thoroughfare of that name." He goes on to surmise that the word comes from the Latin *ballium*, meaning enclosure: that area enclosed by the city wall. Walters (301) adds that the outer wall of a castle is called a bailey. The "Ancient Bailey" to which the judge later refers is a variation on its usual sobriquet "Old Bailey."

Middlesex Sessions: This refers to the magistrates' courts at the Sessions House in Clerkenwell (99, 177, 283, 300). Middlesex was the county in which London was located. It and parts of other adjoining counties were later administratively absorbed by the area of Greater London (166). Goodman (87) says *Sessions* is short for "Quarter Sessions, "the quarterly sittings totaling about 100 days. In

Chapter II

general such courts handled only limited civil and criminal cases.

Gurneys [At length I became as rich as the Gurneys]: A family of Quakers who formed a banking house in Norwich in 1770 (178). In about 1800 they opened a branch in London. It became the world's greatest bill-discounting house and was known as "the bankers' banker," taking business away from the Bank of England. The Gurneys went public in 1865, forming a joint stock company with limited liability. In 1866 the London branch failed, in debt £11 million. The Gurney family, however, remained wealthy — which was probably at least in part the inspiration for Gilbert's later jabs at limited liability companies (as in *The Gondoliers* and *Utopia Limited*) (103). The Norwich branch prospered and was taken over by Barclays in 1896 (48). As an aside, you might want to know that a Gurney relative invented those light carriages on which you recline while being whisked about in hospitals (43).

Incubus [An incubus then I thought her]: The OED (229) gives several definitions, among the kindest of which is "A person or thing that weighs upon and oppresses like a nightmare." In medieval times it denoted a demon who had his way with women when they slept. The word derives from the Latin *incubare*, to lie on (which also gives us *incubate*). To complete this discourse, perhaps you should know that the female equivalent of an incubus is a succubus. Gentlemen: Beware!

Fudge [Though all my law be fudge]: *Fudge* is a colloquialism dating back at least to

1700, when it meant a lie (229). By Gilbert's time it also meant anything ridiculous or highly unreliable (56, 115). As a verb it means to obscure the truth (142). Knight (178) says the word was not applied to candy until the end of the nineteenth century.

Pianissimo: Very softly, in a stage whisper.

Patent {Rhymes with latent.} [It is patent to the mob]: Obvious. See also Chapter III.

Mob: Derived from the Latin *mo'bile vulgus* (the fickle crowd), and dating back to the time of Charles II (56).

Job [It was managed by a job]: The OED (228) has as one definition: "A transaction in which duty or the public interest is sacrificed for the sake of private … advantage." Another definition is "any unfair arrangement" (115). For our purposes: a deceitful action or dirty trick.

Nob [my being made a nob]: One dictionary (250) defines this as "A person of wealth or social distinction." Some believe the word is derived from *nabob*, which originally meant an oriental chief or viceroy, but later came to mean a person of great wealth, especially one who had acquired that wealth in India. Others (115, 181, 320), however, maintain that it is short for *nobility*. Prestige (245) interprets it as slang for a person of social distinction.

'Twixt ['Twixt rich and poor]: Short for betwixt, meaning between.

Lower {Rhymes with flower.} [Though the tempest lower]: To threaten or look sullen.

Posies: A posie is defined as a flower, nosegay (bunch of fragrant flowers), or a bouquet.

Passing fair [Though thy beauty rare shame the blushing roses —They are passing fair!]: An archaic meaning of *passing* is surpassingly. Thus, although the flowers are surpassingly beautiful, Angelina is even more so (181, 263, 274). Brewer (56) opines that the expression comes from the Dutch word *passen*, to admire. See entry for "Passing" in Chapter X.

Vernal [O'er the season vernal]: *Vernal* refers to springtime. The phrase refers to youth.

Substantial damages [Come, substantial damages!]: Ledbetter (184) says that exemplary damages (i.e., high enough to serve as a warning to others) could arise only in matters of breach of promise and then only when aggravated by seduction. Goodman, however, says he cannot confirm this; he believes it simply means heavy compensation (143).

My lud!: "My lord," or "m'lud" are standard forms of address to a judge in a British court of law (184).

Supercilious [wear a supercilious smile]: A smile that is at once haughty, contemptuous, proud, disdainful, and indifferent. Really packed with insolence! Shipley (266) thinks the word is derived from the Latin *cilium*, eyelash. (When speaking disdainfully you tend to lift the eyebrow.) See also Chapter IV.

Camberwell [Camberwell became a bower]: A rather prosaic working-class residential suburb of London, on the south — and therefore unfashionable — side of the Thames (251). Ledbetter (184) says it was in earlier times a pleasant residential area, the birthplace of Robert Browning, and locale where Mendelssohn once stayed. It later became industrialized and heavily populated.

Bower: This could mean either a shelter of leafy branches, a summer house, or an arbor.

Peckham [Peckham an Arcadian Vale]: The twin of Camberwell. See above. Oliver Goldsmith once taught there in a boy's school (184). Until about 1850 Camberwell and Peckham were villages separated from London by open fields (142).

Arcadian Vale: Arcadia was a mountainous part of Sparta, famous in song and story for its contented, simple-living people and admiring sheep. *Vale* means valley.

Otto [Breathing concentrated otto!]: Derived from *attar of roses*, i.e., perfume made from rose petals. Knight (178) says some 250 pounds of roses are needed to make a single ounce of attar.

Watteau [An existence à la Watteau]: Idyllic pastoral setting, as in the paintings of Jean-Antoine Watteau (1684-1721).

Trousseau {TRUE-so} [For the maid had bought her *trousseau*]: A bride's collection of clothing, linen, and the like, suitable for her new status as a married woman (from the French word for bundle). That's not the kind of bundle Angelina is looking for now.

Perjured [Oh, perjured lover]: One who has told a lie. In this case, it means one who has been untrue to his oath of fidelity (15).

Cologne [water from far Cologne]: Cologne water: *Eau de Cologne*. Cologne is a major German city on the Rhine. The toilet "water" in question is made by adding aromatic oils to alcohol. It was first produced commercially in Cologne, and no fewer than three companies there claim to being the originator. Ledbetter (184) says Cologne water is now made in France by descendants of its creator. By tradition Cologne water is dabbed on the face or waved under the nose of any lady who has fainted. For an exhaustive treatise on its composition, see *The Encyclopedia Americana* (105) or Bradley (48).

Submission [with all submission]: Due respect.

James the Second [In the reign of James the Second]: The son of Charles I, James II succeeded to the throne in 1685 but abdicated in 1688, when William of Orange forced him out. His was a short, bloody reign, but the Counsel would have us believe that he left his mark on matrimonial law.

Nice [A nice dilemma]: If we interpret *nice* in the conventional sense we can conclude that the judge is indulging in irony (as in "a nice mess"). On the other hand, as Asimov (11) says, *nice* is used by lawyers in the older sense of requiring careful thought and examination. That seems the more likely interpretation.

Breach [A breach 'twill surely be]: A breach of promise: In legal matters, a failure to carry out a promise of marriage. *Breach* means to break.

Chapter II

Prepossessing [I'm not prepossessing]: Attractive, likely to make a good first impression.

Abatement: A mitigating factor. This is from a pair of lines that are in the score but are omitted from some versions of the libretto. The complete verse, as found in *The Savoy Operas* (131), is sung by the jury as follows:

> We would be fairly acting,
> But this is most distracting!
> If, when in liquor, he would kick her,
> That is an abatement.

Furies [All the legal furies seize you]: See "Semi-despondent fury" above.

Attorneys [Barristers, and you, attorneys]: At the time the opera was set (early 1870s) the person briefing a barrister in the Court of the Exchequer would have been an attorney. Shortly thereafter, however, the Judicature Act merged the solicitors and attorneys, and the former title was adopted (178).

Shelf [Put your briefs upon the shelf]: This should not be taken literally; the judge is telling both parties to shelve (i.e., lay aside) their pleadings.

Knell [The knell is sounded]: A slow ringing of a bell at a funeral.

Doated [On you he's doated]: Bestowing excessive adoration.

Moated [To castle moated]: Protected by a deep encircling ditch, probably filled with anything but *Eau de Cologne*.

Tether [In marriage tether]: A rope or chain used to keep an animal from straying. This is not to be taken literally.

Snob: [The defendant is a snob]: Brewer (56) says this means, "not a gentleman; one who arrogates to himself merits which he does not deserve."

Fob [I'll reward him from my fob]: A small waistband pocket. Since the pocket is a small one, we may infer that the reward was perhaps only loose change. "Another insult, and, I think, a light one!"

Chapter III   The Sorcerer

Having shown what could be done with *Trial by Jury*, Carte found financial backers and organized the Comedy Opera Company to pursue his dream of English musical theater. He then contracted with Gilbert and Sullivan to write their first full-length comic opera: *The Sorcerer*, which opened at London's Opera Comique on November 17, 1877. The opera was at least moderately successful and ran for 178 performances.

The Sorcerer is historically significant in that it set the pattern and style that made the succeeding operas so successful. Gilbert's control over the acting company and his firm insistence on disciplined teamwork were innovations that were then badly needed in British theater. He also brought into the company such stalwart performers as George Grossmith, Rutland Barrington, and Richard Temple. These performers (and soon others) stayed with the company for many years, and Gilbert and Sullivan obligingly wrote many roles specifically to suit their talents.

The Sorcerer's plot involves an engaged couple who want everyone to be as happy as they, and so the groom-to-be brings in a "family sorcerer" to administer a love potion to the entire village. As you might expect, the love potion works, but everyone falls in love with the wrong partner. All is made right in the end, however, as the sorcerer breaks the spell by the expedient of giving himself up to the powers of evil — in an appropriate puff of smoke. (You will soon learn that the Gilbert and Sullivan operas do not hinge on strongly convincing conclusions.)

CHARACTERS AND SETTING

Sorcerer: A person who is supposed to exercise supernatural powers through the aid of evil spirits (250).

Pointdextre {POIN-dexter} [Sir Marmaduke Pointdextre]: This is a family name that implies a thoroughly Norman, hence presumably noble, ancestry. Nobility is further implied by the fact that the name is actually a heraldic term. Bradley (47) informs us that "the dexter point is the top right-hand corner of a coat of arms as carried by its bearer; i.e., the top left-hand corner as seen by a spectator."

Baronet [an Elderly Baronet]: A baronet holds a hereditary position ranking between a knight and a baron, but without privilege of sitting in the House of Lords. See also Chapter X.

Grenadier Guards: A grenadier was originally a soldier trained to throw grenades. The grenades were carried in a shoulder bag and were rather heavy. Moreover, the grenadiers were often called upon to lead the charge. For these reasons British grenadiers had a reputation for both strength and bravery. When the grenade ceased to be used, the grenadiers maintained their existence as crack companies of their battalions. According to the 1910 edition of *The Encyclopædia Britannica* (103), "In the British service the only grenadiers remaining are the Grenadier Guards." Prestige (245) reveals what is perhaps most important, which is that, "officers in the Grenadier Guards were drawn from the aristocracy, and needed a substantial private income. Alexis is thus wealthy and aristocratic."

Vicar [Vicar of Ploverleigh]: There are various definitions of this term just within the Church of England. Let us simply say that Dr. Daly is the clergyman of the local parish.

Notary: Also known as a *notary public,* this is a public officer authorized (among other duties) to certify documents and to record the fact that certain persons swear that something is true. Some authorities (47, 245, 274) believe the signing of the marriage contract (in which the notary plays an important part) is a take-off of similar scenes in grand opera, such as *The Barber of Seville* and *Lucia di Lammermoor.*

Betrothed [betrothed to Alexis]: Informally pledged in marriage. In the first act Alexis and Aline advance their intent to marry from a moral commitment to a legally binding, irrevocable contract (18). Going as far back as Roman times we find that betrothals were not to be taken lightly (27). The same was true in the fifteenth century. Fry (121) states that Edward V, just two months after succeeding to the throne, was declared illegitimate because his father, Edward IV, had been betrothed to Lady Eleanor Butler when he married the boy's mother, Elizabeth

Chapter III

Woodville. The teen-aged Edward V and his younger brother were shortly taken by their uncle (Richard III) to the Tower of London for "safe keeping," and shortly thereafter disappeared.

Sangazure {SANG-ah-zhoor}: Lady Sangazure's family name throbs with vibrations suggesting royal lineage. It means "blue blood" in French. Her title, Lady, implies any of a long list of possible noble associations.

Partlet [Mrs. Partlet — a *Pew-opener*]: Mrs. Partlet's personality and social standing both are implied in her family name, which the OED (229) defines as "A word used as the proper name of any hen, often *Dame Partlet;* also applied like 'hen' to a woman." Bosdêt (43) says the name first surfaced in English literature as "Pertelate" in Chaucer, and has medieval connections with a village priest's mistress. Surely this racier reference has nothing whatsoever to do with the good, virtuous and amiable Zorah Partlet.

Pew-opener: Partridge (233) gives us a clue. He defines a pew-opener's muscle as one in the palm of the hand "because it helps to contract and hollow the palm of the hand for the reception of a gratuity." From this we infer that a pew-opener was an impoverished parishioner who was allowed to gather tips by escorting well-heeled worshipers to their family pews and holding the pew doors open for their benefit. (If you don't already know the word, a pew is an enclosed church bench.)

ACT I

Elizabethan [Sir Marmaduke's Elizabethan mansion]: Pertaining to the time of Elizabeth I, who reigned from 1558 to 1603. Elizabethan architecture is described as a mixed style, transitional between Gothic and Renaissance, with classic designs worked into the decadent Gothic style (75).

Knells [Forget your knells]: The sound of slowly rung bells at funerals or other mournful occasions.

Lay [Of mournful lay]: A song.

Green [at the feast on the green]: Since the setting is given as the exterior of Sir Marmaduke's mansion, we can infer that this particular green is his palatial lawn.

Plighted [plighted to Aline]: Firmly committed, implying that Alexis and Aline have a formal understanding that marriage will ensue. That is not yet legally binding, but will be as soon as the party can be convened and the agreement signed and notarized (18).

Amatory numbers [charged with amatory numbers]: *Amatory* pertains to love, or anything causing love, or anything having to do with lovers. *Numbers* refers here to musical compositions or poetry.

Madrigals [soft madrigals]: A madrigal is a song with parts for several voices, sung a *cappella* (that is, without accompaniment).

Curate {CURE-uht, but CURE-ate sounds better in the context} [I was a fair young curate then!]: In the Church of England, an assistant to a rector or vicar.

I WAS A PALE YOUNG CURATE THEN!

Parish [then half a parish trembled]: A district that has its own clergyman.

Gilded [Fled gilded dukes and belted earls before me]: Associating nobility with gold belts apparently dates back to Roman times. Gibbon (124) mentions that in the time of the Emperor Constantine military commanders called dukes and counts were distinguished by gold belts. Even today a "gilded youth" is defined as a young man of wealth and fashion (75). That definition could as well apply to dukes, even old ones. Dukes, earls, and other noble titles are comprehensively dealt with under "Characters and Setting" in Chapter VII.

Belted [belted earls]: "This refers to the belts and spurs with which knights, etc., were invested when raised to the dignity" (54). In addition see above for Edward Gibbon's observation.

Stepped [as good a girl as ever stepped]: Mrs Partlet presumably means Constance is as good a girl as ever set foot on this earth. Gillette (135) reminds us that in *H.M.S. Pinafore* we find Ralph loyally speaking thus of Captain Corcoran: "A better Captain don't walk the deck."

Take [Oh, I take you.]: Understand.

Fogy [I am an old fogy now]: Brewer (56) says that properly speaking the term applies to military pensioners, but Dr Daly simply means he's an old goat.

Comely {KUMM-lee} [the young maidens of the village are very comely]: Good-looking.

Tush {Make it rhyme with gush.} [But tush! I am puling!]: "An expression of impatience, contempt, or rebuke" (115). We might say "pshaw!"

Puling {Rhymes with fueling.}: Whining, whimpering, or needlessly complaining.

Plighting [most auspicious plighting]: Act of becoming engaged to be married.

Obleege [will you obleege me]: Oblige, i.e., do a favor.

Clerkly {clarkly} [In clerkly manuscript]: Neatly copied in a big round hand.

Sol {Rhymes with doll.} [Ere Sol has sunk …]: Another name for the Roman god of the sun, corresponding to the Greek Helios. In this case Dr. Daly simply means the sun. Lemprière (187) tells us that "according to some ancient poets, Sol and Apollo were two different persons. Apollo, however, and Phoebus and Sol, are universally supposed to be the same Deity."

Reverie: Dreamy thoughts about pleasant things or, better yet, pleasant people of the opposite sex.

House [the House of Sangazure]: A family, usually one with prestigious ancestors.

Helen of Troy: King Menelaus's young wife who eloped with that cad Paris and so triggered the Trojan Wars. Hers was "the face that launched a thousand ships" and won her the undying affection of the Worshipful Order of Hellenic Shipbuilders. She was reputed to be the daughter of Zeus and Leda.

Escutcheon: The word originally meant a shield. It more generally refers to the shield-shaped surface on which a family's coat of arms is displayed. Prestige (245) suggests that what is meant is an *escutcheon of pretence:* "The small escutcheon bearing the arms of an heiress placed in the center of her husband's shield" (229).

Menials: Low ranking domestic servants.

Protest [I protest I am mighty well]: To assert.

Palpitating [With a heart palpitating]: Beating rapidly: pitty pat!

Cloy [May their love never cloy]: Become tiresome, excessive.

Aurora [As Aurora gilds the day]: Dawn, after the Roman goddess of morning.

Apostrophe [I find some satisfaction in apostrophe like this]: An address, usually a digression, to some person or personification that may or may not be present.

Portal [Take me to thy portal]: The expression means "Take me as thy bride."

Execute the deed: We are indebted to Evans (111) for this explanation. "To execute a deed is to sign, seal and deliver the legal document. To sign speaks for itself. To seal is to impress your own personal seal … on seal-

Chapter III

ing wax … (you then) place the forefinger of your right hand on the seal and say 'I deliver this as my act and deed.' Until you do that the deed has no legal effect. If you are a tenor or soprano you may sing the words." The modern meaning is simply to sign a legal document with the intention of being bound by its contents (142).

Deliver [I deliver it as my Act and Deed]: This expression is explained in the immediately preceding entry. Knight (179) notes that what is being delivered symbolizes a legal "deal" rather than a physical handing over of the property itself. Shakespeare used it in a sense of stating, reporting, or making known (82).

Quiver [See they sign, without a quiver]: Without hesitation.

Maxim [the truth of that maxim]: A general rule or proverb.

Panacea {pan-uh-SEE-uh} [the panacea for every ill]: A cure-all.

Evangel [oh, evangel of true happiness]: One who bears good news.

Mechanics' Institutes: Rees (251) explains the term as follows:

> "Mechanics" were not technicians but simply labourers at or near the very bottom of the social scale. The institutes … were charitable establishments where these people were taught to read and write and where the rudiments of Victorian education were instilled. A variety of penny publications was brought out weekly by several organisations dedicated to the purpose, and there were of course the "penny readings." Alexis' speech commencing with "I hope so …" is a parody of the wide range of subject matter offered in these places to largely uneducated and frequently illiterate audiences. It is really all a matter of terminology: Bottom the weaver and his companions in *A Midsummer Night's Dream*, a carpenter, a joiner, a bellows-mender, a tinker, and a tailor, were all "mechanicals."

George Grossmith, the original D'Oyly Carte comic baritone, started his career as an entertainer in mechanics' institutes. In his autobiography (146) he offers a good descrip-

tion of them. Bosdêt (43) adds that the institutes were established with funds donated by Queen Adelaide, wife of William IV (who reigned from 1830 to 1837).

Workhouses: Poorhouses (no longer in use in England).

Navvies {Rhymes with have ease} [I have addressed navvies]: Laborers on the construction of roads, canals, and other civil works. The word is a truncation of *navigator*, the name given at first to the men who dug the canals, then called "navigations." The term was later extended to apply to laborers in other civil works (55, 115, 251).

Countesses [what do the countesses say?]: In Britain a countess is the wife of an earl.

St. Mary Axe: A street in the older part of London. Wells refers to it later as "Simmery Axe," that being its common pronunciation. Terry (285) mentions that the street at one time housed conjurors' shops. The peculiar name comes from a church that was built on the street some time before 1197. The church was called St Mary the Virgin and St Ursula and the Eleven Thousand Virgins.

Duffy (99) and McCann (206) relate two versions of an ancient tale about a certain king of England who gave his daughter Ursula and 300 (one says 11,000) of her handmaidens permission to travel abroad (one says to marry Atilla the Hun). In any event, while on the continent Atilla slaughtered them all with three axes. Bosdêt (43) says the atrocity occurred in A.D. 393, and one of the axes was brought back to London as a souvenir of the second Crusade. The church was built to enshrine the relic but it was dedicated to St Mary as well as Ursula. The church was converted into a warehouse in the siixteenth century and later destroyed. What happened to that revered axe remains a mystery. For the sake of scholarly integrity I have to add that Tillett (291) has reason to believe the story about Ursula is mythical in its entirety.

Philtre: A love potion. (Now we're getting into the heart of the plot.) At this point Gilbert drags in a laborious pun on the word filter: an earthenware jar for purifying drinking water. When the opera was written

(1877), theater managers were in the habit of leaving the house lights up. Audiences could buy copies of the librettos, which they were fond of reading word-for-word throughout the show. Being thus informed, they could tell the difference between *philtre* and *filter*. Modern audiences cannot, and directors could do us a favor by omitting that particular exchange altogether.

Steep [to steep the whole village]: Saturate.

Hercules: In classical mythology Hercules was a hero noted for gigantic strength and virility. The role is traditionally played by the smallest member of the troupe, perhaps a child.

Necromancy: Magic. Specifically a supernatural procedure for foretelling the future by communicating with the dead.

Wishing caps: In folklore, caps that empower the wearer to make wishes come true (75).

Divining rods: Hand-held devices, often hazel or willow twigs, for locating subterranean water or minerals, such as gold, silver, or pirates' chests. Everything else having been tried without success, one wonders if divining rods might not be used to locate the lost music for *Thespis*.

Counter-charms: The OED (229) defines this as, "Anything that counteracts, or neutralizes the influence of a charm." Surely, you could have inferred as much; but I went to the trouble of looking it up, so there it is.

Amulets: Objects worn on the person to bring good luck or ward off the devil. Shipley (266) says the word derives from Latin *amolire letum* (to turn away death). Brewer (56) on the other hand says it comes from the Arabic word *hamulet*, meaning that which is suspended.

Nativity [We can cast you a nativity at a low figure]: Meaning we can determine the exact position of the planets at the time of your birth. This is what an astrologer does in casting your horoscope.

Horoscope [a horoscope at three-and-six]: A diagram of the heavens at a given time, and used by astrologers to tell fortunes.

Three-and-six: Three shillings and sixpence, or 17.5 percent of a pound sterling.

Abudah chests [Our Abudah chests, each containing a patent Hag]: Abudah was the central character in a pseudo-Persian fairy tale by James Ridley, included in his book *Tales of the Genii* (255). Abudah was a wealthy and charitable merchant whose nights were disturbed: "For no sooner was the merchant retired within the walls of his chamber, than a little box, which no art might remove from its place, advanced without help to the center of the chamber, and opening, discovered to his sight the form of a diminutive old hag, who with crutches hopped forward to Abudah, and every night addressed him in the following terms …" (Her nocturnal castigations admonished him to seek out "the talisman of Oromanes," which would bring true contentment — which turned out not to be the case; but we've told you enough to explain the term Abudah chest more thoroughly than you really wanted to know.)

Patent: *Patent* has several meanings. It may, for example, mean either obvious or protected by patent rights. In the present context the second meaning is patently correct; it's more commercial and fitting to Mr. Wells's approach to commercial sorcery. Our British friends often pronounce it PAY-tent. Evans (111) explained: "Scientists and lawyers call it — correctly —'pat-tent.' Nearly everyone else calls it 'pay-tent,' usually meaning not an actual legal patent but just an ingenious device." See also Chapter II.

Hag: A hag is, in this case, a presumably mechanical sorceress who (by some undisclosed means) can prophecy disasters.

Spring complete [with spring complete]: This means the Abudah chest comes completely equipped with a spring — presumably to activate the patent hag.

Aladdin lamps: In *The Arabian Nights*, Aladdin acquired a magic lamp that when rubbed produced a genie to do his bidding.

Chapter III

Prophetic Tablets: These are flat surfaces, perhaps of wood, each containing an array of various symbols that, when correctly interpreted, allow one to predict the future. Rees (254) adds that these may contain chemicals producing "magic fire," generating colored flames and smoke.

Change of Ministry [from a change of Ministry down to a rise in Unified]: In England, the term "change of Ministry" usually implies a complete change of government, with one party replacing the other (257). In a broader interpretation, much more modest changes, such as the replacement of a single cabinet member, might be understood (142, 254). Within the context, the first interpretation seems more appropriate. Turnbull (294) says the term is now obsolete.

Unified: British government bonds. On opening night, in 1877, the term "Turkish stock" was used. The late George Applegate (8) reported that Turkey was then borrowing from some of the western countries of Europe, "which would, I suppose, cause *her* stock to rise and fall from day to day." In modern American productions some well known stock might well be mentioned. How about General Motors, or Exxon, or perhaps the Dow Jones average?

[**Note:** Now we come to John Wellington Wells's self-introduction, often looked upon as the first of the G&S list (or patter) songs that have become perhaps the most distinguishing and popular feature of the Savoy operas. A patter song is a comic number depending for its humorous effect on rapid enunciation of words (158). The word *patter* is most commonly thought to derive from *pater-noster*, the first two words of the Lord's Prayer said with a Roman Catholic rosary. Brewer (54) states, "When saying mass the priest often recited in a low, rapid, mechanical way until he came to the words 'and lead us not into temptation,' which he spoke clearly and deliberately."]

Melt a rich uncle in wax: Dunn (100) and Walmisley (299) concur that the expression relates to a medieval superstition that one could effect the death of a person by melting his or her waxen image. Rossetti's poem "Sister Helen" tells of a woman who, mad with jealousy, gradually melts her ex-lover's waxen image for three days and nights, starting on the morn of his scheduled wedding to another woman.

Djinn [the resident Djinn]: In Arabian mythology, spirits of supernatural powers. Also spelled genie or jinnee. Djinn is the plural of djinnee, in case you ever come up against one. In Arabian mythology such spirits were created two thousand years before Adam and Eve (55). The resident djinn would be a collection of such supernatural creatures available to do your bidding on a full-time basis.

Simmery Axe [Number seventy, Simmery Axe]: The authentic Londoner's pronunciation of St. Mary Axe.

Posthumous shade {POSS-cheh-muss} [And for raising a posthumous shade]: *Posthumous* refers to conditions after death. *Shade* has many meanings. The most likely one here is ghost. *Raising* pertains to calling up from the grave.

Returns [unbounded returns]: Another word for profit, nice work for a prophet. Hyder (162) writes that Gilbert was alluding to the popular Victorian business slogan: "Small profits, quick returns," which was, in turn, a play on the Roman S.P.Q.R. (*Senatus populusque Romanus*: the Senate and people of Rome).

Proclivity [Humour proclivity]: A natural tendency.

Oracular [Answers oracular]: Here's a term teeming with mystic significance. It can mean an infallible guide. It can also mean an equivocal pronouncement. It is derived from the oracles at Delphi, priests or priestesses who claimed to transmit the voices of the gods. They protected their reputations by giving ambiguous advice. See also Chapter IV.

Bogies [Bogies spectacular]: Hobgoblins: persons or objects of terror (54). What some of us used to call "boogie men."

Tetrapods [Tetrapods tragical]: Morningstar (216) explains that Gilbert was referring "to the tetrapody form of a logaoedic verse, a great favorite of Greek tragedians." (Logaoedic means the verse is made up of long and short syllables in certain well-defined sequences.) A tetrapody is a verse of four metrical feet (6). (In poetic matters a "foot" is a patterned group of syllables.)

[**Note:** In some editions of the libretto the sequence of the last three items is reversed.]

Astronomical [Facts astronomical]: The word pertains to the study of the heavenly bodies. Asimov (11) believes that Gilbert really meant *astrological*, but needed a word to rhyme with *comical*. Asimov may be right. On the other hand might we not argue that Gilbert meant facts in large numbers?

Reflectors [And that, without reflectors]: This pertains to the mirrors often used in stage illusions.

Spectres [gaunt and grisly spectres]: Ghosts.

Grisly: Ghastly.

Shrouds [He can fill you crowds of shrouds]: Interpret this as meaning he can provide you with many ghosts, each clothed in a burial wrap.

Rack [He can rack your brains]: To torture by stretching.

Gibberings [gibberings grim and ghastly]: Senseless chattering, like a lecture on medieval monetary practices in Faroffistan.

Organity [Changes organity, with an urbanity]: The OED (228) has it as "The condition of having organs, or being organic." We presume in changing organity the resident Djinn is simply using his supernatural powers to assume a different form.

Urbanity: Refined elegance, *savoir-faire*.

Satanity: Pertaining to Satan, who (according to Jewish and Christian beliefs) is the chief adversary of man, a.k.a. the devil.

Inanity: A senseless frivolity.

Tautology [Barring tautology]: Needless repetition. "Posthumous shade" and "a panacea for every ill" are two handy examples.

Demonology: The study of demons (evil spirits) or of beliefs about the same. Witchcraft would be an example.

'Lectro-biology: I should have taken this to mean simply electro-biology had not Rees (251) called to my attention Merivale's autobiography (213) in which *electro-biology* is described at some length. It was merely hypnotism under another name. The early practitioners seemingly believed that electricity was involved, hence the misleading terminology.

Nosology [Mystic nosology]: Study of diseases. Asimov (11) and Huston (158) suggest that *mystic nosology* may be the curing of illness through magic. Stedman (274) thinks it more likely that it pertains to curing illnesses that are caused by magic.

Philology [Spirit philology]: Study of language and the origin of words.

Puffing [We are not in the habit of puffing our goods]: Exaggerating the worth.

Philanthropical [purely philanthropical motives]: Pertaining to love of mankind shown through generous deeds. A thousand-dollar gift to your local Gilbert & Sullivan troupe would be a good example. Make that annual.

Wood [we should strongly advise your taking it in the wood]: Buying it by the barrel.

Chapter III

Pipes [pipes and hogsheads for laying down]: Wine containers, generally of 126 U.S.-gallon capacity.

Hogsheads: These are wooden barrels of 63 U.S.-gallon capacity.

Laying down: Storing for future use. This entry and the three preceding it are common terms in the wine wholesaling business.

Army and Navy Stores: Rees (251) explains that this is "A very smart emporium on Victoria Street. It is still there. Anyone might shop there, but officers could become members and obtain discount." For further details see Goodman (140).

Carouse [to carouse in a few minutes]: To revel. Although we normally associate the word with excessive drinking, the villagers presumably expect to sip nothing stronger than tea.

Incantation: A set of charm words that, when spoken at the right time (usually midnight) in the right place (a graveyard will do nicely), and in the right tone of voice (funereal preferred), will perhaps cast a magic spell, call up one or more demons, or otherwise produce supernatural effects and scare you half to death. Gilbert was presumably well acquainted with the impressive incantation scene in von Weber's grand opera *Der Freischütz.*

Sprites [Sprites of earth and air]: The sprites of earth were goblins, those of air were sylphs.

Shoals [Come here in shoals]: Crowds.

Noisome [Noisome hags of night]: Offensively disgusting and disgustingly offensive. They smell awful, too. Ugh.

Hags: Witches or sorceresses (56), but not to be confused with that mechanical hag from the Abudah chest.

Imps [Imps of deadly shade]: Miniature devils or demons.

Pallid [Pallid ghosts]: Pale.

Shell [echoed in every shell]: Every sea shell.

Fell [Ye demons, fell, with yelp and yell]: Villainous.

Set us free — our work is done: Knight (178) explains that spirits may be set free after performing important tasks for their master.

Mustard and cress [Now for the mustard and cress]: These are tender sprouts grown from mustard and cress seeds, served together as a garnish or salad.

Rollicking [the rollicking bun]: Jovial, care free, and high spirited. A rollicking bun is one accompanied by generous quantities of strong waters. In real life Gilbert is said to have confided to George Grosssmith (the fellow who created most of the comic baritone parts): "If you promise me faithfully not to mention this to a single person, not even your dearest friend, I don't think Shakespeare rollicking" (240). See also Chapters V and VI.

Sally Lunn: A plain, light tea-cake, which is split, toasted, buttered, and served usually with jam. Named after a late-eighteenth century street vendor in Bath. If you want the recipe, see Applegate's mouth-watering opus (9). Papa (232) reports that close cousins of Sally Lunns are sold in New Orleans, where they are known as *pain à la vielle tante.*

Brindisi {BRINN-dee-zee} [Tea-cup brindisi]: A toast, from the Italian word for the same. Every Italian opera had to have its drinking song — but none, we vouch, with tea. Perhaps the most rousing brindisi of all is the one in Verdi's *La Traviata,* first produced in 1853. Rees (254) reports that Verdi's opera was on the boards in London at the time *The Sorcerer* was produced, so it was surely well known to many in the Savoy audiences. See also Chapter XIV.

I will go bail for the liquor: Read: I will guarantee the quality of the tea. See also Chapters VIII, IX, and XIII.

Jorum [At brewing a jorum of tea]: A jorum is generally taken to mean a large punch bowl or at least a large portion of liquor (66). "A jorum of tea" is a typical

Gilbertian twist, an oxymoron. The roots of *jorum* are uncertain but it may derive from the Biblical Jeroboam, "a mighty man of valour … who made Israel to sin" (54). This led somehow to *jeroboam*, meaning a large bowl, or goblet, or wine bottle. Those of you who take your drinking seriously can probably work thish into a convershayshun.

Caddy [tea-pot, kettle, caddy, and cosy]: A caddy is a box, often ornamental, containing canisters of tea. Stedman (273) explains that caddies were generally kept locked so that only the mistress of the household had access to the precious leaves. Bosdêt (43) says the word is derived from *kati* a Malaysian unit of weight somewhat over a pound. The term came to be applied to the special airtight tin boxes sized to hold that amount of tea, which were used to ship the leaves to England.

Cosy: A cloth jacket for keeping a teapot warm. Often called a tea cosy.

Plot [Toil, sorrow, and plot]: Conspiracy.

Three spoons to the pot: The normal allotment of tea is one spoonful per person to be served, "plus one spoon to the pot." A generous allotment would allow two spoons to the pot. Dr. Daly, however, tends to get carried away; he tosses in *three* spoonfuls. This is really living! (And it's someone else's tea.)

Alloy: An addition to a material reducing its purity.

Tillage [Peace-bearing tillage]: The normal meaning has to do with cultivation of the land. We can interpret it as the figurative land that is ploughed, i.e., tilled (276), to produce a harvest of love.

Garner [Great garner of bliss]: A storehouse.

ACT II

Dark lantern: A lantern with a sliding shutter for confining the emission of light. The burglar's trademark. The term also appears in Chapter V.

Manifest [manifest its power]: To reveal, to make plain.

Meet [I did not think it meet]: Appropriate.

Pedigree [A dame of lengthy pedigree]: Line of ancestors.

K.C.B.: Knight Commander of the Bath: an order of chivalry. Bathing is thought to have been part of a purification ritual introduced in the eleventh century (225). Bradley (47) notes that this is but one of three classes within the Order of the Bath, this being the middle one. Ranking above it is the Grand Cross of the Bath (G.C.B.), and below it the Companion of the Bath (C.B.). [See entries for the same term in Chapters IV and XIII.]

Doctor of Divinity: A person who has received the highest educational degree in theology. See also Chapter V.

Q.C. [And that respectable Q.C.]: The initials stand for Queen's Counsel: "a barrister of seniority and experience who has been granted this title in recognition of eminence in the law. The colloquial phrase of becoming a Q.C. is 'to take the silk,' because a barrister who is a Q.C. wears a silk gown, whereas other barristers wear a 'stuff' gown" (244). On their appointment they are called "within the bar" and thereafter sit on the front row of the court, which is separated from other advocate rows by a wooden bar in the older courts (142). When a queen is replaced by a king, all those Q.C.'s become K.C.'s (257).
Shepherd (263) notes that in this opera the Q.C. title apparently belongs to the notary, which seems strange because notaries are of a separate profession. Donkin (257) explains that some barristers are also notaries, and even one who was a Q.C. would be honored to officiate at a betrothal ceremony uniting the parish's two foremost families. Burgess (60) hypothesizes that Mr Wells is using the term ironically.

Al-fresco-ly [All fast asleep, al-fresco-ly]: Outdoors. *Al fresco* is Italian for "in the cool."

Approbation: Approval.

Where be oi, and what be oi a doin': Bradley (48) states that these accents imply

Chapter III

that Ploverleigh is located in the western part of England, probably in Dorset (a.k.a. Dorsetshire) not far from the Devon border. (See map on page 36.) On the other hand, Joseph (166) thinks those accents more indicative of Somerset (just north of Dorset). He points out, too, that Wellington and Wells are two small towns in Somerset. Walters (302) would settle for "Mummerset," a term for an unspecified western region.

Guineas [I've guineas not a few for you]: A monetary unit equal to £1.05 (i.e., one pound, one shilling). In this case read: I've plenty of money for you. The coin was last issued in 1813, but the term remained in general use long thereafter. It took its name from the African country that was its source of gold. See also Chapters VI and VIII.

Nectar [My cup is not of nectar]: In Greek mythology, the drink of the gods.

Rector [Our kind and reverend rector]: A Church of England clergyman in charge of ecclesiastical affairs of a parish. Constance may be using the term loosely as a favor to Gilbert who wanted a rhyme for *nectar*. Dr. Daly is clearly the *Vicar* of Ploverleigh. A Rector holds the equivalent position and authority, but there is a significant difference in the way their incomes are handled (75). Walters (302) says the terms are interchangeable in today's common parlance.

Snuffy [He's dry and snuffy]: This may mean soiled with grains of snuff or (colloquially) irritable and cross (75). It may also mean tipsy (115). In the context I should vote for the first interpretation. If he is dry can he also be tipsy? In the next line he is called ill-tempered, so *irritable and cross* would be wasted.

Blind young boy: The context clearly implies Cupid (Eros), who is referred to by Shakespeare as "This wimpled, whining, purblind, wayward boy," "The blind bow-boy," and "Her [i.e., Venus's] purblind son and heir, Young Adam Cupid" (82). Shakespeare is also quoted as saying, "Love looks not with the eyes but with the mind and therefore is winged Cupid painted blind."

Vaunted [thy vaunted love]: Boasted.

Solaced [not unlikely to be solaced]: Comforted and cheered.

Heverythink: West country language for "everything."

Estimable [your estimable father]: Worthy of admiration.

Minx [I'm no saucy minx]: In Gilbert's day the term meant a flirt or a harlot, or anything in between. Today it merely implies little more than an impertinent woman, and that may come close to Mrs. Partlet's intent.

Hussies [Hussies such as them]: A word of contempt for a woman, ranging from slight (36) to extreme (294) depending on the degree of venom in the voice.

Widdy [a clean and tidy widdy]: A corruption of *widow*.

Lowering {Rhymes with cowering.} [Why do you glare at one with visage lowering?]: Threatening. Applegate (8) argued that the *one* in the quotation is likely a typographical error dating back to the earliest editions of the libretto. See Allen (3). A few of the newer editions substitute *me*. The old D'Oyly Carte Opera Company consistently used *me*, and also changed *glare* to *gaze*. Their example seems worth following.

One Tree Hill [I often roll down One Tree Hill]: In the first edition of this book I listed seven "One Tree Hills" within reasonable distance of London. I also noted the widespread disagreement among various authorities as to which one of those Gilbert may have meant. Since then, George Williams (317) has submitted a rather poor photocopy of a cartoon by Thomas Rowlandson (1756-1827). Entitled "The centre of attraction at Greenwich Fair: One Tree Hill," it presents a wild and bawdy scene, which we have carefully copied and reproduced below. As you will note, among other disreputable actions, it shows several couples rolling down the slope while locked in close embrace. Some of the well-fed "ladies" with legs akimbo offer no evidence whatsoever of wearing undergarments. This surely is the sort of social activity that should revolt a person of Lady Sangazure's refined tastes. In my opinion

those other six hills are out of the running. This conclusion is strengthened by Rees (254) who has uncovered an 1865 comic drama named *One-Tree Hill*.

> Act 1 is set in "Greenwich Park, Summit of One-Tree Hill."
> *Enter a young husband and wife.*
> *Annie:* Tom, you won't do anything to oblige me.
> *Tom:* Why, haven't I brought you here today to roll down the hill if you like?
> For I suppose that is one of your reminiscences of happiness.

[**Note:** For those of you who don't know London, Greenwich Park is in the southeast environs of that city. The fair had become such a nuisance that it was closed down in 1870 (161).]

Rosherville [I sometimes go to Rosherville]: This refers to Rosherville Gardens, a lower class amusement park, described as follows by Brewer (54): "In Victorian times 'the place to spend a happy day.' These gardens were established by Mr. Rosher in disused chalk quarries at Gravesend. A theatre, zoological collections, and music formed part of their attraction, and the gardens were particularly favored by river excursionists." Hardwick (149) contributes the titillation that the Gardens "were notorious for the number of prostitutes who used them to ply their trade." Goodman (140) may be consulted for a definitive exposition on the gardens.

Abjure [abjure my lot!]: A strong term meaning to disclaim. Strictly speaking abjure means to abandon an allegiance to a cause, break an oath, and so forth.

Mésalliances {MACE-ahl-ee-AHNS} [To foster mésalliances through the nation]: French for mismatches. This is from the original libretto as recorded by Allen (3), and is not used in modern versions.

Sovereign law [Thine uttered will is sovereign law to me!]: A law subject to no overriding laws.

Flageolet: A small, non-reed wind instrument with a mouthpiece and six holes, usually without keys. The instrument, a variant of the recorder, was invented in 1599 by Juvignay, an instrument-maker in Paris (89). See also Chapter VII.

Pillage [hearts to pillage]: Plunder or steal.

Love's tillage [What a worker on Love's tillage]: Interpret as: What an aid in Cupid's work. This is a somewhat different interpretation of tillage as used earlier in the libretto.

Magic fell [Its magic fell]: Fell here is an adjective, so the term means villainous magic.

Perfidy: [Thy perfidy all men shall know]: Treachery or breach of faith.

Instance [This poor child drank the philtre at your instance]: Urging, or insistence.

Chapter III

Colonial Bishopric [the congenial gloom of a Colonial Bishopric]: A district under the ecclesiastical jurisdiction of some overseas bishop. Knight (178) comments that many of those overseas dioceses were lacking in amenities, and such an appointment was originally tantamount to exile.

Ahrimanes {Ahri-MONN-ees or Ah-RIM-enees} [must yield up his life to Ahrimanes]: In Persian mythology, the personification of evil, somewhat analogous to Satan. For a closer look at the old boy, read Byron's *Manfred* (65). Rees (251) observes that Ahrimanes is none other than the Oromanes already mentioned under our discussion of Abudah chest. Rees (254) also explains that Ahrimanes was a name familiar to English audiences because he was portrayed in a popular opera by Balfe.

Take stock [we take stock next week]: To inventory the goods still unsold. (Somehow, that very small prophet was going to be unavailable to carry out the task.)

Co. [It would not be fair on the Co.]: The company. {As printed, the word would be pronounced Ko, and it may be that in Gilbert's time that would have been conventional. For modern audiences, however, make it KUM-penny.}

English Counties Mentioned in the Lexicon
(Names and borders are as of a century ago.)
Reference: Bartholomew (29).

H.M.S. PINAFORE

Chapter IV   H.M.S. Pinafore

H.M.S. *Pinafore* was Gilbert and Sullivan's first great joint success, and it brought them outstanding fame on both sides of the Atlantic. The show opened at the Opera Comique on May 25, 1878. Although initially well received, an exceptionally hot summer kept audiences away until Sullivan started playing selections from the show at promenade concerts for which he was the musical director. That turned the tide; the opera went on to run for more than 570 performances, and it has been one of the most popular works on the musical stage ever since.

In *H.M.S. Pinafore* Gilbert satirizes British class consciousness and pokes fun at a First Lord of the Admiralty who knows little about ships — which just happened to be true to life in England at the time. In *Pinafore*, too, Gilbert firmly established the style of producing humor by treating a thoroughly ridiculous situation in a thoroughly serious manner. He added to the effect by insisting on accurate settings and costumes, and by rigidly restraining actors who wanted to ham up his lines or engage in any sort of slapstick. *H.M.S. Pinafore* remains a joy as well as a landmark in the history of musical theater.

CHARACTERS AND SETTING

H.M.S.: His, or Her, Majesty's Ship. Signifies a ship of the Royal Navy.

Pinafore: A child's dress or apron. Allen (3) says there is reason to think that Gilbert had originally named the opera *H.M.S. Semaphore* (anything nautical to rhyme with "one cheer more") but changed it to *Pinafore* at Sullivan's suggestion. Naming a fighting ship after such an unprepossessing item of apparel must have appealed to Gilbert's sense of the ridiculous, particularly as it contrasted with such formidable names as *Goliath*, *Audacious*, *Minotaur*, and *Majestic* (which were in Nelson's fleet). Then give three cheers for Sir Arthur's part of the libretto! An incidental note: Shipley (266) imagines that the term arose from a mother's admonition, "Don't spot your dress. Here's something to *pin afore* it."

Rt. Hon. [The Rt. Hon. Sir Joseph Porter, K.C.B.]: *Right Honourable* is a prefix accorded certain high-echelon politicians, judges, and others distinguished for their public service who have been appointed members of the Queen's Privy Council (243). *A Privy Council* is "a body of advisors, theoretically selected by the sovereign, whose function it is to advise the sovereign in matters of state" (250). Despite the elaborate uniform invariably affected by Sir Joseph, the First Lord of the Admiralty is not an admiral, but a politically appointed civilian responsible for managing the navy. Prestige (243) notes that in the traditional D'Oyly Carte productions his uniform "was that of a Privy Councillor, with the badge of a K.C.B., to both of which he was fully entitled." Hyder (160) adds the warning that he should never wear epaulettes because they are accouterments reserved strictly for military officers.

Speaking of Privy Councilors, I am reminded of Queen Victoria's favorite Prime Minister, Benjamin Disraeli. When asked how he managed to get along so well with her, Disraeli replied, "I never refuse; I never contradict; I sometimes forget" (203).

K.C.B.: Knight Commander of the Bath. In England, one of the highest orders of knighthood. "Bathing as a purification ritual was probably introduced in a religious context with knighthood in the 11th century" (225). See also Chapters III and XIII.

Ralph [Ralph Rackstraw — Able Seaman]: Our hero's Christian name should be pronounced *Raif*. Remember that Buttercup's second act revelation includes these lines:

> In time each little waif
> Forsook his foster-mother,
> The well-born babe was Ralph —
> Your captain was the other!!!

Rackstraw: The other seamen on the *Pinafore* are given nautical-related surnames, and we wonder if Gilbert intended the same for Ralph. The word is uniformly avoided by all ordinary dictionaries that come to hand. I did, however, find a 1921 seaman's manual (31) that defined *rack* as slang for a berth. See also Gibson (125). So I propose that Ralph's surname might refer to straw-filled ticking. Hyder (161) comments that, although the

Chapter IV

other sailors have seagoing names, "Ralph is a man set apart. Anyway, Gilbert never liked tenors." In any event, Gilbert might have derived quiet pleasure in assigning a seaman such a bucolic-sounding name, for the expression "to rack straw" means to pitch straw into a storage rack. Knight (177) says "This was a demonstration of Ralph's rustic background in opposition to Josephine's supposed superior social status." Kesilman (47) agrees that *Rackstraw* implies humble origins, but disagrees with the bucolic association. He points to Josephine's lament about what life would be like with Ralph. In it she describes a squalid urban setting.

Able Seaman: A sailor certified as possessing all-around nautical capabilities; one step above the lowest rating, or ordinary seaman. Such seamen are more often referred to as "A.B.'s," short for *able bodied* seamen.

Deadeye [Dick Deadeye]: A deadeye is a round block of wood with three holes drilled through the flat face. They are used in pairs as a crude block-and-tackle to maintain tension in the shrouds supporting a mast. Deadeye is clearly a superb name for a one-eyed character.

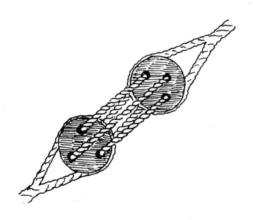

Bobstay [Bill Bobstay]: A bobstay is a wire, rope, or chain running from the end of the bowsprit diagonally downward to the stem of the ship. Its function is to keep the bowsprit from being pulled upward by the tension in the forestay. See picture on page 49.

Boatswain's Mate: A boatswain is a non-commissioned naval officer who supervises work ordered by a higher ranking officer. The word is usually pronounced "bosun." A boatswain's mate is his assistant. Brewer (56) says the "swain" comes from the Saxon word *swein*, meaning a boy or servant.

Becket [Bob Becket]: A becket is a short length of rope used to secure coils of line, spars, oars, etc. For convenience, it is usually formed with an eye (loop) at one end and a hook at the other.

Midshipmite: The OED (228) defines this as a sailor's perversion of *midshipman*. The latter is defined as "in the navy, the designation of a rank intermediate in the line of promotion between that of naval cadet and that of the lowest commissioned officer (i.e., in the British navy that of sub-lieutenant, in the U.S. navy that of ensign)." Another definition is "a diminutive midshipman" (115). As traditionally cast, the midshipmite is indeed a little mite of a lad — a Gilbertian visual pun.

Bumboat (Buttercup is identified as a *bumboat woman*): A boat that goes from ship to ship in a harbor, selling articles to seafarers. Bosdêt (43) suggests the term was derived from the fact that the boats developed from scows that, in the seventeenth century, had been used to transport dung out to sea, hence the disreputable name.

ACT I

Portsmouth [on the Portsmouth tide]: The chief naval base in Great Britain.

Men-o'-war's men [Hail, men-o'-war's men]: A man-of-war is a naval vessel, and the second "men" refers to her ratings, i.e., her unlicensed crew.

Jacky [I've snuff and tobacco, and excellent jacky]: This one is controversial. Most authorities are split between *gin* (8, 115, 228, 234, 251, 254, 299, 301) and *chewing tobacco*.

(21, 98, 147, 149, 286). Green (145) ventures that it is rum-soaked chewing tobacco. Gilbert, in his Bab Ballad "The King of Canoodle-Dum" (127), tells of a cannibal king who orders that "every lady, and every lady's lord should masticate jacky (a kind of tobaccy), and scatter its juices abroad." All this leads me to conclude that Buttercup's *jacky* is most likely chewing tobacco soaked in gin or rum.

Treacle {TREE-kul} [I've treacle and toffee]: The mundane meaning is simply molasses — which is the residual product of the sugar refining process. But the word has an older and more romantic meaning: an antidote for the bite of wild beasts. Venice treacle, for example, was a compound of 64 drugs in honey — which sounds like the electuary mentioned in *The Yeomen of the Guard*. See Brewer (54). Paulshock (238) avers that the best treacles always included "chopped, powdered, or distilled vipers, as well as opium, honey, and a slew of other ingredients, many very rare and difficult to obtain." She adds that "the original recipe called for periods of storage for up to ten years to allow all 50 or so ingredients to ferment and blend … " I think that is all very interesting; but I also think Buttercup was selling molasses, or something like it, and not that vile medicine.

Soft tommy: Grand Pierre (144) defines this as baker's bread. Sailors use the term in contradistinction to biscuits (115).

Chops: Slabs of meat with the bone still attached.

Conies: The term can mean either rabbit meat or rabbit fur. In the context, meat seems more likely.

Polonies: Collins (75) says this is "A kind of partly-cooked sausage." Hyder (161) says the word is a corruption of *Bologna*, the city of its origin. The American corruption is *baloney*.

Spithead [the reddest beauty in all Spithead]: The sheltered stretch of water between Portsmouth and the Isle of Wight.

Dissembled [I have dissembled well]: She means she has used various artifices to improve her figure and complexion. Another

interpretation is applied to the same word in the second act.

Canker-worm [there may lurk a canker-worm]: A destructive grub or caterpillar. Buttercup is speaking figuratively and hinting at her dark secret. Her words remind us of Shakespeare's lines in *Twelfth Night*: "She never told her love, but let concealment, like a worm i' th' bud, feed on her damask cheek."

Three-cornered [And I'm three-cornered, too, ain't I?]: Dick Deadeye is usually portrayed as permanently bent at the waist and with one shoulder carried higher than the other in a deformed, almost triangular configuration.

Madrigal: The word has several meanings. In this case it means a lover's lament set to music.

Minstrelsy {MIN-strelsey}[The pearl of minstrelsy]: The art or practice of a wandering poet or musician.

Menial [To do her menial's duty]: A menial is the humblest sort of servant, one assigned to do the most degrading tasks. Proofreading lexicons is a depressing example.

Foremast hand: A common sailor. The term derives from the practice of housing the officers aft (i.e., near the stern) and the common seamen in the forecastle. See page 49.

Quarterdeck: That part of the upper deck extending from the main mast (near midlength) to the stern. The officers, being accommodated in the stern, consider the quarterdeck "their" territory. Unlicensed sea-

Chapter IV

men avoid the quarterdeck unless called there in the line of duty. See page 49.

Fore-yard arm [who lays out on the fore-yard arm]: Please turn to page 49. Item No. 6 is the fore mast, and Item No. 7 is one of the fore-yard arms: i.e., a yard arm on the fore mast. Sailors must "lay out" on the yards in order to handle the sails. See Item No. 11.

Main-truck [he hoists his flag at the main-truck]: The very top of the main mast — the highest point of the entire ship, and a suitable place for the highest officer to display his flag. See page 49, Item No. 8.

Hoists ... his slacks: In his children's version (132) Gilbert explains that "hoisting his slacks" means hitching up the waist-band of his trousers to put them in their proper place.

Peer [Though related to a peer]: In general, a nobleman. More specifically, "a member of any of the five degrees of the nobility in Great Britain and Ireland, namely duke, marquis, earl, viscount, and baron" (250). As Asimov (11) observes, when one is related to a peer, one finds ways to work it into the conversation. See also Chapters VII, XII, XIII, and XVI.

Hand [I can hand, reef, and steer]: In this case, *hand* means to take in and furl a sail. See the OED (228). The expression "hand, reef, and steer" is an old nautical cliché describing the skills required of an able seaman.

Reef: Reduce the area of a sail exposed to the wind by partially furling it. Item No. 9 shown on page 49 is an example of a reefed sail.

Ship a selvagee [and ship a selvagee]: Smyth's *Sailor's Work Book* of 1867 defines selvagee as "a strong and pliant hank, or untwisted skein of rope-yarn marled together, and used as a strap to fasten round a shroud or stay, or slings to which to hook a tackle to hoist in any heavy article." This is as quoted in the OED (228). To *ship a selvagee* is to place it in working position.

Ancestral timber [That ever blossomed on ancestral timber]: The family tree.

Tackle [She does not seem to tackle kindly to it.]: From the context, the word means *take*, i.e., accept. The question is how it should pronounced. I have always heard it pronounced, on stage, to rhyme with shackle. Yet, I wonder. Seamen traditionally pronounce it TAY-kill in "block-and tackle" and similar applications. If Corcoran elects to pronounce it the authentic seagoing way (TAY-kill) the audience will more easily understand the meaning; so why not?

Own [Sad are the sighs that own the spell]: Acknowledge.

Venerate: To regard with reverence.

Gilded [Not to some gilded lordling?]: Brewer (54) defines *Gilded Youth* as "Wealthy and fashionable young men, principally engaged in the pursuit of pleasure." That seems reasonably close to what Captain Corcoran must have had in mind. In his children's version (132) Gilbert adds a footnote: "I should have thought he would have liked a gilded lordling, but you never can tell."

Fie [Oh fie!]: Brewer (56) avers that the exclamation is appropriate when reproving something exceptionally dirty or indecent.

Solecisms {SAHL-eh-sizms} [he would commit solecisms that society would never pardon]: A solecism is a badly worded, ungrammatical expression that may range from the absurd to the vulgar. Or it may mean a breach of etiquette. Again, in his children's version Gilbert has Corcoran aver, "He would drop his h's and eat peas with a knife." Brewer (55) says the word comes from the Greek *soloikos*, which means to speak incorrectly, and derives from the town of Soloi, the residents of which spoke a debased form of Greek.

Barge [Sir Joseph's barge is seen]: This would be a large oar-propelled boat with cushions within a wood or canvas shelter in the stern for the honored passenger's comfort — and that of his guests.

Poop-deck: A deck forming the top of a superstructure in the aft part of a ship. The term is derived from the Latin *puppis*, meaning the stern of a ship. See page 49 Item No. 5.

Barcarolle: The original meaning was a boating song of the Venetian gondoliers, but now it means any boating song. *Barca* is Italian for boat.

Nine-pounders [Bang-bang the loud nine-pounders go]: Cannon firing a nine-pound ball. This was a relatively small cannon, but well suited, as in this case, to firing blanks as a salute. British ships of the period carried batteries of cannon firing balls weighing 9, 18, or 32 pounds (7). But, this brings up the question of to what degree the Royal Navy fired salutes for a civilian bureaucrat such as Sir Joseph. Gilbert, in any event, has given him a "bang-bang" and Sullivan has given him accompanying thumps on the tympani.

Royal N.: The Royal Navy.

Pennants dipping: Pennants are long, narrow streamer-like flags flown at the mast heads of a war ship. Dipping them is a form of courteous salute to an approaching dignitary. See page 49, Item No. 10.

Writs [I served the writs with a smile so bland]: To serve a writ means to deliver a summons ordering a person to appear in court (142). To be effective, a writ must be delivered to the recipient's hand (60).

Articled clerk {Make that second word rhyme with bark.}: An apprentice who has signed articles of indenture (or covenant) to a law firm. The apprentice is bound to serve for a fixed number of years, during which time he (or she) learns law. Burgess (60) says that at the time the opera was written the articled clerks paid a fee for the privilege, whereas today they are paid a salary.

Pass examination: An examination to be successfully completed before becoming a solicitor (112). The term *solicitor* is explained in Chapter II.

Institute: Terry (286) explains that "The Incorporated Law Society's Hall … was colloquially known as the Law Institute." Bradley (46) states that the Law Society is the governing body for solicitors and handles the qualifying examinations for entry into the profession. Goodman (140, 141, 142) adds that the Institute is situated in London's Chancery Lane, No. 113, indeed.

Pocket borough: A borough is a town represented in Parliament (167). A pocket borough was one that was effectively under the voting control of an individual or family. British laws now make the term obsolete.

Fettered: Chained at the ankles. More broadly: shackled.

Patronize {The pat in *patronize* rhymes with rat.} [Don't patronize them, sir]: Assume the air of a superior to one you are addressing.

Smarter [There's not a smarter topman in the navy]: Ralph isn't claiming superior intelligence, but he wants to be known as an agile (and probably highly motivated) seaman.

Topman: One of those agile sailors sent aloft when work needs to be done high in the rigging (311). See page 49, Item No. 11. Massie (201) says these men, "had been picked for their quickness, agility, and courage and they had fierce pride in their ability and their ship's standing."

Hornpipe [Can you dance a hornpipe?]: A lively jiglike dance performed solo and traditionally favored by sailors. Its name was derived from a folk clarinet formed of two ox horns, one housing the reed and the other forming the bell (250). Kravetz (181, 182) says "When I was a lad" is actually composed in the form of such a dance, as is the fast section of "A British tar."

MS. music: Music manuscript.

Grog [see that extra grog is served out]: Grog is rum thinned with cold water. Prestige (245) says the standard mix is one part rum, two parts water. The OED (229) traces the word back to an admiral named Vernon, who habitually wore a grogram

Chapter IV

(grosgrain) cloak. He was nicknamed Admiral Grogram. After he instituted the water-and-rum drink in the British Navy, his foreshortened name was applied to the drink. Knight (178) says before the admiral's time the crew drank their allowance of brandy or rum clear. He adds that grog was abolished in 1970.

Ship's company: The crew, not the visitors.

Seven bells: That could be at 3:30, 7:30, or 11:30, either AM or PM. It would occur half an hour before the changing of the watch.

Tack [You're on a wrong tack]: Read: You're headed in the wrong direction.

Messmates [Messmates, ahoy!]: The term "mess" can mean a space where meals are served on shipboard. *Messmates* refers to the group of seamen who eat together, thus implying social equality. See also Chapter X.

Tar [A British tar is a soaring soul]: This is a slang term for a common sailor, sometimes in the form of *Jack Tar*. The OED (229) proposes that it derives from *tarpaulin*, (heavy canvas such as is used in sails). Indeed, in the 1600s a seafarer was at times referred to as a "tarpaulin" (115).

Furl [and his brow should furl]: Read: wrinkle.

Tang [the tang of a tyrant's tongue]: The first meaning of *tang* is a strong taste or flavor. Another meaning pertains to a sharp projection on any sort of hardware. Let us interpret it here as a sharp, acidic tongue.

Antithetical [a combination of antithetical elements]: Directly opposed.

Cimmerean {sih-MEER-ee-an} [the Cimmerean darkness of tangible despair]: Homer told of the Cimmereans, who dwelt in a land "beyond the ocean stream," where the sun never shone. In post-Homeric times the Cimmereans were an ancient people who lived on the shores of the Black Sea, from which comes the name (54).

Ganglion [I am but a living ganglion of irreconcilable antagonisms]: The OED (228) assures us that a ganglion is a tumor, or a knot on a nerve forming a center from which nerve fibers radiate, or a class of organs that includes the thymus gland, the thyroid body, and the adrenals. *The Random House Dictionary* (250) uses similar terms but adds "a center of intellectual or industrial force, activity, etc." I have heard the word used as meaning a snarl. Several of my knowledgeable friends (265, 273, 289, 326) opine that Ralph's nervous system was immobilized by conflicting signals into a quivering pulp. Prestige (243) on the other hand believes that Ralph was carried away and simply used an impressive-sounding word in the wrong place. Occam and I tend to support Prestige.

Jove's armoury: Bolts of lightning, the favorite weapon of Jove, also known as Jupiter, the supreme deity in Roman mythology.

Adrift [cuts my hopes adrift]: Literally broken from moorings, out of control, and at the mercy of wind and tide.

Ensign {En-sin} [Has hung his ensign high above]: The literal meaning is the national flag displayed aboard a ship. The poetic meaning (which applies here) is that the sun (Apollo's ensign) is high in the sky and shining away.

Roundelays [In dreamy roundelays]: Simple songs with recurring themes, often associated with circle dances.

Bated breath [With bated breath and muffled oar]: *Bated* is short for "abated." *With bated breath* is defined as "breathing restricted from fear, *etc.*" (75). Shakespeare uses the expression in *The Merchant of Venice*.

Muffled oar: To ensure quiet rowing, with little splashing from the oars, oar blades may be wrapped (and so muffled) in cloth.

ACT II

Regent [Bright regent of the heavens]: An acting ruler.

Sixes or sevens [why is everything either at sixes or at sevens?]: The origin of this phrase (more commonly "sixes and sevens") is obscure. It applies to a state of confusion; or of persons, unable to come to an agreement. Brewer (55) says the phrase comes from dicing. Another explanation proposes that the term arose from the ranking in importance of medieval guilds in London. The tailors and the skinners had equal claims to sixth rank in annual processions. To compromise the conflict they agreed to switch sixth and seventh places each year. The expression has been found in literature dating about as far back as 1340 (115).

Court martial: In this case a gathering of naval officers convened for the trial of a person charged with violating naval law. (We think Sir Joseph is bluffing.)

Staunch {Rhymes with launch.} [you are staunch to me]: Firm, constant, loyal, true, and trustworthy — like a Boy Scout.

Fain [I would fain see you smile]: Gladly.

Aloof [You hold aloof from me]: The term means to maintain a distance, and is derived from a nautical expression meaning to stay upwind (56).

Highlows [Highlows pass as patent leathers]: Highlows are variously described as high shoes reaching over the ankles, and as low boots. In the present context we can take them as being workaday shoes.

Jackdaws [Jackdaws strut in peacock feathers]: Walters (301), who is an ornithologist as well as a Savoyard, explains that *jackdaw* is "the English name for *Corvus monedula*, a small species of crow. The allusion is to Aesop's fable of the jackdaw who dressed himself in peacock feathers to appear better than he really was, and was rejected both by his own kind and those whom he sought to emulate."

Logs [Storks turn out to be but logs]: Brewer (54) reminds us that this alludes to Aesop's fable of King Log and King Stork (1, 2). In the story, some frogs asked Jupiter to give them a king. Jupiter responded by throwing a log in the water. The frogs didn't admire the log's style and asked Jupiter for a more active leader. The replacement was a stork, who proceeded to eat his subjects. Moral: be satisfied with a passive ruler.

Bulls [Bulls are but inflated frogs]: This pertains to Aesop's fable of the frog and the ox (8, 170). In the story a mother frog wants to impress her children by making herself as big as an ox that is grazing nearby. She puffs herself up beyond the bursting point, and the story comes to a sudden climactic and tragic denouement: Pop!

Drops the wind and stops the mill: The windmill will stop when the wind dies. I presume, this is another hint to the captain that he may be in for a change, and not for the better.

Turbot and brill [Turbot is ambitious brill]: Turbot and brill are related varieties of flatfish. The turbot, however, is a distinctly bigger and tastier fish, and more fashionable. One serves turbot at dinner parties but (horrors!) never brill. Knight (177) mentions that brill have scales while turbot do not.

Farthing [Gild the farthing if you will]: A British coin of minimum value, withdrawn from circulation in 1960 (294), it was worth a quarter of a penny (under the old system). "Farthing" means one fourth (56). Bosdêt (43) states that gilding a farthing was a common method of deceiving foreigners and drunks since, if well done, it could easily pass for half a sovereign.

Oracular: An equivocal pronouncement. See also Chapter III.

Once a cat was killed by care: From an old expression, "Hang sorrow — care'll kill a cat." Brewer (54) ascribes this to Ben Jonson's *Everyman in His Humour* (a play produced in 1598). There's a moral: Although a cat has nine lives, care can wear all of them out.

Wink [Wink is often good as nod]: Brewer (54) cites the proverb, "A nod is as good as a wink to a blind horse." This can be taken to mean a hint is useless if the other party does not catch on.

Spoils the child who spares the rod: From the Biblical injunction, "He that spareth the rod hateth his son," or the more recent, but now unfashionable "Spare the rod and spoil the child."

Chapter IV

Lambs [Thirsty lambs run foxy dangers]: This brings to mind Aesop's fable of the lamb who was accosted by a wolf while drinking from a stream. The story ends with the wolf eating the lamb (8, 170). Captain Corcoran is such a ganglion of irreconcilable antagonisms at this point that he can't tell fox from wolf.

Dogs are found in many mangers: This alludes to Aesop's fable about the dog who insisted on napping in the straw that was intended for the ox's meal. The disappointed ox observed that people sometimes begrudge to others what they cannot themselves enjoy.

Paw of cat the chestnut snatches: This alludes to the ancient fable about the monkey who persuaded a cat to pull chestnuts from the fire. The cat burned his paw in so doing, while the monkey ran away and ate the nuts. The term "catspaw" has come to mean someone who is used for another's benefit.

Worn out garments show new patches: Knight (177) recalls the Biblical saying, "No man putteth a piece of new cloth into an old garment."

Only count the chick that hatches: This is from the ancient advice about not counting chickens before they're hatched. Evans (113) says the expression is derived from one of Aesop's fables, although there is also the possibility that the fable was derived from the advice.

Catchy-catchies [Men are grown-up catchy-catchies]: After mouthing a string of platitudes, Corcoran uncorks this mystic expression. Some authorities (21, 149, 286) hypothesize that the term refers to babes in arms. (That's what you say when you toss the kid up and catch him, we hope.) Rees (251) ventures the opinion that the term is derived from what you say when you tickle a baby under the chin: "Kitchi-kitchi." Halton's guess is that the allusion is to a game of tag (147), while Walmisley (299) and Dunn (100) hedge their bets and suggest either alternative. Let's just say men are nothing but oversized kids.

[**Note:** In his children's version (132) Gilbert follows the Captain/Buttercup duet with this comment:

Captain Corcoran — though very uneasy at her portentous utterance — was rather disposed to pat himself on the back for having tackled her on her own ground in the matter of stringing rhymes, and (as he thought) beaten her at it. But, in this he was wrong, for if you compare her lines with his, you will see that whereas her lines dealt exclusively with people and things who were not so important as they thought themselves to be, his lines were merely chopped-up proverbs that had nothing to do with each other or with anything else.]

Dissemble [I'll dissemble]: The OED (229) defines *dissemble* as "To alter or disguise the semblance (of one's character, a feeling, design or action) so as to conceal, or deceive as to, its real nature." I have heard it argued, however, that it should be defined in the narrower sense of pretending that some fact is not true; the opposite, *to feign*, is to pretend that something is true when it is not. For example, Buttercup is dissembling when she hides what she knows about the captain's babyhood: Sir Joseph is feigning when he pretends to be of exalted birth. (That he started his career sweeping floors and polishing handles reveals his humble origins.)

Creep on apace [The hours creep on apace]: Gilbert has fed Josephine an oxymoron to deliver. The OED (229) defines *creep* thus: "To move softly, cautiously, timorously or slowly; to move quietly and stealthily so as to elude observation; to steal." It defines *apace* as "With speed; swiftly, quickly, fast." Consider her extreme youth and forgive her.

"Blue and white" ["Blue and white" Venetian finger glasses]: This presumably refers to the oriental ceramics that were then all the rage in England. But where do "Venetian finger glasses" come in? They were more likely to be red or orange. Stedman (274) and Walters (302) believe there should be a comma after "blue and white." I think they are right.

Finger-glasses: Finger bowls (for rinsing fingers after a meal).

Gillow's [And everything that isn't old, from Gillow's]: A smart London store for furniture and gewgaws. Walters (301) adds that the store is now named Waring and Gillow.

Pudding basin [dinner served up in a pudding basin]: This implies that family members will not eat off individual plates, but will convey food directly from a communal basin to their mouths exactly the way Chekov describes the everyday life of Russian peasants (73). Irish peasants ate that way as well (89).

Brown right hand: This implies an outdoor life indicative of lower class working conditions.

Organs [Where organs yell]: Josephine is complaining about the loud, incessant, and crude decibels arising from a grind organ (sometimes called a barrel organ). For an illustration see the entry for "Organ boys" in Chapter VIII.

Lordship [Though his lordship's station's mighty]: Sir Joseph was First Lord of the Admiralty, a political appointment (245). One must not assume that he was a peer of the realm. He would not be correctly addressed as Lord Porter, or even Lord Porter, K.C.B. Being a social climber, however, he probably did nothing to discourage people from committing that solecism.

Jurisdiction [I admit the jurisdiction]: The bounds of legal authority.

Elysian [The prospect is Elysian]: Delightful. Elysium was the Greek equivalent of Heaven, where "the shades of the virtuous lived a life of passive blessedness" (75).

Cat-o'-nine-tails: A whip made of nine lead-tipped leather thongs joined at a handle. The traditional persuader of the British navy, it was abolished in the Royal Navy in 1879 (201). Bosdêt (43) says the expression "not room enough to swing a cat" refers not to a real cat, but to a cat-o'-nine tails. Brewer, in the 1895 edition (55), says it refers to a once-popular sport of swinging cats by their tails. In the 1970 edition, however, the cat-o'-nine tails version is favored (42). In short, we really don't know. Forgive this digression.

Boat cloak: A long cloak worn by ships' officers.

Pull ashore: Means to pull on the oars and row ashore

Hymen [Hymen will defray the fare]: The Greek god of marriage and nuptial solemnities (75).

Defray: Cover the cost.

Supercilious sneer: A facial expression effected by curling the upper lip or turning up the nose (or both), showing proud and haughty contempt. See also Chapter II.

Meanest [The meanest in the port division]: The lowest in rank or pecking order.

Port division Presumably refers to the port watch. Ship's crews were in those days divided into two groups for alternating work. These were called the port and starboard watches.

Epauletted scorn [The butt of epauletted scorn]: The term is one coined by Gilbert to mean the scorn shown by ships' officers. Epaulettes are those shoulder decorations, usually with tassels, worn on naval officers' uniforms.

Quarter-deck derision [The mark of quarter-deck derision]: This refers to the sneers of officers.

Mould [Above the dust to which you'd mould me/him]: Cast down.

Roosian, Proosian, and Itali-an: These mis-pronunciations may be interpreted as typical British disdain, if not contempt, for "them furriners."

Reprobation [In uttering a reprobation]: A scolding, or good chewing-out.

Damme {Rhymes with clammy.} [Why, damme, it's too bad!]: A contraction of damn me! (Shocking!)

Ribald {Rhymes with nibbled.} [Go, ribald, get you hence]: A vulgar person who uses coarse language.

Celerity [To your cabin with celerity]: Haste. Contrary to popular rumor, celerity is not a young woman. Note lower case c.

Chapter IV

Fo'c'sle {FOKE-sill} [love burns as brightly in the fo'c'sle]: Correctly fo'c's'le: the sailors' usual way of speaking of a forecastle, a raised deck in the bow of a ship. In medieval ships the forecastle was an elevated platform in the bow from which archers could shoot at the enemy. Protection was afforded by a wooden bulwark (wall) on which shields were often hung. Extending somewhat above the bulwarks, the collective shields resembled the castellated top of a castle wall, hence the term "forecastle." See Item No. 1 on the next page.

Fell [with this sailor fell]: Villainous.

Telephone: Bell invented the device in 1876. The first London exchange opened two months after the opera opened (7).

Baby-farming [I practiced baby-farming]: Collins (75) defines a baby farmer as "one who, for a fee, accepts on a relatively large scale the care of infants but is indifferent as to their welfare." Wilson (320) maintains that Buttercup could not be accused of being "indifferent as to their welfare." He notes that "except for her one great carelessness, Buttercup seems quite an affectionate, matronly sort of woman." Wilson is probably right in defending Buttercup, but Kanthor (169) produces evidence that baby farmers, in general, had a thoroughly rotten reputation. Knight (178) believes most of the babies were illegitimate.

Nussed [Two tender babes I nussed]: Buttercup's way of pronouncing *nursed* to make it rhyme with *crust*. Gypsy blood makes one a natural poet, or poetess, as the case may be. Or at least it confers poetic license. (Actually, *nuss* was a commonly used pronunciation among the lower classes of that period.)

TWO TENDER BABES I NUSSED

Patrician: A person of noble birth.

Waif: A homeless or neglected child.

A PLUMP & PLEASING PERSON

ALWAYS READY for a KNOCKDOWN BLOW

H.M.S. Pinafore

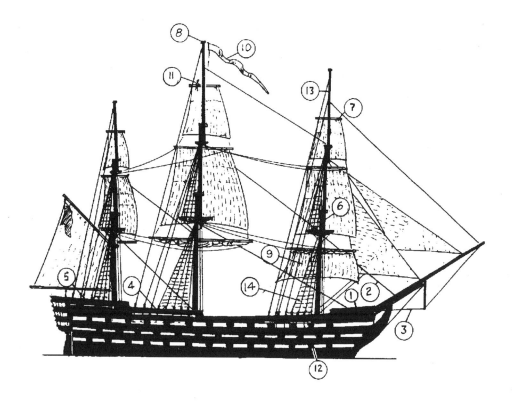

Some Nautical Terms

1. Fo'c's'le
2. Forestay
3. Bobstay
4. Quarterdeck
5. Poop deck
6. Fore mast
7. Foremast yard arm
8. Main truck
9. Reefed sail
10. Pennant
11. Topman
12. Gun port
13. To'gall'n'm'st
14. Shrouds

THE PIRATES OF PENZANCE

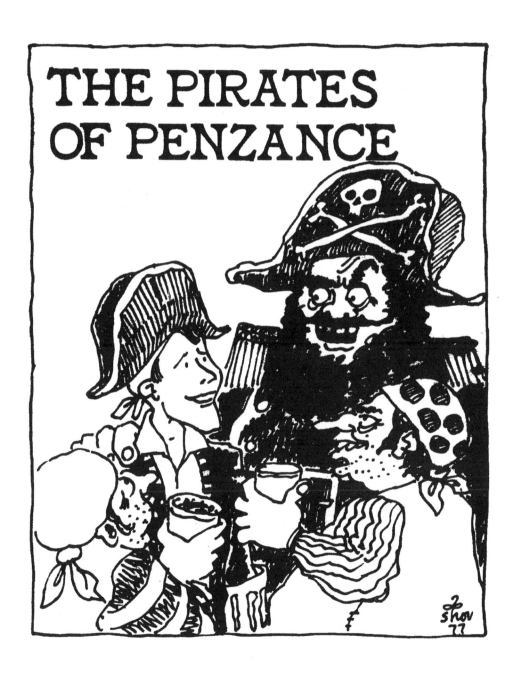

Chapter V The Pirates of Penzance

During the initial run of *H.M.S. Pinafore*, Carte clashed with his backers, and the Comedy Opera Company was dissolved — with hard feelings on both sides. Carte formed a partnership with Gilbert and Sullivan and the triumvirate went on to produce *The Pirates of Penzance*. Ever since *Pinafore*, the company had been distressed by American entrepreneurs who had been producing unauthorized Gilbert and Sullivan operas without paying royalties. Carte decided the best way to solve that problem would be to open their new show in New York rather than London. So the trio came to New York and opened *The Pirates of Penzance* at the Fifth Avenue Theater on December 31, 1879. The opera opened in London's Opera Comique the following spring and had a run of 363 performances — considerably less well received than its predecessor but still a great success.

The story line satirizes the Victorian proclivity toward an excessive devotion to duty, even when such devotion leads to ridiculous actions. This illustrates another Gilbertian brand of humor: the ultimate result of carrying a good thing too far. Sullivan's music is generally described as a parody of Italian opera, nowhere better illustrated than in the famous number where the pirates belt out "With cat-like tread, upon our prey we steal," as they stomp across the stage.

CHARACTERS AND SETTING

Penzance: Even in Gilbert's time this was a well-known resort town on the southwest tip of England, equivalent perhaps to America's Cape Cod.

Major-General: A British army officer of the lowest grade of general officers, ranking just below a lieutenant-general (229). Stone (284) mentions that in the U.S. Army the rank of brigadier general is yet lower than that of major general.

Cornwall: A county in the extreme southwestern corner of England, known for its rocky, picturesque coast.

ACT I

Sherry: A fortified Spanish wine made from grape juice twice fermented. This seems a rather elegant beverage for a band of cutthroats, but it has the virtue of rhyming with merry. Walters (302) suggests that "pirate sherry" may really have been rum. On the other hand, Kravetz (182) and Turnbull (294) think that Gilbert is hinting at what is revealed in the end, which is that the pirates are all noblemen who have gone wrong. Drinking out of glasses is another clue. Kravetz also suggests that their being noblemen explains why they never attack a party weaker than themselves. Not cricket, you know.

Bumper [Let the pirate bumper pass]: A glass or mug so full that, courtesy of surface tension, it bumps up in the middle (56).

'Prentice [For today our pirate 'prentice]: Apprentice; one bound to a master for a given period to learn a trade or art.

OUR PIRATE 'PRENTICE

Indenture [Rises from indenture freed]: A service contract. In days of yore, before copy machines changed our lives, contracts were written and signed in duplicate on the same parchment, which was then torn, or cut in a zig-zag line, down the middle, each half going to one of the signers. The indentations could later be used to prove that the two parts belonged together — which explains how

Chapter V

contracts came to be called "indentures." Isn't this exciting?

Scent [Strong his arm and keen his scent is]: Samuel is referring to Frederic's sense of smell, not his lack of personal daintiness. Hyder (161) opines that reference is being made to Frederic's skill in sniffing out treasure-laden ships.

Scuttling [a keener hand at scuttling a Cunarder or cutting out a P. & O. never shipped a handspike]: Deliberately sinking a ship by knocking holes in her bottom.

Cunarder: A ship of the Cunard fleet, presumably a passenger liner.

Cutting out: To isolate and capture or destroy one ship of a fleet.

P. & O.: A ship of the Peninsular and Oriental line, presumably a passenger liner.

White Star: A well-known steamship line later associated with the ill-fated *Titanic*. This term is used rather than "P. & O." in the first night edition (3).

Handspike: A wooden pole used as a lever, usually in a capstan. To ship a handspike means to insert it into the capstan. (A capstan is a reel on a vertical axis, used to pull in lines.)

Pilot: A person qualified to guide a ship entering or leaving a harbor.

Breakers [on breakers always steering]: Waves distorted by shallow water, as over a reef or close to shore. Read: always making disastrous mistakes.

Hear, hear!: An Englishman's expression of approval or even approbation. Brewer (55) explains that at one time disapproval of a speaker was indicated by humming. To offset that, those in favor of the speaker cried "Hear him," which eventually became "Hear, hear!" See also Chapters VII, IX, and XVI.

Mercantile navy: The totality of a nation's ships and seafarers engaged in commerce, more commonly called the merchant marine.

Top of the tide [Well, it's the top of the tide and we must be off]: High tide. Getting a sailing ship out of port is greatly eased if you wait until the tide is running out, which phenomenon invariably occurs shortly after high tide.

Sally [sally forth]: To set out on a voyage or excursion.

Circumspect: Taking regard of all aspects of a situation. In short, prudent.

Custom House [Can it be Custom House?]: This refers to the customs bureau, charged with collecting import or export taxes. (It is somewhat equivalent to the U.S. or Canadian Coast Guards, but includes on-shore patrols.)

Dower [What is such a dower]: Contribution of wealth (or, in this case, affection) a woman brings to a marriage.

Take heart of grace: Brewer (54) defines this as meaning to pluck up your courage. It may be based on Paul's teaching that we should rely on God's grace (His freely granted favors) for strength. Moral courage was at one time believed to reside in the heart (55).

Lowers {Rhymes with cowers.} [Take heart; no danger lowers]: Threatens.

Tether [Free them from their tether]: A rope or chain to keep an animal from getting away. Figuratively: "Give them their freedom."

Glass [The glass is rising]: Barometer.

Pianissimo [the Girls continue chatter *pianissimo*]: Very softly.

Homely duty: Domestic life.

The Pirates of Penzance

Felicity: Contentment.

Parsonified, conjugally matrimonified: Some of Gilbert's finest creations, which you may interpret as referring to marriage before a parson. These serve to remind us of Bierce's definition of *marriage*: "The state or condition of a community consisting of a master, a mistress and two slaves, making in all, two" (39).

Doctor of divinity: A person who has earned the highest educational degree in theology. See also Chapter III.

Caravanserai [Ere your pirate caravanserai proceed, against our will, to wed us all]: A strongly protected Arabian hostelry with a large courtyard for caravan beasts of burden. Perhaps the best interpretation we can place on it is to call it a poetically embroidered form of *caravan* — which we can interpret broadly as a gathering of wayfarers, in this case piratical rovers. We may also suspect that Gilbert was digging deep for something (anything!) to rhyme with *Wards in Chancery*.

Wards in Chancery: Wards of the Court of Chancery, i.e., persons under that court's protection. This perhaps explains why Major-General Stanley could be the father of so many lovely girls all between the ages of 18 and 22. How he managed to have this charming collection farmed out to him has never been explained. Bradley (48) advances what seems to me to be a rather unlikely hypothesis; but you may look it up if you're curious.

Marathon [From Marathon to Waterloo]: In 490 B.C. the Athenians and Spartans defeated the Persian army in a decisive battle on a plain near the village of Marathon, about 26 miles north-east of Athens.

Waterloo: Napoleon met his final defeat in 1815 in a battle against British and Prussian forces just south of the Flemish town of Waterloo.

[**Note:** The allusion here is to Creasy's book, *The Fifteen Decisive Battles of the World from Marathon to Waterloo* (81), first published in 1851.]

Categorical [in order categorical]: According to type or class. Creasy presents his fifteen battles in chronological order, so the major-general has seemingly taken the trouble to rearrange them by type (e.g., naval vs land) before committing them to memory.

Equations, both the simple and quadratical: A simple equation is one in the form of $Y = aX + b$, where Y is the unknown value, X is a variable value, and a and b are fixed values. For example if you want to convert a temperature reading from centigrade to Fahrenheit, you would use this simple equation:

> Degrees Fahrenheit = (9/5) times (degrees centigrade) + 32.

A quadratic equation is one in which the highest power of the unknown quantity is a square. *Quadratical* is a Gilbertian original term, but his meaning is clear.

Binomial theorem: A *theorem* is a mathematical statement that can be proven to be true. A *binomial* is an algebraic expression containing two terms joined by a plus or minus sign. A + B and A - B are two examples. The *binomial theorem* is a general equation for finding the product of a binomial expression multiplied by itself any number of times.

Hypotenuse: A *hypotenuse* is the longest leg of a right triangle, i.e,. the one across from the 90 degree corner. The "many cheerful facts" alludes to the Greek philosopher and mathematician Pythagoras (582-507 B.C.) and his theorem, which states that you can find the square of (the length of) the hypotenuse by summing the squares of the lengths of the other two sides.

Integral and differential calculus: The calculus is a useful branch of mathematics that approaches problems by considering the behavior of small increments of the object under study. Integral calculus finds cumulative values such as areas or volumes. Differential calculus deals in differences in values such as rates of change. For a comprehensive exposition, see Asimov (11).

Chapter V

Beings animalculous: Adjective form of *animalcule*: a minute or microscopic animal. Antonie van Leeuwenhoek, who first observed bacteria, called them *animalcules* (little animals) (89).

Sir Caradoc: The name Caradoc and variations such as Caradog and Garadue are not uncommon in various British encyclopedias (93, 103, 104, 223, 288). In the context, however, the exceptionally valorous Sir Caradoc of King Arthur's round table is the strongest candidate.

Acrostics [I answer hard acrostics]: A composition, often in verse, in which the first (or perhaps last) letters of the lines form a word or phrase when taken in order. Brewer (54) explains that the word comes from the Greek *akros* for outermost, and *stichos* for line of verse. We are sure Major-General Stanley knew this, and so you should, too.

Paradox [I've a pretty taste for paradox]: A statement that sounds self-contradictory or absurd, and yet is in fact correct.

Elegiacs {ell-eh-JIE-acks} [I quote in elegiacs all the crimes of Heliogabalus]: Stedman (273) kindly provides this definition and commentary — with guidance from the OED (228): "This refers to the classical verse form, the elegiac, in which elegies (mournful verses) were written. The elegiac distich consisted of an hexameter and a pentameter, and the metre was dactylic. So it is appropriate for the major-general, because it is classical and also relatively difficult and abstruse; but I suppose he had a classics master at school who made him put things into elegiac verse!" Cameron (66) adds that setting a passage into Latin elegiacs was a standard exercise for English schoolboys. Dealing with the life and fate of Heliogabalus was no doubt considered a cautionary lesson. But press on.

Heliogabalus: Roman emperor A.D. 218-222. His name is also spelled *Elagabalus*. He imposed the worship of false idols upon the Roman world, appointed misfits to high office, and executed more than his share of dissident generals. Above all, he outraged public opinion with his openly homosexual orgies. He was killed by the Praetorian Guards after a short but newsworthy reign.

See the paragraph on the fellow in Chapter XIII. More crimes exposed to the public gaze!

Conics {Rhymes with tonics.} [In conics I can floor peculiarities parabolous]: Study of the geometric properties of a cone cut by imaginary planes (i.e., parabolas, circles, ellipses, and hyperbolas).

Floor: To conquer, as in wrestling.

Parabolous: Pertaining to parabolas. Gilbert's variation on *parabolic*.

Raphaels [I can tell undoubted Raphaels from Gerard Dows and Zoffanies]: Paintings by the Italian master Santi Raphael (1483-1520). Some of his murals adorn the Vatican. He is looked upon as the first of the great religious painters. Some Victorians looked upon him as a symbol of the start of the decline of art. Our next chapter has more to say about how they revolted against his influence.

Gerard Dows: Dutch painter from Leyden (1613-75). A student of Rembrandt, famous for his rich coloring and excellence of detail. *Dow* is an anglicized version of his real name: *Dou*. Stedman (274) comments that his paintings were not at all like Raphael's.

Zoffanies: Johann Zoffany (properly *Zaufelby*): Bavarian-turned-British painter (1733-1810). One of the original members of Britain's Royal Academy, founded in 1769.

The *Frogs* [the croaking chorus from the *Frogs* of Aristophanes]: A witty comedy produced in 405 B.C. in Athens. The framework for the story involves the god Dionysus's descent into hell to find a competent poet, there being none left on earth. This leads to a comical competition between the shades of Aeschylus and Euripides, each finding fault with the other's works. This competition inspires much ribald commentary from Dionysus. "The whole is enlivened by the grotesque costumes and the *brek-ke-ke-ke coax* refrain from the chorus of frogs, whose original habitat was the precinct of Dionysius in the marshes" (105). Now you, too, know something about the croaking chorus from the *Frogs* of Aristophanes. How many of your neighbors can make that claim?

Aristophanes: Greek writer of satiric plays, some more ribald than others. He lived around 450-380 B.C.

Fugue: Let me avoid this thicket by quoting Elson (102): "It is a composition in the strict style, in which a subject is proposed by one part and answered by other parts, according to certain rules." By *subject* he means a musical theme (tune). By *parts* he means different musical instruments or singers. The major-general, you may be sure, could not by himself do justice to a fugue by humming. But, who among the pirate band was about to challenge him on that delicate point?

Washing bill [I can write a washing bill in Babylonic cuneiform]: A laundry list.

Cuneiform: Wedge-shaped writing (on clay tablets) of ancient Babylon, etc. It is possible that the reference was inspired by an exhibition of Egyptian and Assyrian antiquities that had recently been exhibited by Sir Henry Creswicke Rawlinson (207).

Caractacus: An early British king who fought a series of delaying battles against the Roman invaders in the first century A.D. Whether he ever wore a uniform is open to considerable doubt (302). Bradley (48) avers that his usual battle dress was simply body paint. His final defeat, in A.D. 47, led to his capture. Taken before the Roman emperor Claudius, his eloquence won him his pardon. His children became Christians and introduced that religion into Britain.

There is some confusion about his name. Bradley (46) says *Caractacus* was the Roman translation of the British name *Caradoc* (but not to be confused with the Sir Caradoc of Arthurian legend mentioned earlier in the song). Perhaps it is a coincidence, but his final defeat occurred "probably at Caer Caradoc," in the region of Shropshire (105). Further light (or is it shadow?) is cast by *The Encyclopædia Britannica* (104), which insists that the name should be spelled *Caratacus*. I have a feeling this is more than you really thirsted to learn.

Mamelon [when I know what is meant by "mamelon" and "ravelin"]: A hillock or mound, presumably a low earthen wall or fort, in the present context. Brewer (56) defines it as a mound in the shape of a woman's breast, making this perhaps the raciest word in the entire canon.

Ravelin: A detached outer-work for protecting the ramparts of a fort.

Mauser rifle: A firearm featuring a repeating magazine. It was invented by a German, Paul von Mauser (105), and was used by the Prussian army (48).

Chassepôt rifle {SHAHS-POE} (A term used rather than "Mauser rifle" in earlier editions): A French Army rifle introduced in 1866 (89).

Sorties [When such affairs as sorties and surprises]: A sortie is a sudden movement of troops from a besieged place to attack the besiegers.

Surprises: Sudden attacks without warning.

"Commissariat": The army's supply department.

Tactics: The science of positioning military units to best advantage against an enemy. From the Greek phrase *ta taktika*, meaning matters of arrangement (266).

Sat a gee [You'll say a better Major-General has never *sat* a gee]: Stedman (273) assures us that in nineteenth-century England "gee" was a commonly used slang word for horse. Farmer and Henley (115) say the same. Walters (301) adds that in England "gee-gee" is still a popular children's word for a horse. Expressions such as "sat a horse with skill" were not uncommon a hundred years ago (208). So "sat a gee" simply means rode a horse.

Malediction: A curse. Quite the opposite, we can assure you, of the benediction you receive in church.

Valedictory: A farewell.

[**Note:** The last two terms are from a verse that was supposedly used on opening night (3) but which has since been dropped. It is sung by the pirates after the major-general sings about telling a terrible story:

Chapter V

If he's telling a terrible story,
He shall die by a death that is gory —
One of the cruelest slaughters
That ever was known in these waters;
And we'll finish his moral affliction
By a very complete malediction,
As a compliment valedictory,
If he's telling a terrible story.]

For what, we ask, is life ... : You don't need to have those words explained; I merely want to call to your attention the presence of those commas around *we ask*. A good lesson here on the importance of punctuation and careful proofreading..

Gildest [Thou gildest e'en the pirate's trade]: Make more attractive.

Emollient: Something that soothes or assuages — like reading this book.

Auspiciously [Should it befall auspiciously]: Under favorable circumstances. Abundantly propitious.

Dimity [We display to lace and dimity]: A thin cotton fabric reinforced with corded stripes, popular for dressmaking in those days. The allusion, of course, is to the ladies who wear "lace and dimity." The word comes from the Greek *dimitos*, meaning double thread (55).

ACT II

Martial [that martial cheek]: Military or warlike.

Darksome [darksome dangers]: The OED (229) says this is "now chiefly a poetic synonym of *dark*, of vaguer connotation." (I dare say you might have guessed.)

Escutcheon [for having brought dishonour on the family escutcheon]: A family shield displaying heraldic insignia.

Tarantara: Simulated sound of a trumpet. In a letter to Sullivan dated August 6, 1879, Gilbert explained that the word serves as a "talisman" to help the police maintain their courage. (The stage directions instruct the policemen to hold up their truncheons to imitate trumpets or bugles when they sing the word) (181).

Emeutes {eh-MUTES} [For when threatened with emeutes]: From the French word *émeutes*, meaning riots.

Heart in boots {BEUTS} [And your heart is in your boots]: In low spirits. Brewer (56) says the expression suggests that your heart or spirits have sunk into your boots allowing you to run away.

Cornish [and every Cornish daughter]: Pertaining to Cornwall, the county in which Penzance is located.

Alloy [mercy should alloy]: Diminish or make less extreme.

Cranks [For cranks and contradictions queer]: Twists of language. Example: A cross-eyed cyclops. Most meanings of *crank* pertain to something bent (266).

The Pirates of Penzance

Astronomer Royal: "Official title of the head of the Greenwich Observatory, established 1675" (75). Bradley (46) says the title has not been used since 1972.

Tremorden Castle: General Stanley's baronial mansion. Bradley (48) says, "This is a fictitious location, but a perfectly plausible name for a place in Cornwall. The Cornish word *tre* means hamlet or homestead and is found at the beginning of many place names in the county." One example is pointed out by Aurora (18): Trematon Castle, near Saltash, in Cornwall.

Dire [my vengeance dire]: Horrible, dreadful, calamitous, disastrous, threatening, formidable, or immoderately fierce. (How can such a short word have so many elongated synonyms?)

Roundelay [This joyous roundelay]: Originally a round or country dance, the term has come to mean a short, simple song (273).

Sooth [He will be faithful to his sooth]: Pledge.

Family descent: Pride and sense of honor arising from a long and distinguished family heritage.

Constabulary [constabulary duty]: Pertains to *constable*. The term has several meanings all concerning the maintenance of law and civil order.

Coster [When the coster's finished jumping on his mother]: *Coster* is usually defined as short for *costermonger*: a street vendor of fruit, fish, vegetables, and so forth. The examples of usage shown in the OED (229) strongly imply that costermongers enjoyed a reputation for uncouth, bullying behavior.

Knight (177) calls attention to the line from Shakespeare's *Henry VI*: "Virtue is of so little regard in these costermonger times." Samuel Johnson, in his 1756 dictionary (165), defines *coster-monger* as a seller of apples. Bosdêt (43) says they originally sold only French apples, which were far juicier than English apples and enjoyed a much longer shelf life. But, I wander.

Rollicking: Carefree, boisterous , and hearty. See also Chapters III and VI.

Poaching [on the manor poaching]: To poach means to trespass onto another's property to take game or fish without permission. Here we can interpret it as meaning to encroach or invade. The *manor* would be the grounds of Tremorden Castle.

Plate [We are not coming for plate or gold]: Objects such as tableware made of precious metal. See also Chapter XII.

Crowbar [Here's your crowbar and your centrebit]: A heavy metal rod, tapered and bent at one end, and used to force open doors or windows.

Centrebit: A device used to cut out circular plugs in wood or metal. Bradley (48) suggests that burglars use such tools to cut holes in doors, thus allowing the burglar to reach through and release internal locks or bolts.

Life-preserver [Your life-preserver — you may want to hit!]: Brewer (54) says this is "a loaded short stick for self-defence." In his Sherlock Holmes story "The Adventure of the Beryl Coronet," Conan Doyle mentions someone who "took down a life-preserver from the wall" (in order to intimidate the intrepid detective). The incident is shown in an illustration that appeared when the story was first published. It shows a club a little over a foot long with about a three-inch diameter knob on the working end (96). Three of Gilbert's revised Bab Ballad cartoons show robbers equipped with similar weapons (126). A copy of one is shown below. In his Bab Ballad "Gentle Alice Brown" Gilbert includes these lines: "He took a life-preserver and he hit him on the head / And Mrs Brown dissected him before she went to bed." Given that clue, I would argue

Chapter V

with Brewer about their function being confined to self-defense. They were perhaps called "life-preservers" because they could stun a victim without killing him — equivalent to a blackjack. Halton's view is much the same, except that he mentions a flexible shaft (147).

Silent matches: Friction matches as we know them have gone through many evolutionary developments since their invention in the early 1800s. Until the 1860s all matches had an unfortunate tendency to ignite with a tiny explosion, often spewing about bits of burning phosphorus. The most effusive specimens were referred to as "sneezy" matches. The problem was first solved, apparently, by an Austrian firm. Their matches were "distinguished above all others for excellence of quality and elegance of form, as well as for their ready inflammability, noiseless regular combustion, without scattering of the inflammable mass" (95). Not too long thereafter, the Diamond Match Company in the United States offered for sale a new variety of match called "Lu-Mets: The new silent lighters — Heads don't fly —Contain no phosphorus" (53). That is presumably the sort of thing Gilbert had in mind when he has Samuel pass out "silent matches."

Dark lantern: A portable light source with a sliding shutter for confining the emission of light.

Skeletonic key: Refers to a skeleton key: one "with part of the webs filed away, designed to open or pick a lock by avoiding the impending wards" (75).

Falsehood unatoned: A barefaced lie.

Dale: Valley, or at least a low place between hills.

Rover [Yet, the breeze is but a rover]: Strictly speaking, one who wanders. In this case a fickle flirt.

Doing and undoing: The expression can have many meanings. Asimov (11) suggests that it means cheating and seducing. He may be right, but apparently the censorious Lord Chamberlain took a more benevolent view, perhaps something akin to kiss and tell.

Rogue [That the rogue could tell]: The word has many interpretations ranging from a mischievous rascal down through a sly knave or cheat. In the context I think "sly knave" is about right.

Peignoirs: Dressing gowns.

Unshriven [Is he to die, unshriven — unannealed?]: Unconfessed and unabsolved.

Unannealed: Without having received extreme unction (i.e., last rites).

Trow [for well we trow]: Believe.

Central Criminal Court: Pirates, fittingly enough, would be brought to trial under admiralty law. In England those cases were tried at the Central Criminal Court, more commonly known as "Old Bailey," at the corner of Old Bailey and Newgate Streets in

The Pirates of Penzance

central London. See Goodman (140) for details.

Mien [with humbled mien]: Demeanor, appearance, or general bearing.

Bar [Away with them, and place them at the bar]: Take them to court and confine them in the dock (142).

Hymeneally [Hymeneally coupled, conjugally matrimonified]: Married, after Hymen, the god of marriage. This is from the closing scene as presented on opening night (3) but now seldom used.

House of Peers: A peer is "a member of any of the five degrees of nobility in Great Britain and Ireland, namely duke, marquis, earl, viscount, and baron" (250). The House of Peers, more usually known as the House of Lords, is one of Britain's two legislative bodies, the other (and more influential) being the House of Commons. All English peers of age 21 or older are qualified to sit in the House of Lords. In Gilbert's day only limited numbers of peers from Ireland and Scotland were qualified (245). (At the present time the House finds itself being pushed toward drastic reform.)

PATIENCE

Chapter VI Patience

For his next libretto, *Patience*, Gilbert chose to poke fun at the "aesthetic" craze that had then been in vogue in England for a couple of decades. For full enjoyment of the work you should know something about the aesthetic movement. Its progenitors included William Morris (poet and designer), Edward Burne-Jones (painter), James Whistler (painter), Dante Gabriel Rossetti (poet and artist), and Algernon Swinburne (poet). They formed a closely-knit group with uniform convictions about the dreary constraints of Victorian art, design, and literature — and the new direction in which they ought to steer it. They elevated the search for beauty above all other aims in life and thus came to be referred to collectively as "the aesthetes." The writers sought freedom from stuffiness and extreme respectability. The painters wanted to rescue art from the traditions of the Renaissance religious painter Raphael, whose style still influenced accepted artists of the day. They sought inspiration in earlier, romantic themes, often with story-telling composition enhanced with elaborate decorative detail. It was this harking back to earlier styles of art that gave them the popular name "Pre-Raphaelites," a designation that was often applied to the writers as well.

The aesthetes were unquestionably talented. Their free-thinking proclivities, however, often led to bizarre affectations in attire, speech, and life style. Moreover, they attracted a large following of admirers who mimicked their superficial behavior but lacked the talent to emulate their commendable works. Gilbert's jibes were not directed at the talented work of the aesthetes. Rather, they were directed at their eccentric affectations and, most of all, at their ranks of mindless admirers.

At the time Gilbert was writing the libretto, Oscar Wilde, a recent Oxford graduate, was determined to make a name for himself as an aesthete. He carried the bizarre features to new extremes and probably served in part as one of Gilbert's targets. His advocacy of knee breeches for men and Grecian costumes for women is still reflected in most productions of the opera. He became strongly identified with the opera, especially when D'Oyly Carte paid him to go on a lecture tour of North America so the American public would know what the fun was all about.

Nevertheless, each of the aesthetic poets in *Patience* appears to bear characteristics attributable to several of the Pre-Raphaelite brotherhood, as well as to Oscar Wilde.

You should also know that for a period during his work on the opera, Gilbert intended to feature two rival curates (based on his Bab Ballad *The Rival Curates*) rather than two rival poets (272). Traces of those clergymen are still to be found in the libretto.

For a nicely summarized explanation of the aesthetic movement and *Patience*, see Williamson (318). For more complete expositions see Fido (119), Ellmann (101), Beerbohm (32), Stedman (272), Forty (120), and Von Eckardt (297).

The opera opened at the Opera Comique on April 23, 1881. The following October 10 it was transferred to a new theater, the Savoy, which Carte had designed and built specifically for the Gilbert and Sullivan operas. This was the first theater to be illuminated throughout by electricity, although a gaslight system was also included just in case the new gadgetry should fail. (The theater still stands, and has recently been rebuilt after a disastrous fire.) *Patience* was well received and ran for 578 performances.

Although *Patience* was highly topical, it has remained popular because the affectations satirized in the opera live on today in the arts, in politics, and in nearly every walk of life. Gilbert's memorial on the Thames Embankment carries the words "His foe was folly and his weapon wit." That was never more true than when he wrote *Patience*.

CHARACTERS AND SETTING

Dragoon Guards: Cavalry soldiers. According to the OED (229) the term is derived from *dragon* because the soldiers were originally equipped with an early form of musket that "breathed fire like a dragon." Another source (6) says the term arose because the pistol hammers were shaped something like dragons. In any event, when first formed, dragoon guards were infantrymen who did their fighting on foot, but rode horses for quick deployment. Bierce (39) defines a dragoon as "A soldier who combines dash and steadiness in so equal measure that he makes his advances on foot and his retreats

Chapter VI

on horseback." Like the Duke of Plaza-Toro. *The Encyclopædia Britannica* (103) explains that the scheme of alternating between horse and foot eventually developed into all-horse-back operations, i.e., cavalry. Cavalry units were of three types: heavy, medium, and light, each suited to its own special duties. At one end of the scale large men on large horses formed the heavy cavalry and they were often called heavy dragoons, hence "Dragoon Guards." See also Chapter III.

Duke [The Duke of Dunstable]: The highest order of nobility in Britain's peerage. The word derives from the Latin words for a leader: *dux*, or *duc* (266).

Dunstable {DUNST-ible}: A market town in a southern corner of Bedfordshire, north of London. At the time the opera was written, Dunstable was known as a center for printing and straw hats.

Fleshly [*a Fleshly Poet*]: Fleshly can mean corporeal, corpulent, gross, or sensual. We can assume that Gilbert meant that Bunthorne (or at least his poetry) was sensual, i.e., carnal — in a Victorian way—as opposed to the idyllic poetry of Grosvenor; whereas the term when later applied to the Dragoon Guards ("They are fleshly men of full habit!") surely implies *gross*. Under the entry "The Fleshly School" in Brewer (54) we read of Robert Buchanan's violent published attack on the poetry and literary methods of Swinburne, Rossetti, Morris, and others of their ilk. Buchanan apparently coined the term, with Rossetti particularly in mind.

Grosvenor {GROVE-nerr}: Bunthorne's rival, Grosvenor, takes his name from a London art gallery that opened in 1877 and became famous for its association with the aesthetes. More on this later.

Idyllic {ih-DILL-ick} [*an Idyllic Poet*]: An idyll may be, among other things, a poem or narrative of simple perfection and loveliness.

Solicitor [Mr. Bunthorne's Solicitor]: A legal advisor. In England there are two classes of lawyers: barristers and solicitors — all of which is explained under the heading "Barrister" in Chapter II.

ACT I

Concords [To weeping concords tune thy roundelay!]: Harmonies.

Roundelay: An air or tune in three parts, in which the first strain is repeated in the others (75).

Cynosure {SIGN-oh-sure or SIN-oh-sure} [the very cynosure of our eyes and hearts]: Center of devotion. Brewer (54) says the term derives from the name of the North Star. Cameron (66) explains that *cynosure* is the Greek word for "dog's tail," which was the ancient name for the constellation Ursa Minor, or the Little Dipper. As you may recall, the end of the Little Dipper's handle is the North Star.

For the nonce: For the moment; i.e., temporarily. See also Chapters VIII and XI.

Transcendentality [There is a transcendentality of delirium]: Pertaining to a condition of being abstruse, mystical, and perhaps with an intuitive feeling for divine truths. Remember that the aesthetes held that beauty transcended all other considerations in life.

Transfiguration [it is aesthetic transfiguration.]: A change in external appearance, from being plain or ugly to being radiant or beautiful, or both.

Full habit [They are fleshly men, of full habit!]: This can be interpreted as gross men of vulgar tastes: boors, oafs, and lumpkins. Hyder (161) says that "of full habit" is an old expression meaning fat. This is borne out in Captain Marryat's novel *Peter Simple* (200) in which a 250-pound man is described as having a "full habit of body."

Etherealized [our tastes have been etherealized.]: Rendered spiritual and attuned to celestial philosophies.

[**Note:** The next 51 entries are from the Colonel's song "If you want a receipt." If you are in a hurry you can skip right past them and not miss a thing as far as understanding the plot is concerned. Look for the row of asterisks on page 71.]

Receipt: An older term for a cooking recipe. The word was also used to indicate a list of medical ingredients (217).

Heavy Dragoon [Known to the world as a Heavy Dragoon]: See "Dragoon Guards" under Characters and Setting at the start of the chapter.

Lord Nelson [The pluck of Lord Nelson on board of the *Victory*]: Vice-Admiral Lord Viscount Horatio Nelson (1758-1805): English naval hero. Under his command British naval forces inflicted a major defeat on the French and Spanish fleets off Cape Trafalgar in 1805. Nelson, who lost his life in the battle, is memorialized by a statue on an exceedingly tall pedestal in London's Trafalgar Square.

Victory: Nelson's flagship at Trafalgar, and still preserved as a museum ship at Portsmouth. To G&S fans she is best known as the prototype for *H.M.S. Pinafore*. Gilbert and Sullivan visited the *Victory* in 1878 and Gilbert made sketches of the rigging and deck arrangements for his forthcoming nautical opera.

Bismarck [Genius of Bismarck]: Otto von Bismarck (1815-98): the creator and first chancellor of the newly united German Empire (1871). Before the "Iron Chancellor's" time, the German people were divided among what Winston Churchill described as "pumpernickel principalities."

Fielding [The humour of Fielding — which sounds contradictory]: Nearly all writers on the subject propose that this refers to Henry Fielding (1707-54), a London magistrate, playwright, and novelist, best known for his novel *Tom Jones*. Since his literary works contain a considerable measure of wit, why did

Gilbert imply there was something contradictory about Fielding's humor? Dunn (100), Hardwick (149) and Prestige (245) opine that Gilbert was making a pun on the term "fielding" as used in the game of cricket, and which is not considered much fun. (It is roughly equivalent to playing in the outfield in baseball.) Turnbull, for his part, thinks Gilbert simply wanted a word to rhyme with *Victory* (294).

Paget [Coolness of Paget about to trepan]: Sir James Paget (1814-99), a British surgeon and pathologist who taught at St Bartholomew's Hospital in London (77).

Trepan: To cut a circular plug out of someone's skull, preferably not your own.

Jullien [the eminent musico]: Virtually everyone who has essayed to define the colonel's catalog (100, 147, 149, 177, 273, 281, 286, 299) agrees that this refers to Louis Antoine Jullien (1812-60), an eccentric and flamboyant conductor whose parents loaded him down with 41 names. Born in France, he emigrated to England to escape his creditors. There he organized an orchestra and produced many promenade concerts, a concept that he originated. Berlioz (38) refers to Jullien's "incontestable and uncontested character of madness." His portly form and gorgeous waistcoats were often the butt of *Punch* cartoons. We also learn that "he would conduct Beethoven symphonies with a jewelled baton, and wearing a new pair of white gloves presented to him on a silver salver" (93). He finally returned to France but was thrown into debtors' prison, where he soon died, insane. In his 1890 book *Songs of a Savoyard* (130), Gilbert substituted this line: "The grace of Mozart, that unparalleled musico." Stedman (274) doesn't like the change. She says Jullien's flashy, shallow character more closely reflects that of the dragoons. Nevertheless, it would make sense to use his revised lines in modern performances because Mozart's name is known to everyone, while old Whatsisname's is not. But, while you are at it, make it read "The grace of a Mozart, unparalleled musico" so it will scan.

Musico: One definition in the OED (229) is a musician, and that is probably what Gilbert meant.

Chapter VI

Macaulay [Wit of Macaulay, who wrote of Queen Anne]: Thomas Babington Macaulay (1800-59), distinguished English writer and statesman. Although his writings were formidable, he did manage to turn some neat, witty phrases. Here, for example are lines from a letter to a Mr. Ellis dated September 3, 1850: "Dear Ellis, Here I am lodged most delightfully... I wish that I may not, like Will Honeycomb, forget the sin and sea-coal of London for innocence and haycocks. To be sure, innocence and haycocks do not always go together" (292). The reference to Queen Anne is either Gilbert's little joke or a dead giveaway that he never finished reading Macaulay's great history. At the very start of his monumental series *The History of England* (192), Macaulay stated that his aim was "to write the history of England from the accession of King James the Second down to a time within the memory of men still living." That would certainly have included Queen Anne, who died nearly a century before Macaulay was born. But, by the time Macaulay had worked his way up to Queen Anne's reign, old age had slowed him down and he simply lacked the energy and will to go on (292).

Queen Anne: Queen Anne, the last of the Stuarts, reigned from 1702 (succeeding William and Mary) until her death in 1714. England and Scotland were united to constitute Great Britain during her time on the throne. She bore seventeen children, but only one survived infancy — and he died at the age of ten. She is described as having few talents (250). Whether she deserved it or not, Anne seems to have developed a colorful image. Just in going through Brewer (54), we discover these revealing titilations: (i) Her nickname was Brandy Nan; (ii) To form "Queen Anne's fan," place a thumb on your nose and wiggle your upward-pointing fingers; and (iii) A favorite Jacobite toast during Anne's reign was to the "little gentleman in velvet," referring to the mole that raised the molehill that tripped King William's horse and led to William's injury and eventual death. Despite all this, she was "identified with cultural stirrings that were later fadishly acclaimed" (118). During her reign decorative arts came to full flower, and Queen Anne style furniture was characterized by well-proportioned, elegant lines and attractive veneers (121), so Bunthorne is at least partially justified in claiming that "the reign of good Queen Anne was Culture's palmiest day."

Paddy [The pathos of Paddy, as rendered by Boucicault]: This probably embodies the typical poor Irishman portrayed in Boucicault's plays. It might also refer to Boucicault's roles in his own plays. See next entry.

Boucicault {BOO-si-ko}: Dion Boucicault was an Irish playwright and actor who was well known in Gilbert's day. Traveling in both the United Kingdom and America, he wrote or adapted about 400 farces, comedies, and melodramas — in some of which he acted with great success. Several of his plays had Irish settings (105). His play *The Colleen Bawn* was one of Queen Victoria's favorites, and history records that she attended no fewer than three performances. Two days after the queen attended the third performance, her mother died, and within a year so did Prince Albert. Throughout the rest of her life she consented to having a few entertainments staged within the palace, but she never again made a public appearance in a theater (258).

Bishop of Sodor and Man [Style of the Bishop of Sodor and Man]: Sodor is an ancient name for the Hebrides (islands off the west coast of Scotland). The Isle of Man is much farther south, in the Irish Sea. The most likely candidate for the Colonel's intent would appear to be Rowley Hill, D.D. (1836-87), who was made Bishop of Sodor and Man in 1877. *The Dictionary of National Biography* (93) says that "He discharged his duties with great zeal and success."

D'Orsay [The dash of a D'Orsay]: Count Alfred Guillaume Gabriel D'Orsay (1801-52) was a French dandy who married into the English nobility and became the center of a fashionable artistic and literary circle in London. He was "long *arbiter elegantarium* of English society and was considered an accomplished artist and sculptor." In 1849 he fled to Paris to escape his creditors (77). Walmisley (299) divulges many juicy details about D'Orsay's private life that would bring the blush of shame to the cheek of modesty.

Quackery: Fraudulence. Aurora (15) argues that D'Orsay was irresponsible and unrealistic, but not the quack that the colonel implies.

Dickens: Charles Dickens (1812-70): Eminent English novelist, author of *Oliver Twist*, *A Tale of Two Cities*, and *A Christmas Carol*, among other famous works. Gilbert adapted *Great Expectations* for the stage, and looked upon Dickens as one of his favorite authors (240). See also Chapters X and XIII.

Thackeray: William Makepeace Thackeray (1811-63): Another English novelist, who was nearly as popular as Dickens in his day. He was the author of many satirical journal sketches and such famous novels as *Vanity Fair* (287). One of his books was *The History of Samuel Titmarsh and the Great Hoggarty Diamond*. I dare say you never heard of it.

Victor Emmanuel: Presumably refers to Victor Emmanuel II (1820-78), King of Sardinia, who united Italy in 1861 after decades of war with Austria and the troops of Pope Pius IX. He became the first king of Italy and was widely admired.

Peveril {Rhymes with several}: Sir Geoffrey Peveril was the hero of Sir Walter Scott's historic novel *Peveril of the Peak* (262), in which the action takes place in the Peak Region of Derbyshire and on the Isle of Man. The remains of Peveril Castle still stand.

Thomas Aquinas: An Italian religious leader, scholastic philosopher, theologian, and writer of the thirteenth century; one of the great pillars of the Roman Catholic faith and founder of the Dominican Friars. He lived from ca. 1225 to 1274, and was canonized in 1323.

Doctor Sacheverell {suh-SHEV-erell}: Henry Sacheverell (ca. 1674-1724) was an Anglican clergyman who became the center of a religious dispute with political overtones during the reign of Queen Anne. He was charged with seditious libel and adjudged guilty. He was, however, given a light sentence: a three-year suspension from preaching. His troubles were triggered by a seditious sermon that earned the distinction of being burned by the common hangman (54, 55).

Tupper: Martin Farquhar Tupper (1810-89) was a popular, but abominable English poet. His *Proverbial Philosophy*, published in 1838, sold nearly two million copies; yet he was a favorite target of contemporary parodists, including Gilbert, who mentions Tupper slightingly in two of the Bab Ballads. Gilbert also published in *Fun* a mock testimonial to Tupper written in "dog Latin" (66, 127). Despite general critical disdain, Tupper must have been in Queen Victoria's good graces because he was commissioned to write verses for one of her family entertainments (258).

Tennyson: Alfred, Lord Tennyson (1809-92): English baron and Poet Laureate 1850-92. His epic poem *The Princess* was the basis for *Princess Ida*. His best known work, perhaps, is *Idylls of the King*.

Daniel Defoe: English novelist and journalist (ca. 1660-1731). Best known for his novel *Robinson Crusoe*.

Anthony Trollope: English novelist (1815-82) whose many novels generally dealt with upper middle-class families in country settings. Among his best-known works are several novels set in the imaginary English cathedral town of Barchester.

Mr. Guizot {gee-ZOE}: François Pierre Guillaume Guizot (1787-1874), erudite and versatile Frenchman who made his mark as statesman, educator, and historian. He published several books, held important ministerial posts, and was ambassador to Britain.

Fusible: Capable of being melted or liquefied.

Pipkin: A small baked clay pot.

Crucible: A bowl in which metals, ores, etc., can be melted.

Residuum: Latin for "residue."

Paragon [for this soldier-like paragon]: A model of perfection as, for example, a well-presented Savoy opera.

Czar [Get at the wealth of the Czar]: Emperor of Russia, who in 1881 was Alexander II, the one who sold Alaska to the United States. The Czars were known for their great wealth, often ostentatiously displayed.

Aragon [The family pride of a Spaniard from Aragon]: A region in the north-east of

Chapter VI

Spain. It was an independent kingdom from A.D. 1035 until it merged with Castile in the fifteenth century. During its independence it conquered and ruled over many neighboring or far-flung provinces and city states, such as Naples. The "family pride" presumably pertains to the many noble families with unsullied blood lines that originated in Aragon. I dare say Pooh-Bah himself liked to think he had ancestral roots in the region.

Mephisto [Force of Mephisto pronouncing a ban]: Mephisto is presumably the Prince of Darkness, also known as Mephistopheles (as in *Faust*).

Ban: A curse invoking evil consequences.

Lord Waterford [A smack of Lord Waterford, reckless and rollicky]: Probably refers to Lord Charles (1846-1919) of the Beresford family, the Marquis of Waterford, in Ireland. The family had a reputation for daring and, often, notorious shenanigans. Massie (201) avers that Henry Beresford, the third marquis, was killed in a hunting accident and that the fifth marquis was hopelessly crippled by a fall from his horse. By the time his younger brother, Lord Charles, had reached middle age "He had broken his chest bone, his pelvis, his right leg, his right hand, a foot, one collarbone three times, the other once, and his nose in three places." Lord Charles entered the navy in 1859 and rose rapidly by force of his strong personality, fiery enthusiasm and reckless courage that made him the idol of the fleet. Massie goes on to recount Charles's amazing military and political exploits that reinforce the adage that truth is stranger than fiction.

And here's one more exploit: On April 13, 1878, when Gilbert and Sullivan traveled to Portsmouth to inspect *H.M.S. Victory*, who should meet them as they arrived but none other than Lord Charles Beresford (325).

Rollicky: Derived from *rollicking*, meaning boisterous and free-spirited. See also Chapters III and V.

Roderick [Swagger of Roderick, heading his clan]: There are several possibilities here. The last king of Ireland, Rory O'Connor, was also known as Roderick. The last Visigothic king of Spain, Don Rodrigo, was the center of many colorful legends, which entered English literature and in which he was known as Roderick. But how many Spanish kings have any clans to lead? The strongest candidate, by far, is Sir Walter Scott's Roderick Dhu, of "haughty mien and lordly air." He was the overbearing Highland chieftain in Scott's poem "The Lady of the Lake" (261). Confronting a lonely young Englishman, a rival for the hand of fair Ellen, the lady of the lake, Black Roderick:

> Then fixed his eye and sable brow
> Full on Fitz-James: "How say'st thou now?
> These are Clan-Alpine's warriors true;
> And, Saxon, — I am Roderick Dhu!"

Paddington Pollaky: Most authorities agree this refers to a highly successful and internationally famous private detective whose office was at Paddington Green (in London). His real name was Ignatius Paul Pollaky (140).

Odalisque [Grace of an odalisque on a divan]: A concubine in a Turkish harem. Strictly speaking, an odalisque was simply a female Turkish slave. Undraped odalisques reclining on divans were popular subjects of erotic paintings of the day. One example by Ingres (in the Louvre) is named *Odalisque*. There she is, artistically clothed in only a head-wrap and bracelet, gracefully reclining upon what we may suppose to be a divan.

Hannibal: Carthaginian general and tactical genius who lived about 247-183 B.C. He is best known for leading his troops and elephants over the Alps to attack Rome. After many military successes in Italy he was finally defeated without ever taking Rome. He returned to Carthage but went into exile, where he died by his own hand.

Sir Garnet: This is Sir Garnet Wolseley, who in the 1870s was the leader of successful military campaigns against native African leaders both on the Gold Coast and in South Africa. He was later made a viscount and now is generally referred to as Lord Wolseley. In 1887, when he was Field Marshal, he agreed to come to a rehearsal of *Ruddigore* to check the authenticity of the military uniforms worn by the bucks and blades. A more urgent matter came up, however, and he had to send

Patience

a substitute (139). What could possibly have been more urgent?

Hamlet: "The melancholy Dane," tragic protagonist of what many believe to be Shakespeare's greatest play.

The Stranger: The protagonist of a then well-known play by August (or Augustus) Friedrich Ferdinand von Kotzebue (1761-1819), translated from German into English by Benjamin Thompson.

Manfred: The most likely candidate is the gloomy hero of Lord Byron's dramatic poem of the same name (65). This character, supposedly Byron's self-image, lived as a recluse in an Alpine castle, haunted by remorse for his incestuous role in his sister's suicide. (Byron is suspected of carrying on with his stepsister.) A less likely candidate is the Manfred who was king of Naples and Sicily in the thirteenth century. Halton (147), Terry (286), and Darlington (86) favor that interpretation; but Byron's unhappy protagonist fits the "not very much of him" context considerably better. Moreover, if you read the poem you will easily be convinced that Gilbert was well acquainted with it. You will meet such old *Sorcerer* friends as "Spirits of earth and air," (close enough to "Sprites of earth and air") and "Appear!— appear! — appear!" and even wicked old Ahrimanes is featured. Then, from *Ruddigore*, we meet "What wouldst thou with me?" and "ho! without there!" Further evidence is found in an early outline of *Patience* exhumed from the British Museum by Stedman (272). In this, Gilbert describes "two grim and portentous middle-aged females dressed in heavy black — who stand about in gloomy Manfred-like attitudes..." This can only be Byron's Manfred. Moreover, Gilbert has a character disguised as Byron's Manfred in his burlesque *La Vivandière* (273).

Beadle of Burlington: This is almost assuredly the beadle (uniformed attendant) who maintains decorum in the Burlington Arcade (shops) off Piccadilly. Bryson (58) says it was the world's first shopping mall. The arcade is still in business and still maintains a corps of retired military officers who serve as beadles, uniforms and all. Goodman (140) shows a picture of one.

Richardson's show: In his book *Sketches by Boz — Illustrative of Every-Day Life of Every-Day People* (90), Charles Dickens describes this traveling theatrical troupe as he witnessed it at the Greenwich Fair: "This immense booth, with the large stage in front, so brightly illuminated with variegated lamps, and pots of burning fat, is 'Richardson's,' where you have a melodrama (with three murders and a ghost), a pantomime, a comic song, an overture, and some incidental music, all done in five-and-twenty minutes."

Mr. Micawber: A character in Dickens's *David Copperfield*. He was a shiftless fellow, but always full of unjustified optimism. Why the colonel dragged him in is not clear — unless it was for the optimism; but we should have thought that Paget, about to trepan, would have supplied more than enough of that commodity.

Madame Tussaud {too-SO}: Marie Tussaud (1760-1850) was a Swiss who learned wax modeling in Paris and founded her now-famous London wax museum in the early 1800s.

(And that ends the catalog of names from the Colonel's song.)

*   *   *   *   *   *

Thousand a day [to be a duke, with a thousand a day!]: This refers to the ducal income, largely from tenants, amounting to a thousand pounds per day.

Toffee: This is much like what Americans call taffy, a chewy candy made, usually, from brown sugar or boiled-down molasses with butter mixed in. Some American versions of the libretto substitute "candy" (181).

Adulation: Excessive flattery.

Abject: Contemptible.

To a T! [That describes me to a T!]: "Exactly; to a nicety; as true as an angle drawn with a T-square" (115).

Snubbed: Treated with contempt. See also Chapter VIII.

71

Chapter VI

Thorough-paced [A thorough-paced absurdity]: Complete and unmitigated.

Flushing [Blushing at us, flushing at us]: Glowing with color. Blushing is generally linked with embarrassment; flushing has a broader meaning — quite aside from its association with indoor plumbing — but here it simply means much the same as blushing.

Fleering [fleering at us, jeering at us]: Mocking or scorning.

PRETTY SORT OF TREATMENT

County family: Collins (75) defines this as "an ancestral family having long associations with a particular county." Rees (251) adds that the term has strong snobbish connotations. These lovesick maidens are socially acceptable and want Bunthorne to know it. They are members of the gentry, ranking just below the nobility. The honorific "Lady" given to at least four of the group is another clue that these ladies are clearly of the upper crust.

Clay [who despises female clay]: As earth is the Biblical material for the human body, *clay* is a figurative expression for the body, as distinct from the soul. Bunthorne is using it to imply that the girls are mere mortals. "Clay" was a clergyman's favorite word.

Deign: [Deign to raise thy purple eyes]: Condescend.

Poesy [heart-drawn poesy]: An archaic synonym of poetry (229).

Transcendental lore [That some transcendental lore]: Learning in matters far above ordinary comprehension: mystic, obscure, and fantastic.

Supplicate [This we supplicate]: Beg humbly and earnestly.

Fleshly [a wild, weird, fleshly thing]: In this case the word means sensual.

Precious [very yearning, very precious]: The word has a remarkable range of meanings: (i) of great monetary value, (ii) of great moral or spiritual value, (iii) affecting a fastidious delicacy, and (iv) colloquially, an intensive of something bad, e.g., a precious mess. Bunthorne probably had (ii) in mind. A few lines later the Lady Saphir also uses the word. She, too, probably meant version (ii), but Gilbert meant (iii) or (iv). Take your pick.

Faint lilies: The Pre-Raphaelite painters were particularly attracted to lilies as symbols of beauty and purity. Many of their paintings show languorous maidens holding lilies while apparently thinking of nothing at all.

(The next seven entries are from Bunthorne's poem "Oh, Hollow! Hollow! Hollow!" which Patience mistakes for a hunting song because fox hunters by tradition cried "Hallo!" when sighting the prey.)

Amaranthine {am-are-AN-thine} [Quivering on amaranthine asphodel]: The word is from the Greek: *a*, meaning "not," and *marainein*, meaning "fading," hence when combined: unfading (66).

Asphodel: "Any of various liliaceous plants of the genera *Asphodelus* and *Asphodeline* native to southern Europe ..." (6). A second meaning is a lily or daffodil. In Greek mythology, asphodels were the ever-blooming flowers that grew in the Elysian fields. Rees (251) adds that the plant is also the source of a potent diuretic, meaning a medicine that turns on the waterworks — and we don't mean tears.

Calomel: Mercurous chloride, a medicine used as a laxative. (It's also used in the treatment of a certain unmentionable disease, but we're sure that's *not* what Bunthorne had in mind. He may have been a fleshly poet, but he wasn't *that* fleshly.) Shipley (266) says the word derives from the Greek *kalos* (fair) + *melas* (black) because it is a white powder that turns black when exposed to light.

Historical aside: The American explorers Lewis and Clark started on their expedition with no fewer than fifty dozen patented calomel pills, the composition of which included six parts of mercury to one part of chlorine, and jalap (a dried root with purgative proclivities of its own). The combination was described as awesome. Indeed, to the man in the street the pills were affectionately referred to as "thunderclappers" (5).

Plinth [When from the poet's plinth]: Square slab forming the base of a column or pedestal. We can interpret this as Bunthorne's reference to being on a poet's pedestal.

Colocynth: Believe it or not, colocynth is a strong purgative made from the pulp of a kind of cucumber. The phrase "amorous colocynth" is an example of advanced oxymoronism.

Aloe: A purgative derived from the juice of the aloe plant.

Uncompounded pills: Pills containing but a single medicinal ingredient. In this case they are simply derived from plants.

As you may have surmised by now, Bunthorne's entire poem stresses the incompatibility of medicinal and poetic aspects of flowers (7). So we may now ask the profound philosophical question: Does "Hollow! Hollow! Hollow!" refer to the emptiness of life, or the physical condition of the body cavity after extensive purgative medicinal ministrations? Aurora (16) and Papa (231) take this up at length. Rees (251) notes that medical science was rather limited in those days:

> Purgation was pretty standard for anything. I will bet that nobody, but nobody in the Savoy audience had got through life without being purged at least several times. They [referring to the purgatives mentioned above] were standard medicine known to all and stocked by every apothecary. They were prescribed unmixed (uncompounded) with other substances. This much established, I leave it to you to diagnose the cause of the writhing of the lithe-limbed maid, and to decide why the first comment on the poem (by Angela) is "How purely fragrant!"

And, if that is not enough, Rees calls to our attention this poem by Oscar Wilde, which is typical of what Gilbert was parodying:

> …And sweet to hear the shepherd
> Daphnis sing
> The song of Linus through a sunny dell
> Of warm Arcadia where the corn is gold
> And the slight lithe-limbed reapers
> dance about the wattled fold.

> And sweet with young Lycoris to recline
> In some Illyrian valley far away,
> Where canopied on herbs amaracine
> We too might waste the summer-trancèd
> day … .
> from "The Burden of Itys"

Empyrean {em-puh-REE-en} [You are not Empyrean]: "The highest heaven, or region of pure elemental fire" (75). Keep in mind that Bunthorne and his admirers are not true aesthetes, but only blind followers and mimics. They use such high-flown language without really understanding the meaning.

Della Cruscan {DEL-a-KRUS-kan} [You are not Della Cruscan]: The original Della Cruscans were members of a Florentine academy of the sixteenth century dedicated to purifying the Italian language. The term was also used by a group of late-eighteenth century English poets who lived in Florence and wrote in affected aesthetic style.

Early English [would at least be Early English]: English language and literature between A.D. 1250 and 1500, also Gothic architecture in vogue in England during the thirteenth century (75). Bradley (47) says the style was favored by the Pre-Raphaelites.

Primary colours! [Red and Yellow! Primary colours! Oh, South Kensington!]: These are the fundamental pigments, red, yellow and blue, from which all the others (orange, green, violet, and brown) can be derived by combining. The aesthetes usually preferred rather subdued and somber mixes.

South Kensington!: This is somewhat obscure, but the consensus of my more knowledgeable friends (140, 243, 247, 251, 265, 273) is that the reference is to the bohemian inhabitants of that part of London.

Chapter VI

Quoting Prestige (243): "South Kensington was, and still is, the centre in London for art museums, the Royal College of Art, and the area where those so inclined live or (if students) lodge. *Punch* of the period made frequent references to the outré aesthetic habits of the denizens of South Kensington." Rees (251) makes these comments: "South Kensington and the immediately adjacent Brompton were not only the sites of more than one 'art school' but also the abode of many of the more aesthetically inclined. Gilbert lived on the fringe of this area at The Boltons during the 1870s and '80s and it was here that he wrote the libretto of *Patience* ... Aesthetes were probably two-a-penny in some of the streets nearby and Gilbert doubtless had plenty of opportunity to study them *in situ*." The aesthetes of that day would certainly look upon primary colors as lacking in sophistication. To Jane's "Oh, South Kensington!" might be added: "Forgive these hopeless Philistines."

Cobwebby gray: This presumably alludes to Whistler's extensive use of muted grays and blacks, as in that famous picture of his mother.

Bloom [with a tender bloom like cold gravy]: The dull, cloudy coagulated surface of once-warm gravy.

Hessians [a lover's professions, when uttered in Hessians]: Knee-high cloth boots with tassels, long worn by Hessian troops (229).

Veriest: Most extreme.

Chaste [handsome and chaste]: Simple in taste and style (an unlikely adjective to apply to those gaudy dragoon uniforms, but let it pass).

Peripatetics: Pertains to the philosophy of Aristotle, who believed in teaching while ambulating about. In the present context one need infer no Aristotelian influence other than the walking-talking aspect.

Dirty greens [I do *not* care for dirty greens]: This is an apparent allusion to the affected attire of some of the aesthetes. Stedman (274) says they showed a preference for sage green (green mixed with gray).

Platitudes [I am not fond of uttering platitudes]: Mundane remarks, especially those uttered in a pompous manner.

Stained-glass attitudes: This may call attention to Morris and Burne-Jones, both of whom worked in stained glass, a medium that tends to depict figures in stiff attitudes. On the other hand it may be a hold-over from those rival curates.

Germs of the transcendental terms: Fundamentals of mystic jargon.

Palmiest day: Most flourishing period (229).

Empress Josephine: Empress of France 1804-09; first wife of Napoleon Bonaparte. Bradley (47) says, "She held a brilliant court and helped confirm the reputation of Paris as the artistic capital of the world." To this DeLorme (88) adds that Josephine also held brilliant courts in Strasbourg and Mainz; she founded a conservatory with great teachers, and is known to have encouraged Cherubini and Le Sueur. Barker (27), on the other hand, maintains that her brilliant court was ostentatious and often empty show. "Bunthorne was trying to emphasize the absurdity of condemning all that is recent by picking a correspondingly absurd climatic point for the last stage of 'good' art." Other historians (109,

218) mention that her rustic upbringing was such that she found it necessary to employ a full-time tutor to bring her cultural prowess up to the level of her imperial position.

Born in Martinique in 1763, Josephine started life as Marie Josephine Rose Tascher de la Pagerie. While still in her teens she married the vicomte Alexandre Beauharnais, who was executed as an anti-revolutionist fifteen years later. After two years of widowhood, she married Napoleon, but he had their marriage annulled after eight years. She nevertheless lived on in style until her death in 1814.

Spleen [must excite your languid spleen]: Asimov (11) explains that the spleen is a small organ near the stomach. In times gone by the spleen was believed to be the seat of various emotions. A man with a "languid spleen" would be unable to work up much enthusiasm for loving a woman.

An attachment à la Plato: Friendly, but without sexual overtones. Plato (ca. 427-347 B.C.) was a Greek philosopher, a pupil and friend of Socrates. He advocated a love of the idea of beauty, evolving from a physical desire for a person through love of physical beauty and later of spiritual and ideal beauty.

French bean: The term has been variously defined as what Americans call an ordinary string bean (perhaps with the pod sliced along its length), kidney bean, wax bean, or scarlet runner (75, 229, 238, 250, 290).

Philistines {FILL-is-tines, or -tins} [Though the Philistines may jostle]: Uncultured wealth-worshippers who have no interest in the arts. Brewer (54) has a nice outline of the etymology of the word, which has overtones of friction between town and gown. The term was popularized in England by the poet, essayist and critic Matthew Arnold (1822-88).

Apostle [you will rank as an apostle]: A leader of reform. Dixon (94) suggests that this may have been a sly reference to the Apostles Club, a well known but exclusive intellectual society formed in Cambridge in 1820.

Piccadilly: A well-known London street of prestigious hotels and shops. "The street's name is believed to be derived from certain collars of the seventeenth century made by a fashionable tailor who called his home 'Piccadilly Hall' "(77). Goodman (140) says the collars were starched and were thought to be called "pikadils."

Poppy or lily: Poppies, as well as lilies, figured in some of the Pre-Raphaelite paintings. The line about walking down Piccadilly alludes to the popular notion that Oscar Wilde had a habit of parading down the street holding a lily. Did he really do so? Ellmann (101) finds reason to think so; but Fido (119) quotes Wilde to the effect that he (Wilde) said he had never done such a thing, but had nevertheless convinced the world that he had, which was far more difficult. Does that settle the issue? Not unless you have confidence in Wilde's veracity.

Elysian Fields: In Greek mythology, "the abode of the shades of the virtuous dead in the nether world where the inhabitants lived a life of passive blessedness" (75). See also Chapter IV.

Bilious [I am not as bilious as I look]: Suffering from trouble with the bile or liver, which may turn the skin yellow. (Eating butter with a tablespoon may be to blame.) The word also means peevish and disagreeable. Perhaps Bunthorne means he is not as ill-tempered as his complexion might indicate. See also Chapter XIV.

Touch-and-go jocularity: Light-hearted jesting.

Aceldama [this black Aceldama of sorrow]: Brewer (54) tells us this is from the Aramaic and means "Field of Blood." Figuratively, it is used for any scene of great slaughter. The name was applied to a potter's field near Jerusalem used from Biblical times until the seventeenth century. According to Matthew (XXVII: 7, 8), when Judas repented betraying Jesus, he gave his thirty pieces of silver back to the chief priests and elders and went out and hanged himself. The chief priests concluded that they could not put such "blood money" into the treasury, and so they used it to buy "the potter's field to bury strangers in. Therefore that field has been called the Field of Blood to this day." In Acts I: 18,19, however, we find that Judas "bought

Chapter VI

a field with the reward of his wickedness; and falling headlong he burst open in the middle and all his bowels gushed out. And it became known to all the inhabitants of Jerusalem, so that the field was called in their language Akel´dama, that is, Field of Blood." With all that as preamble, let us venture the opinion that Bunthorne meant the word in its figurative sense — if he meant anything at all.

{Now how should you pronounce the word? No one knows how the classics pronounced the letter c, nor is there agreement about which syllable should be emphasized. In short, you have a choice of at least four acceptable pronunciations. To me, ass-el-DOM-ah sounds best within the context, and Cameron (66) prefers it too. He points out, however, that some dictionaries give a-SEL–da-ma, "which accords with the rules of Latin accent, since the word came into the King James version through Latin."}

Eros [Oh, forgive her, Eros!]: The Greek god of love.

Abstraction [the abstraction of refinement]: The essence.

Hey ... willow waly O: Filler words, commonly used in ballad refrains. *Willow* has many melancholy associations including the famous "I'll hang my harp on a weeping willow tree," Desdemona's willow song, and the tale of that poor little tom-tit in *The Mikado.* Waly means "alas" or "well-a-day!"

Fain [I would fain discover]: Gladly.

Chronos: Father Time in Greek mythology, often identified with the Roman god Saturn.

Florentine: Pertaining to the city of Florence, one of the great centers of art during the Renaissance.

Pandaean {pan-DEE-enn} [Gaily pipe Pandaean pleasure]: Pertaining to Pan, the Greek god of pastures, forests, flocks, and herds — and pan pipes.

Double pipes: A double pipe is more correctly called an "aulos," one of the two major musical instruments of classical Greece. An aulos comprised two oboe-like instruments joined at the upper end and strapped behind

A TRUSTEE for BEAUTY

the player's neck. Such instruments were frequently used to accompany stage productions. You may also see them in paintings of classical celebrations (105, 323).

Daphnephoric bound: Before we wrestle with this term we need to provide some background. To begin with, in Greek mythology Daphne was a young virgin. Pursued by Apollo, she was saved from a fate worse than death by her father — or mother, depending on which source you believe — who changed her into a laurel tree. Daphne, then, is the personification of virginal timidity. She is also the personification of the laurel tree, whose leaves and boughs are associated with Apollo. He, in turn, appropriated laurel wreaths and garlands for poets (hence the term "poet laureate"). Derived from that we have *Daphnephoria*, a periodic festival held in Thebes in honor of Apollo. The festival featured a procession, the chief figure in which was called the "Daphnephoris" (meaning laurel bearer), a youth, the priest of Apollo, who wore a long, splendid robe, a crown, and wreaths of laurel. He was preceded by another honored individual who carried a sort of maypole decorated with laurel and flowers. The Daphnephoris held onto the laurel, and he in turn was followed by a band of maidens carrying garlands and singing hymns to Apollo (103). This parade must certainly have been in Gilbert's mind when he wrote the stage directions for the finale of Act I. Bunthorne enters wearing a crown of roses; he is bound up in garlands by which Angela and Saphir lead him. He is followed by the women's chorus, who are described as "dancing classically." We could imagine "a Daphnephoric bound" as referring to the bound-up poet. Prestige (244) says he finds this suggestion attractive. Cameron (66) believes that Gilbert most likely had in mind the gentle, graceful little leaps of a poet laureate. Aurora (18) endorses this. The connection with the virginal Daphne, of course, may also suggest timid hops of maidenly shyness. Here, there are two difficulties. One is that to me the verb "bound" implies a vigorous exertion more appropriate to a stag than to an aesthetic poet or a gentle maiden (although you might argue that a bound might be involved in trying to escape from Apollo). The other is that Green (145) confesses that in all his years with the D'Oyly Cartes he never saw anyone leaping about. All this leads me to think that Gilbert meant bound as a leap, but that Sullivan took it to mean "bound-up," and so implied no jumping about in his score. Wright (323) suggests that Gibert might have intended both meanings as a pun. We must keep in mind the final, and perhaps most likely, possibility that in mouthing the words, the rapturous maidens didn't know, themselves, what was meant. Let us, then, Daphnephorically bound on to the next term, which promises to be as prosaic as this one has been poetic.

Raffled: A raffle is a special kind of lottery in which many people each pay a fixed amount, but only one is awarded the prize. *Raffled* makes a verb of it. The more general term, *lottery*, allows awarding of more than one prize.

Martial [dews each martial eye]: Warlike.

ON THE ADVICE OF MY SOLICITOR

Avidity: Eagerness.

Diffidence: Shyness.

Blue-and-white: Oriental ceramics that were then all the rage among the aesthetes,

especially Whistler. They ranked in popularity with lilies and peacock feathers.

Terra-cotta-ry: Stedman (274) notes that Gilbert is using the example of pot/pottery to make a plural of terra-cotta, unglazed earthenware such as the familiar everyday flower pot.

Lottery [You may draw him in a lottery]: See "Raffled" above.

Guinea [Put in half a guinea]: Guineas were gold coins first issued in 1663 and initially valued at £1.00. In 1717, owing to changed relative values of silver and gold, the guinea's value was adjusted to 21 shillings, i.e., £1.05. The coin was no longer minted after 1817, when it was supplanted by the 20-shilling (£1.00) gold sovereign. Ever since then, however, certain prices have been quoted in those imaginary guineas, principally because of the snob appeal (105). As for "half-guineas," they are but another example of Bunthorne's transcendental imagination. See also Chapters III and VIII.

Fortune: Chance or luck personified as a goddess who capriciously doles out Life's lots.

Make a clearance [Of this bold girl I pray you make a clearance]: Get rid of her!

Without alloy: Undiminished in value by impurities.

Tutti: Everybody sings!

Comeliness {COME-lee-ness}: Good looks.

ACT II

Glade: A clearing in a woods.

Forsooth: In truth.

Puling: Childish or whimpering, hence immature.

"Dim her eyes": Why is the expression in quotation marks? Because it is a euphemism derived from "Damn your eyes!" (11, 194, 274, 303).

Chapter VI

Gloamings [in life's uncertain gloamings]: In the later years of life.

Well-saved "combings": Loose hairs caught up in a comb and collected (perhaps starting while still young) for later augmenting whatever hair remains.

Lip-salve: Lipstick.

Pearly grey: Face powder. English ladies in Victorian times tried to remain pale because a tanned skin was associated with a working-class existence. They wore long gloves and big hats and carried parasols largely for that reason. Any signs of exposure that crept in despite those precautions were likely to be covered by a dusting of pearly white or grey face powder, the forerunner of the tinted face powders we know today. In Lady Jane's case, the powder would also help hide that mottled complexion she laments. Truly advanced cases might be accorded the stronger treatment of the "pearly-white dye" that Gilbert mentions in his Bab Ballad "King Borria Bungalee Boo" (127).

Beguile: Ensnare.

Incontinently [Or incontinently perish]: Immediately (archaic) (11).

Decalet: A ten-line stanza.

Daisy [a very daisy]: An exceptionally pleasing person or thing. MacPhail (194) invites you to consider "the simple loveliness of the daisy when compared with the languid lily. A nice touch for Grosvenor, often overlooked."

Gentle Jane: Grosvenor's two poems are not at all reflective of the aesthetes. Again, the rival curates (who competed for being most bland) may be to blame (272).

Bluebottles [Or caught bluebottles their legs to pull]: A kind of large fly, about like a horsefly.

Vivisected [Or vivisected her last new doll]: To vivisect is to cut up a living animal for experimental purposes. Dolls aren't really living animals, but the sentiment is well meant.

Earl: In England a nobleman ranking below a marquis and above a viscount.

Carriage [a first-class earl who keeps his carriage]: This noble fellow had no need for livery stables since he maintained his own carriage and stable of horses. Nineteenth century literature is full of allusions to keeping a carriage (45, 287, 293). The implication is usually one of "having arrived," perhaps flaunting an ostentatious life style. Keep in mind that maintaining even one carriage also required keeping one or more horses, a footman or two, a groom, a barn with stables, and plenty of fodder — no easy thing for a city dweller. Hilton (155) mentions that burlesque queen Nellie Farren was once fined thirty shillings for keeping a carriage, a male servant, and armorial bearings without licenses for any of them. See also Chapter XII.

Squirt [A great big squirt]: A syringe (229).

Cayenne-peppered: Teasing Tom sprinkled his sisters' beds with red pepper to cause sneezing. Tush.

Cobbler's wax: Wax that shoemakers put on shoe-sewing thread to make it easier to use. It helps prevent knotting and lets the thread slide through the holes easier. It also strengthens the thread and increases its durability.

Halfpennies {HAY-p'nees}: Large coins (one inch diameter) of little value, ideally suited to Tom's iniquities (314).

Corps de bally {CORE-de-BALLY}: The non-featured dancers in a ballet troupe. In those times actresses and dancers were looked down upon by proper Victorians. As one example, Becky, in *Vanity Fair* (287), is held in low esteem because her mother was a dancer at the opera.

Cloying [This is simply cloying]: Sickeningly sweet.

Drove them home: When a nail is hammered in so that the top of its head is flush with the surface of the board, it is said to be "driven home."

Peripatetic: In Act I, "peripatetic" refers to Bunthorne's philosophies. As used here, however, it refers to the magnet's walking away from the love offered by all those admiring articles of iron or steel.

Mote [Blind to his every mote]: Flaw.

Soliloquize: To talk to oneself.

Damozels: Damsels, dames, maidens, maids, girls, gals, etc., etc., etc., each lovelier than the other.

Spiced [too highly spiced]: The opposite of bland; in this case perhaps skating on the thin edge of respectability, e.g., that "writhing maid, lithe-limbed, quivering on amaranthine asphodel."

Insipidity: Being deficient in taste, spirit, life, and animation. That is, dull, flat, and vapid; not at all like this book.

Your cut is too canonical: *Canonical* pertains to the vestments worn by a clergyman officiating at a cathedral service. Remember that Gilbert at one time meant his rivals to be curates rather than poets. The same goes for *sanctified* (272). *Cut* may refer to Grosvenor's hair style, the shape of his suit, or figuratively the "cut of his jib," i.e., his general appearance. More broadly, it could refer to Grosvenor's personality, which Bunthorne finds too bland. (See "placidity emetical" below.)

Beau ideal: A real or imaginary person who is an ideal of perfection, almost like the present reader.

Morbid: Pertaining to an unhealthy mental state.

Heretical: Contrary to orthodox opinions or beliefs.

Placidity [your placidity emetical]: Mildness.

Emetical: An emetic is a medicine used to induce vomiting.

Ocular: Pertaining to the eye. Here Gilbert means the eye itself. To "stick an eyeglass in his ocular" means to wear a monocle. Asimov (11) cites this as an example of how cultures change. Bunthorne wants Grosvenor to do that so he will look commonplace. Today, a

monocle would have the opposite effect.

Quiddity [full of quibble and of quiddity]: Trifling niceties of speech, resulting usually in pompous and boring drivel (7).

Roly-poly pudding: The OED (229) defines roly-poly as "a kind of pudding, consisting of a sheet of paste covered by jam or preserves, formed into a roll and boiled or steamed." This would not be at all attractive to a fussy aesthete.

Upbraid [we hope you won't upbraid]: Reproach.

Struck [to be "struck" so]: To be immobilized (as in casting a statue). Coins, in manufacture, are said to be "struck."

Inner Brotherhood: The leading Pre-Raphaelite aesthetes often referred to themselves as the Inner Brotherhood (47).

Consummately utter: See "Jolly utter" below.

All-but: Almost.

Botticellian: Pertaining to Sandro Botticelli (1447-1510), an early Italian Renaissance painter. Although Botticelli and Fra Angelico were much admired by the aesthetes, one shouldn't try to find any real meaning in Lady Saphir's ejaculation other than "How arty!"

Fra Angelican: Pertaining to the friar Fra Angelico (1387-1455), another early Italian Renaissance painter.

Jolly utter: A popular bit of semi-meaningless jargon actually affected by the mindless followers of the aesthetes (318). MacPhail (194) says that such expressions were spotlighted by du Maurier's *Punch* cartoons lampooning the aesthetes. Stedman (274) adds that "utter" was an authentic Pre-Raphaelite affectation, but "jolly" was a Philistine word.

Obdurate: Hard-hearted; stubborn; unyielding (75).

Sympathy: There is considerable debate about whether to pronounce the word in the usual way, or as "sympa-THIGH" (to rhyme with "die"). Existing D'Oyly Carte recordings

Chapter VI

make it the former and that makes sense; it doesn't rhyme, but it's easier to understand. David Bamberger (23) finds reason to think that in Gilbert's day both pronunciations were in use, so "simpuh THIGH" may have been what Gilbert had in mind. (He was, after all, a perfectionist in nearly all his rhyming.) So directors can take their choice and have it pronounced "simpuh THIGH" for artistic integrity, or "simpuh THEE" for clarity of meaning; and we suspect Gilbert himself would have found the decision difficult (260).

SOMETHING LIKE THIS SORT OF THING

Narcissus [Ah, I am a very Narcissus]: In Greek mythology Narcissus was an exceedingly vain young fellow who was condemned to fall in love with his own reflection in a pool of water. He died of unrequited love or, in another version, he drowned when he tried to embrace his own reflection.

Premium [insipidity has been at a premium]: In great demand.

Back parting: According to Hyder (161) this is a hair style with the parting going down the back of the head, with the hair on each side combed forward, rather than the now-standard fore-and-aft parting atop the head. In Bradley's view (48) "This would have struck the Pre-Raphaelites as appallingly philistine and prosaic. If they parted their hair at all, it was generally in the middle."

Unmanned [I must not allow myself to be unmanned]: Disheartened, lacking in resolution, and (most unmanly of all) reduced to tears.

Nephew's curse: Don't take this expression too seriously. It's just something Bunthorne borrowed from nineteenth century melodrama to frighten Grosvenor. Or is it? Chambers (72) sees a connection with the apparently beloved aunt whose memory had so affected Bunthorne a few moments earlier.

Adamant: Unyielding, hard as a diamond (like Princess Ida's castle).

Paste [distinguish gems from paste]: Artificial gems made from finely ground glass. Asimov (11) suggests that we interpret this in the figurative sense of telling authentic art from fraudulent.

Idyll: Embodying simple perfection, perhaps in an elevated and polished style. {Exigence of rhyme compels us to pronounce this as "iddle," which in England is acceptable as a second choice to rhyming with idle.}

Stick and a pipe: A walking stick and a pipe for smoking tobacco.

Black-and-tan [And a half-bred black-and-tan]: A Manchester terrier crossed, in this case, with a who-knows-what.

"Hops" [Who thinks suburban "hops"]: Dance halls popular with the lower middle class (245).

"Monday Pops": A series of weekly concerts of light, popular music. Sullivan and Jullien, the eminent musico, both conducted such series. Bradley (47) tells us they were organized by Chappells, the music publishers, and were held in St James's Hall.

Bank-holiday: A civic holiday (usually a Monday) in Britain. They date back to just a decade before the opera was written (48). They were initiated by the banks as days in which the doors were closed while they undertook a quarterly review of the books. They were soon turned into a general day-off from work and then became civic holidays (118). The implication here is that we have a nose-to-the-grindstone fellow who cannot readily escape from work but who likes to mix with the other Philistines on those long, crowded weekends. Not at all like those free-flying aesthetes.

Japanese [A Japanese young man]: Asimov (11) explains that Bunthorne is alluding to his affected admiration for "all one sees that's Japanese."

Lank [A haggard and lank young man]: Drooping; weak and thin (75).

Francesca da Rimini: The ill-fated heroine of the tragic tale of Francesca and Paolo, celebrated by Dante, among others. She is brought in here because of her medieval background, so dear to the aesthetes. (Some editions of the libretto mistakenly substitute *di* for *da*.) Feldman and Barker (118) state that the story was based on actual events and, as the subject of numerous artistic endeavors, became something of a symbol for the aesthetics of medieval romantic sentiment and pathos.

Miminy, piminy: Brewer (54) defines *nimini-pimini* (which is close enough) as "affected simplicity." He ascribes it to advice given to a young lady in *The Heiress* (1786). She is told to practice saying "nimini-pimini" in front of a mirror … "The lips cannot fail to take the right plié." Isn't this a tremendous treasure trove of tantalizing trivia?

Je-ne-sais-quoi {DJUHN-eh-say-KWAH} [*Je-ne-sais-quoi* young man!]: French for "I don't know what," i.e., something (or, in this case someone) who defies cataloging within any of the standard categories. Feldman and Barker (118) relate this to "the ineffable, inexpressible qualities of the æsthetic character."

Chancery Lane: Chancery Lane is the center of London's law courts and law offices. A Chancery Lane young man would be a respectable fellow hoping to rise in the legal profession. He would certainly not be an aesthete.

Somerset House [A Somerset House young man]: Somerset House is a massive building on the Strand (not far from the Savoy Theatre) that houses a goodly share of Britain's unaesthetic bureaucrats. An earlier building with the same name that once stood on the same spot carried many historical associations (140).

Threepenny-bus {THRIP-enny bus} [Threepenny-bus young man!]: Rees (159) and Prestige (245) expect that an aesthete would never mix with the crowd on a bus and would either walk or ride a hansom cab (depending on the state of his pocket); whereas our everyday young man has no such compunctions. Incidentally, buses in those days were horse-drawn and their fares were prominently displayed near the door. Bradley (47) says that in 1900 Gilbert changed the phrase to read "twopenny tube" (i.e., subway).

Greenery-yallery [A greenery-yallery, Grosvenor Gallery]: Some of the aesthetic painters were noted for their fondness for subtle, secondary colors. Smith (269 says the Grosvenor Gallery walls were green and gold (close to yellow). Aurora, on the other hand, takes another tack: Bunthorne's description of himself from "pallid and thin" through various stages to "foot-in-the grave," includes "greenery-yallery" as one descriptive, and his association with the Grosvenor Gallery as another. A nice point.

Grosvenor Gallery: A London art gallery founded in 1877 and known for its displays of paintings by Pre-Raphaelites who were largely unsuccessful in gaining recognition by the Royal Academy. Goodman (140) notes that the aesthetes treated it practically like a club.

Sewell and Cross: A fashionable London firm of drapers (i.e., retailers of yard goods or clothes — either tailor-made or "off the hook"). The firm has long since closed its doors, so don't try to look it up.

Chapter VI

Howell and James: Another fashionable retail firm, no longer in business. Knight (178) says it sold ladies' jewelry, silver smithing, and art pottery as well as clothing. Goodman (85) and Terry locate the shop in Waterloo House (see below).

Particle [A pushing young particle]: I interpret this to mean an ambitious but very subordinate and callow person who is overly-self-assertive.

What's the next article?: From the context we must assume that our steady young man is a sales clerk in a fashionable draper's firm. Having just clinched a sale, our pushing young particle asks his customer what else he — or more likely, she — would like to buy. The expression was a common cliché of that period (273).

Waterloo House: This was a building housing several smart shops. Walmisley (299), Dunn (100), Hardwick (149), and Bradley (47) all state that it was in Cockspur St. and was the location of "Messrs. Halling, Pearce, and Stone, mercers and drapers." Terry (286) and Knight (178) propose that it was in Lower Regent Street. Its location isn't at all important here, so let's move on.

Crotchety: Full of whims or fads (75), and given to expressing them in an aggressive manner (167).

Cracked: Eccentric, perhaps slightly crazy.

Pastoral: Idyllic and bucolic.

Dittoes [an ordinary suit of dittoes and a pot hat]: Webster defines dittoes as "clothes of one material or color throughout." We might interpret this as being subdued and conservative. In most stage presentations, however, these dittoes turn out to be gaudy suits appropriate to racetrack gamblers.

Pot hat: A derby.

Swears and Wells: Formerly a ladies' dressmaking shop. Goodman (140) says the shop was on Regent Street at that time. The name has since been taken over by a chain of furriers.

Madame Louise: A fashionable milliner's shop, which Goodman (140) says was on Regent Street.

Pattering [We're prettily pattering]: Jabbering away without throwing brain into gear. Joseph (167) and Stedman (274) suggest another meaning: bouncy little steps in place of their former Daphnephoric bounds. Take your choice.

Quoting Yum-Yum: Thank goodness that's over!

IT IS NOT INDIGESTION!

GREATLY PLEASED WITH ONE ANOTHER

Iolanthe

When *Patience* completed its run at the Savoy, the triumvirate was ready with another delightful opera, *Iolanthe*, in which we find members of the House of Lords brought into conflict with a lovely company of fairies, led by a buxom fairy queen dressed and accoutered remarkably like Wagner's Brünnhilde. *Iolanthe* opened at the Savoy on November 25, 1882, and had a relatively modest run of 398 performances.

In the following year Sullivan was knighted — not for his highly popular comic operas, but for his serious cantatas and other massive choral works that had won him much fame, but little cash. Under a profit-sharing agreement Gilbert, Sullivan, and Carte had become wealthy through their comic operas; but Sullivan now began to feel dissatisfied. He was convinced that he was meant for bigger things. He also began to resent some of Gilbert's less-than-diplomatic remarks. (The two were never close friends.) Gilbert made matters worse by proposing for their next opera the so-called lozenge plot, in which a magic pill or potion somehow effects major changes in everyone's character. Sullivan bridled at the artificiality of such make-believe and asked Gilbert to try to suggest something more believable and true to life. *Iolanthe* was Gilbert's compromise. Aside from the fairies, the characters in Iolanthe are fairly true to life, and once you accept fairies, their magic powers make all else believable. Nevertheless, The happy collaboration was beginning to show signs of impending rupture.

CHARACTERS AND SETTING

Peer [The Peer and the Peri]: A nobleman of the rank of baron or above and, in this case, a member of the House of Lords. See also Chapters IV, XII, XIII, and XVI.

Peri {Rhymes with cheery}: In Persian mythology, a race of beautiful fairy-like creatures descended from fallen angels and excluded from paradise until their penance is accomplished. A second meaning is a lovely, graceful person (250). Stedman (274) says the word was synonymous with fairy in Gilbert's day. In one of the Philadelphia art museums there is a statue of a peri; she looks just like an angel, wings and all, but is strikingly bare breasted.

Lord Chancellor: In Britain the Lord Chancellor is the highest judicial authority. He is about equivalent to the Chief Justice of the United States (commonly called the Chief Justice of the Supreme Court). He is the Keeper of the Great Seal and, more to the point, is Speaker of the House of Lords. Brewer (56) states that the Lord Chancellor "ranks above all peers except princes of the blood and the Archbishop of Canterbury." Duffy (260) informs us that *chancellor* derives from cancella, the screen from behind which political deliberations were carried out.

Mountararat: A play on words on the Biblical Mount Ararat, resting place of Noah's ark.

Tolloller: *Tol-lol* means just so-so (115) or languid (274) and those terms are presumably a reflection on Tolloller's character.

Grenadier Guards: "An infantryman specially recruited because of fine physique and height" (75). The term is derived from grenade, which is French for "pomegranate." See also Chapter III.

Strephon: Stock name for a rustic lover

Arcadian [Strephon is an Arcadian shepherd]: Refers to Arcadia, a region of Greece associated with simple, rustic pleasures and a peaceful existence.

Ward in Chancery [Phyllis is also a Ward in Chancery]: "A minor under the protection of the Court of Chancery" (75).

Dukes, Marquises, Earls, Viscounts, and Barons: These are the five ranks, in order, of the British peerage. "British dukes rank next to princes and princesses of the blood royal, the two archbishops of Canterbury and York, the Lord Chancellor &c, but beyond this precedence they have no special privileges which are not shared by peers of lower rank" (103). All peers (the word means "equal.") enjoy the right of audience with the reigning monarch, and freedom from arrest in civil cases. English peers are automatically entitled to vote in the House of

Chapter VII

Lords once they reach their twenty first year. Although most of their titles are hereditary and their children are granted titles of courtesy, those children (other than the eldest son) are essentially commoners and have never formed a privileged caste" (105). Ranking below the peers are baronets and knights. A baronet's title is hereditary, a knight's is not. Members of the British nobility (other than the royal family) receive no income from the government. They are expected to survive on the rents derived from the property granted their ancestors or from charging the public to tramp through their estates. They may even find gainful employment. While on the subject of noble titles, we might as well consider what Brewer (56) has to say under the heading "Courtesy Titles." These are titles granted by social custom, but are of no legal value. The courtesy title of the eldest son of a duke is *marquis*; of a marquis: *earl*; of an earl: *viscount*. Younger sons of peers can affix *Lord* to their names, while daughters affix *Lady*.

Palace Yard: The courtyard beside the Houses of Parliament. Terry (286) points out that Private Willis was out of place there, that territory coming under the protection of the metropolitan police.

ACT I

Fairy ring [Round about our fairy ring]: Folklore has it that rings in lawns show evidence of fairy dances. The rings are actually caused by the growth of fungi below the surface. The spawn extends outward at a uniform rate and produces nitrogen, which results in dark rings in the grass (55). Sorry to disillusion you.

Vagaries [We indulge in our vagaries]: Capricious ideas or actions.

Compunction [We reply without compunction]: Without hesitation or remorse.

Lover [That we almost live on lover!]: Leila summarizes her song by singing that fairies could not live without the activity of human lovers (72). I suspect Gilbert would like Leila to swallow the final syllable. Sullivan may

have had that in mind; his music makes it easy to do so. On the other hand, Kravetz (181) suggests that the fairies "are in the habit of buzzing around people in love the way horseflies — you get the idea. Besides, it's a rather nice play on words."

Commuted [commuted her sentence]: Reduced.

Penal servitude: In English common law the term means imprisonment together with hard labor. Under the circumstances of the story, there was no hard labor required, just exile.

On her head: A common Victorian catchphrase meaning "with ease" (298).

Gambol [to gambol upon gossamer]: To leap about in play.

Gossamer: Any filmy substance, such as a cobweb, floating in the air or spread on bushes or grass.

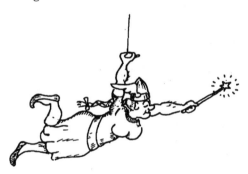

Behest [To thy behest, offended Queen, I bow!]: Command.

Coronet: A small crown.

Flageolet: "A small fipple flute resembling the treble recorder but having usually four finger holes and two thumb holes and a cylindrical mouthpiece" (307). Dr. Daly (Chapter III) was a past master of that delicately modulated instrument, if you'll recall.

Arcadee [songs of Arcadee]: Arcadia.

Bar [At first he seemed amused, so did the Bar]: A collective reference to those assembled at a court of law. See Chapter II for the derivation of the term. When the American Bar Association scheduled a convention in London some years ago, our British friends thought they were to receive a collection of barkeepers. Gilbert could have made something of that.

Bade {bad} [bade me get out]: Ordered.

Servile [A servile usher]: Obsequious, slavish, submissive, and fawning.

Usher: A doorkeeper, messenger, and keeper of order in a court of law.

Crumpled bands and rusty bombazine: The bands are the wide, falling collars worn with clerical, legal, or academic robes. Bombazine is a twilled or corded material made of various combinations of silk, cotton, and wool. It may also refer to a robe of the same material. We may take the "rusty" to imply that the servile usher's robe was past its prime. Black fabric often turns brown with age. Goodman (141) informs us that the bands are a remnant of the links between the law and the Church, while Bradley (48) says that ushers generally do not wear bands.

Chancery Lane: The London site of various establishments related to the legal profession, and many law offices. For details see Goodman (140).

Borough [I've a borough or two at my disposal]: A borough is a town represented in Parliament, corresponding roughly to a Congressional district in the USA. The Queen of the Fairies has enough influence in one or two of these to send whomever she wants to Parliament.

Tory [I'm a Tory of the most determined description]: The Tories were the forerunners of the Conservative party. Now Tory is a nickname for a member of the Conservative party, or at least one who holds conservative views (generally favoring free-market economics with minimum government control). Wilson (319) says that in England government by party first came about in approximately 1680.

Radicals: Those who hold extremely left-wing views, favoring extensive reforms, usual-

ly to be effected by increased government controls.

Division [on a division, they'd be sure to take me into the wrong lobby]: A method of voting in which those in favor of a motion go to one location and those opposed to another. The system is used in Parliament.

Working majority [they're two to one, which is a strong working majority]: In the two-party system, the ruling party needs more than a simple (i.e., one-vote) majority to be sure of carrying all its measures. A working majority involves a considerable numerical edge. Two-to-one would do nicely.

Returned [You shall be returned as a Liberal-Conservative]: Elected.

Liberal-Conservative: This can be interpreted as (i) an independent, (ii) a member of both parties, or (iii) a liberal-leaning member of the Conservative party. In the context, I favor (ii). Just to complicate matters, however, please note that Halton (147) and Terry (285) quote the Queen of the Fairies as saying "Liberal-Unionist," which was a group that splintered off from Gladstone's Liberal party in 1886, some four years after the opera was written. Allen's *First Night Gilbert and Sullivan* (3) shows "Liberal-Conservative." All of which proves that even the durable Savoy operas are subject to change, or even — as in this case — later switching back to the original.

Clean [He's a clean old gentleman]: Brewer (56) gives as one definition: "Free from blame or fault." We may assume that to be Phyllis's opinion of the Lord Chancellor.

Tantantara: Simulated fanfare. Kravetz (181) informs us that Gasophile Sy Miller has a yacht named *Tan Tan Tara*, which tows a dinghy named *Tzing Boom*!

Paragons [Paragons of legislation]: Models of excellence.

Lords [the deuce to pay in the Lords]: The House of Lords. As you may infer from the libretto, Gilbert must have looked upon the institution with amusement. He might have agreed with Lloyd George (at one time prime

Chapter VII

minister) who defined the Lords as, "five hundred men, ordinary men chosen accidentally from among the unemployed" (12).

Hear, hear: An English expression of approbation. See also Chapters V, IX, and XVI.

Counsel [can he appear by counsel before himself ... ?]: A legal advisor. The expression means: Can he send a barrister to appeal to himself on his own behalf?

Arrest of ... judgement: To hold a court decision in abeyance because an error in trial procedure has been discovered (141).

Woolsack: This refers to the Lord Chancellor's traditional seat in Parliament: an oversized red hassock stuffed with wool, symbolic of the nation's former reliance on the wool industry. It is thought to have originated in the fourteenth century (105).

Bar of this House: This alludes to an actual physical barrier (a brass bar or bars) set up in the House of Lords. When Phyllis is induced to present herself "at the Bar of this House," she is figuratively standing or kneeling at the aforementioned barrier. Goodman (142) explains that the House of Lords may sit as a court of law. See Bradley (48) for further details.

Pipes [my pipes and my tabors]: Simple wind instruments such as flageolets, Pandaean pipes, or even bagpipes.

Tabors: Small drums.

Cot [in lowly cot]: Cottage.

Blue blood: This is a colloquial expression for an aristocrat. (Remember Lady Sangazure in *The Sorcerer*?) The OED (229) suggests that the term originated because aristocratic people tended to have untanned skin, making their veins more visible and thus appearing blue in contrast. (A tanned skin was indicative of laboring in the field.)

Belgrave Square: A prestigious residential area of London, just west of Buckingham Palace. Goodman (140) gives a good history, including a picture.

Seven Dials: A convergence of seven streets in what was then a disreputable area of London, near the theater district. The name arises from seven sundials, each facing one of the streets and placed atop a 40-foot column at the convergence. See Goodman (140) for a detailed history and picture.

Riven [With grief my heart is riven]: Torn asunder.

Arcady, Arcadee {ARK-a-DIE, or ARK-a-DEE}: Poetic variations of *Arcadia*, that bucolic region of Greece already defined.

Espoused: Married.

Innately [Proud are we innately]: Inherently proud, like Pooh-Bah.

Manent: This is in the stage directions and means that those named remain on stage. To complete our lesson for the day, *manet* is the singular form; also *exeunt* is plural and *exit* is singular for indicating who is to leave.

Court of Chancery: "The court of the Lord Chancellor of England, the highest court of jurisdiction next to the House of Lords; but since ... 1873, a division of the High Court of Justice" (229).

Chorused [When chorused Nature bids]: Combined. He means every element of nature is speaking, or singing, or both.

Evidence: "Testimony in proof of something" (56). The rules of evidence generally forbid repeating what someone else has said.

Affidavit [an affidavit from a thunderstorm]: A written statement, given under oath before a proper officer such as a solicitor or magistrate, to be used in court.

Said I to myself — said I: An expression possibly derived from a popular song, "Thinks-I-to-myself, Thinks-I," which was in turn derived from a popular novel of the same name published in 1811 (219).

Brief [his attorney has sent me a brief]: A summary of a client's case, prepared by a solicitor for use by a barrister. See also Chapter II.

Dust: "To throw dust in someone's eyes" is an old expression meaning to mislead that person. Sperling (270) says, "In the battle of Honein, the prophet Mohammad supposedly threw dust in the air to confuse his enemies and this apparently successful tactic led to a new turn of phrase."

Exchequer, Queen's Bench, Common Pleas, or Divorce: These were various British courts of justice. Borrowing heavily from Goodman (141): *Exchequer* was one of the superior courts of common law in Westminster Hall. It handled cases involving revenues of the Crown and so forth. (The name dates back to medieval times and comes from the checkered cloth on which the king's accounts were handled.) *Queen's Bench* has since 1875 been the principal (i.e., busiest) division of the High Court of Justice. *Common Pleas* holds exclusive jurisdiction over actions pertaining to real property, and actions between ordinary citizens. (It was apparently merged with *Queen's Bench* a couple of years before the opera appeared.) *Divorce* was "more properly known as the Probate, Divorce and Admiralty Division, 1873-1970." Its full name explained most or all of its work. It is now called the Family Division.

Perjured [Have perjured themselves]: To be guilty of telling a lie while under oath.

Bark [When tempests wreck thy bark]: In its most general sense, a ship. Figuratively, read "when you are in trouble."

Minx [I heard the minx remark]: A saucy girl, at best.

St. James's Park: Bradley (46) says this is the oldest of six royal parks in central London, established by Henry VIII in 1532. It takes its name from the previous owners, the Sisters of St. James in the Field. Goodman (140) adds the telling note that in the 1870s it had become notorious as a hunting ground for prostitutes. What would the Sisters think?

One [and give him one!]: In good Queen Victoria's time, when the opera was written, this could imply nothing more risqué than a kiss. If you wish to make anything more of it, pray go ahead.

Dissemble [Thy fault to dissemble]: Disguise. See same entry in Chapter IV for more details.

Dolce far niente {DOLE-cheh far nee-ENN-teh}: Happy lollygagging, blissful dalliance. Italian for "It is sweet to do nothing" (66).

Festina lente {fes-TINE-uh, (or fes-TEEN-uh) LEN-tay}: Make haste slowly. The motto of the Emperor Augustus (66).

Clay [She moistenèd my clay]: *Clay* refers to the human body, as distinct from the soul. The expression "to moisten or wet one's clay" is cited in the OED (229) as a humorous way of saying "to drink."

Succour [The succour she supplied]: A rescue from distress.

Pipe our eye: Cry (54, 115, 229, 250). This brings visions of fitting one's eyes with pipes to carry a goodly supply of tears from some reservoir. A few lines earlier the peers had been crying over the thought that Strephon might have died in babyhood had not his mother fed him. Since he did *not* die, why should they go on crying? The reason is that they now wish he *had* so he would not be stealing Phyllis from them.

Swain: A rustic lover.

Rankiest: Of highest rank. Another Gilbertian invention.

Countess: In Britain the wife of an earl.

Taradiddle: Good English slang for an outright fib. Fie.

Tol lol lay: These are probably merely filler words. *Tol lol* is used in *The Grand Duke* to mean "just so-so," but any connection with taradiddles is tol lol at best.

Double-dealing [on a career of double-dealing]: Brewer (56) defines this as "professing one thing and doing another inconsistent with that promise."

Chapter VII

"Repente" {reh-PEN-tay}: Gilbert tells us it means "of a sudden." But in what language? Bradley (46) and Asimov (11) say both Italian and Latin.

Paradox: A statement that seems absurd but is in fact correct.

Contradicente {CONE-trah-dee-CHEN-teh}: Latin for "contradicting."

Addled [Perhaps his brain is addled]: Confused. See also Chapter X.

Bearded [Bearded by these puny mortals]: Alludes to the expression "to beard the lion in his lair," which means to defy someone personally and face-to-face. See also Chapter VIII.

Badinage [your badinage so airy]: Playful banter.

Vagary {vay-GARE-ee} [a plague on this vagary]: A capricious idea or action.

Quandary: {Distort to rhyme with vagary} A predicament or state of perplexity.

Chary: Cautious.

Andersen's library: Refers to Hans Christian Andersen's fairy tales, with *library* twisted to rhyme with *fairy*. Hyder (162) points out that in Gilbert's time some English language editions were actually titled *Hans Christian Andersen's Library*.

Ladies' Seminary: A school for refined young women.

Crooks: Shepherds' crooks, those long poles with loopy hooks for snaring sheep. You see them in every Christmas pageant.

Whig: The Whigs were the forerunners of the Liberal party.

Grouse and salmon season: According to Bradley (46) the legal grouse hunting season in Great Britain runs from August 12 (hence "the glorious twelfth") to December 10. The legal fishing season for salmon runs from February 1 until the end of August. The Queen of the Fairies should have made *season* plural, but let it pass.

Friday nights: [He shall end the cherished rights you enjoy on Friday nights]: Here is a well-chewed bone. Some authorities (11, 145, 147, 149, 171, 320) believe the "cherished rights" refer to the privilege of offering private bills, as opposed to those backed by one of the parties. Such a right would be cherished because private bills were likely to benefit the M.P.'s constituency. Other authorities (46, 142, 177, 242, 245, 286, 299) argue that Gilbert had in mind "early rising" (i.e., quitting at 7 PM instead of midnight or later). A key clue in this debate is that when the opera was written (1882) the line read "Wednesday nights." In 1902, however, some amendment to the law apparently caused Gilbert to change the libretto to read "Friday nights." The question then is what was amended? The answer is found in May's authoritative tomes (204, 205). They lead to these conclusions: (i) To begin with, the threat could not have been directed at the House of Lords because they did not meet at all on Wednesdays, so it must have been directed at the House of Commons. (ii) The threat could not have been directed at private bills because in 1882 private bills could be introduced on Tuesdays and Fridays as well as on Wednesdays. (iii) That leaves the threat as being directed at the Commons' custom of "early rising," which in 1902 was indeed changed from Wednesdays to Fridays. So, if only the Commons are under the gun, why do the peers cry "No! No!"? Collegial loyalty I suppose; but Prestige (245) has an alternative explanation: The Scottish and Irish peers who were not among the ranks of Representative Peers were eligible to run for election in the House of Commons. Those peers, at least, would have cause for alarm.

Marriage with deceased wife's sister: This refers to a long-standing legislative feud between the two houses of Parliament. The bill allowing such a marriage was finally passed in 1907, after some half a century of debate. Without such a ban, it was argued, an unmarried woman might be tempted to poison her married sister and then snare her bereaved brother-in-law. A more likely explanation is given by Stedman (273): "Presumably the ban was related to incest — Hamlet is outraged at his mother's incest, she having married her deceased husband's brother. Interestingly enough, marriage with

Iolanthe

deceased wife's sister was permissible in the colonies. In Shaw's *Major Barbara* Adolphus Cusins is legitimate in Australia, but a bastard in England because his father did [that]."

Common Councilmen: Members of the City of London's municipal council, holding a rather modest level of influence and prestige.

Fig [We do not care a fig]: We don't give a hoot (generally enriched with a snap of the fingers). See Chapter XI for sordid details.

Canaille {Gilbert probably wants you to say "kah-NILE" to rhyme with style.} [with base *canaille*!]: French for "the scum of the earth," the kind who profess to loathe the Savoy operas. Ugh!

Plebs [of vulgar *plebs*!]: In ancient Rome, the ordinary people.

The οἱ πολλοί: Hoi Polloi. Greek for the common herd. Halton (147) notes that *οἱ* means "the," so Gilbert is guilty here of a tautology. Nevertheless, it's an accepted idiom.

ACT II

Sentry-go: Guard duty.

M.P.'s [When in that House M.P.'s divide]: Members of Parliament.

Divide: The method of voting described earlier under "Division."

Cerebellum: The back lobe of the brain.

Equanimity {EE-kwah-nimity} [No man can face with equanimity]: Composure.

Blues [in the blues]: Dismayed and dispirited.

A-muck [running a-muck of all abuses]: Attacking without discrimination. Applegate (8) noted that the word is Malaysian (*amok*) and refers to a person who goes into a murderous frenzy and attacks people at random. Brewer (56) proposes a less violent definition: someone who expounds on a subject of which he is ignorant.

Kettle of fish: An old expression indicating a muddle. It dates back at least as far as 1750 (115).

Protegé: Someone under the care or protection of another. There is often an implication that the mentor offers encouragement, too (167).

Pickford [He's a Parliamentary Pickford]: A well-known British moving and delivery company, whose slogan used to be "We Carry Everything." In case you need to know, its present slogan is "The Careful Movers" (284).

Queen Bess [in good Queen Bess's time]: Queen Elizabeth I (1533-1603): Daughter of Henry VIII and Anne Boleyn. During her eventful reign (1558-1603) England gained prestige through the naval exploits of Sir Francis Drake and the voyages of discovery of Sir Walter Raleigh. Her reign, too, is looked upon as England's golden age of literature thanks to the works of Spenser and Shakespeare. One school kid wrote of her: "Queen Elizabeth was the 'Virgin Queen.' As a queen she was a success" (185).

Bays [Yet Britain won her proudest bays]: Alludes to the laurel wreaths of victorious heroes, the bay shrub being a member of the laurel family.

Wellington [When Wellington thrashed Bonaparte]: Arthur Wellesley (1769-1852): The Duke of Wellington. Trained as a military officer he spent eight years in India successfully putting down native insurrections and winning high honors. After a time in politics he was called upon for military service fighting Napoleon's troops in Spain and Portugal. After several successful campaigns he was appointed field-marshal. His armies pushed the French troops back into France and their eventual defeat at Waterloo (in Belgium) in 1815. He was made Duke of Wellington and spent the rest of his life in politics, serving one two-year period as prime minister.

Bonaparte: Napoleon Bonaparte (1769-1821): The famous French military and political leader. From his modest Italian origins in Corsica, he rose to crown himself Emperor of

Chapter VII

France (and scourge of Europe). He spent his final years in exile on the island of St. Helena.

King George [In good King George's glorious days!]: George III (1738-1820), who reigned during the Napoleonic wars and the American War of Independence. History affirms that George III was, indeed, a good man and popular with his subjects. Unfortunately, he was insane during the final nine years of his life. The "glorious days" were those that saw England's triumph over Napoleon.

Representative Peer [give me a British Representative Peer!]: A Representative Peer (note capital R) is one who, in the House of Lords, represents his compatriot Peers in Scotland or Ireland. But is that what Gilbert meant? Possibly not. Quoting Prestige (243):

> I think here Gilbert got confused. In my view the libretto should be printed with a small (lower case) "r" for Representative, which would then clearly make Celia say "give me a typical British peer." I think it most unlikely Gilbert was attempting anything so subtle as to imply that Celia was referring specifically to a Scottish or Irish peer, a group of whom used to sit in the House of Lords as representing the general bodies of Scottish and Irish peers (in distinction from the English and United Kingdom peers, who sat in the House of Lords as of right).

Evans (112), on the other hand, noted that Tolloller and Mountararat both have Irish tenants, so they are probably from Ireland and may, indeed, be Representative Peers. The nice thing about this argument is that few singers can enunciate well enough to allow the audience to distinguish a capital letter from a lower case letter.

Mortify [But I mortify this inclination]: Discipline it. Kill it!

Amorous dove: The term "amorous dove" seems obvious enough, but why relate it to Ovid two lines later? Some say that Ovid likened himself to a dove. Others say the allusion is to Ovid's amorous poetry. A third view is that in ancient times the dove was looked upon as a sensuous and fickle creature, sacred to Venus and hence something of a sex symbol. You are free to accept any or all of these hypotheses.

Type [type of Ovidius Naso!]: One meaning of the word, which applies here, is "a perfect example" (97).

Ovidius Naso {oh-VID-ius NAY-so}: Publius Ovidius Naso (43 B.C. - ca. A.D. 18): A Roman poet, better known as *Ovid*. His literary themes made much of love, with emphasis on physical desire rather than devotion. He is also known for his brilliant interpretations of ancient myths, best represented by his *Metamorphoses*. Ovid's family name, Naso, means "nose." This has led some lexicographers to conclude that Ovid had a big nose. Cameron (66) rebuts this, "While one of his ancestors … may have acquired the name because of his nose, … Ovid's physiognomy was not so distinguished. It was just the family name."

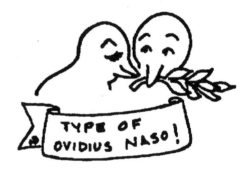

Main [That is the main on which to draw]: The water main leading to a fire hydrant.

Captain Shaw: In Gilbert's day Captain Eyre Massey Shaw (1830-1908) was the well-known and popular leader of the London Fire Brigade. Gilbert knew the good man would be in the Savoy on opening night and the contralto could look right at him. Do you suppose he blushed?

[**Note:** The next five entries are from the De Belville song, which is usually omitted in performance. The words may be found in Reference (126) under "The Reward of Merit," as well as in Allen's *First Night Gilbert and Sullivan* (3). There are in the overture to

Iolanthe some musical phrases that do not reappear in the body of the opera. This is unique in a Savoy opera overture and suggests that the music may have been composed for the De Belville song. It was nicely applied to those words on one occasion by the University of Michigan Gilbert & Sullivan Society.]

De Belville [De Belville was regarded as the Crichton of his age]: The imaginary protagonist of the song mentioned above. He was a man of many talents and virtues, which were ignored until a distant cousin died and he inherited great wealth. In one book (126) he is referred to as "Dr. Bellville," whereas in the other (3) he is "De Belville," perhaps at Sullivan's suggestion; or perhaps the "De" is right and the "Dr." is a typographical error.

Crichton {CRY-tun}: The reference is to James Crichton ("the admirable Crichton"), a young Scottish scholar, adventurer, linguist, and chosen companion of nobility. He was widely admired for his intellectual capacity, beauty, and physical prowess. He lived from 1560 to 1583, going to an early death in an altercation that could have formed the theme of a tragic opera (105).

"Line" [He was a famous painter, too, and shone upon the "line"]: The "line" is where the supposedly best paintings were hung at Royal Academy shows (273).

Ruskin [And even Mr. Ruskin came and worshipped at his shrine]: John Ruskin was an English author, art critic, and social reformer (1819-1900). He was a highly regarded critic and a professor of fine arts at Oxford (105).

Sixpenny Reviews: These were cheap journals of little acclaim. When Gilbert used the poem in Reference (126), he changed the words to "Quarterly Reviews." These were of high intellectual standard and influential (245).

Paramount: Of highest importance.

Unrequited: Unreturned.

Encumbers [my ardent soul encumbers]: Burdens.

Counterpane [First your counterpane goes]: A bed coverlet.

Ticking [nothing 'twixt you and the ticking]: Strong cotton or linen covering for mattresses or pillows.

Harwich {Rhymes with carriage.} [in a steamer from Harwich]: A cross-channel port in Essex about 70 miles northeast of London. See map on page 3.

A STEAMER FROM HARWICH

Bathing machine [something between a large bathing machine and a very small second class carriage]: A horse-drawn wheeled vehicle used as a dressing room by modest Victorian bathers to enter the water without having to parade across the beach. See also Chapter XV.

Carriage: The carriage referred to here was a railroad coach. There were actually three classes of cars in those days.

Penny ice [penny ice and cold meat]: Prestige (243) assures us this is "a quantity of ice cream purchased for a penny from a street vendor."

Sloane Square and South Kensington Stations: These are adjacent stations in the London transit system near where Gilbert

Chapter VII

lived in South Kensington. He claimed, incidentally, that the plot for his short story and, later, play *Comedy and Tragedy* came to him while riding between the two stations (140).

Devon [who started that morning from Devon]: A shire (county) in the southwest of England, just east of Cornwall.

Four-wheeler: Prestige (243) explains that this is a horse-drawn hackney carriage, that is, a vehicle that you could hire. The word hackney is apparently derived from the French *haquenée*, an ambling nag (41).

Round games: Card games in which each player takes his turn in sequence around the table, playing for himself, without a partner.

Clocks [the black silk with gold clocks]: Ornamental stitchings on socks, on each side of the ankle.

Salisbury Plain [crossing Salisbury Plain on a bicycle]: A rolling countryside in the southwest part of England. Its best-known attraction is Stonehenge.

CROSSING SALISBURY PLAIN ON A BICYCLE

Tars [he's telling the tars]: Common sailors. See Chapter IV for derivation.

Cables [from cough mixtures to cables]: Heavy ropes such as those used to anchor ships.

Boot-tree [first take off his boots with a boot-tree]: A boot-tree is a device used to stretch a boot or keep it in shape. That isn't what Gilbert meant; he meant a boot-jack, a notched board used to restrain the heel while extracting one's foot from a boot. The cartoon, which Gilbert himself drew to illustrate the song, shows what he really had in mind.

Greengrocer [From the greengrocer tree]: A retailer of fresh fruits and vegetables.

Apple puffs: Light, baked pastries containing thinly sliced apples and various other delicious components. Never pass up a chance to accept one when served hot, and especially *mit Schlag*.

Three-corners: These are presumably what are more commonly known as turnovers: a triangular, filled pastry.

Banburys: "A special kind of cake first made in Banbury, Oxfordshire" (75). Webster (307) adds that they are tarts with a fruit and raisin filling. Brewer (54) says they are "a spiced pastry turnover." Burgess (60) says they are Danish in origin. I don't know about you readers, but my stomach is beginning to gurgle. Let us move on to less filling matters.

Rothschild [are taken by Rothschild and Baring]: This refers to the Rothschild family of international bankers. The firm was founded by Mayer Anselm Rothschild (1743-1812) of Frankfurt-am-Main. Each of his five sons established banks in different European cities. One of his grandsons, Lionel Nathan Rothschild, was the first Jew admitted to the English Parliament, and his son was made a baron (105).

Baring: An English family of bankers, also with German roots. The brothers Francis and John started the firm in 1770. Francis was made a baron in 1793. Recently a Dutch bank rescued the establishment, which had fallen on hard times (60).

Andante [given *andante* in six-eight time]: Moderately slow — not at all like the bulk of that nightmare song.

Six-eight time: The musical time signature used in most of the songs in the show, including the nightmare song (48).

Maidie [the charming maidie]: A single woman, with modest variation to rhyme with lady.

Shies [He who shies]: To swerve suddenly aside, as a startled horse.

Maravedi [is not worth a maravedi]: An ancient Spanish copper coin worth a fraction of a cent. "Not worth a maravedi" is an old expression meaning worthless (54). The word derives from the Arab family, the Almoravidies, who ruled Cordoba from 1087 to 1147 (266).

In for a penny, in for a pound: Brewer (54) explains this expression as: "Once involved the matter must be carried through whatever obstacles or difficulties may arise — there can be no drawing back."

[**Note:** The next seven entries are from Strephon's seldom-performed recitative and song "Fold your flapping wings." See Allen (3).]

Verity [In verity I wield]: Truth.

Exotic [Crime is no exotic]: Something found only outside one's own country.

Bane [Bitter is your bane]: Something that ruins or spoils. Something poisonous.

Ministry, Cross-Bench, and Opposition: The terms refer in order to the party in power, the Members of Parliament who are unaligned, and the party (or parties) that are out of power.

Drury Lane [Dingy Drury Lane, Soapless Seven Dials]: Drury Lane is in London's theatrical district. The "dingy" speaks for itself. ("Seven Dials" has already been defined.)

Filigree [Fed on filigree]: The literal meaning of the word pertains to delicate, beaded jewelry, which sounds highly indigestible. In *Don Juan* (65), Lord Byron uses these words, in part, to describe a luxurious Arabian Nights repast:

> And fruits, and date-bread loaves closed the
> repast,
> And Mocha's berry, from Arabia pure,
> In small fine China cups, came in at last;
> Gold cups of filigree made to secure
> The hand from burning underneath them
> placed,
> (and so forth).

Those filigrees were presumably intricately woven wire, or ornamentally pierced cup holders (274). In the context, however, the best hypothesis is that Strephon is simply alluding to his fortunate Arcadian background. We may wonder how his mother could have supported him so graciously. After all, she spent her time standing on her head at the bottom of a stream. But, of course, she enjoyed a well-earned reputation for doing surprising things.

Fagin: Refers to the villainous Fagin of *Oliver Twist*, who ran a training school for juvenile thieves.

Coffers [with flowing coffers]: Chests for money or other valuables.

But does your mother know you're . . . : This was a common catch phrase in Gilbert's day: "Does your mother know you're out?" Brewer (54) says it is "A jeering remark addressed to a simpleton." In the present context it has a double meaning.

Suppliant [a suppliant at your feet]: Someone who is pleading. See also Chapter XI.

Aiaiah! Willaloo!: Fairy language expressing grief and woe. Take my word for it. It parodies the Rhine-maidens' "Wallala weila weia," etc. in *Das Rheingold*. The parody is underscored when the Queen of the Fairies is decked out like Brünnhilde.

Chapter VII

Duchesses, marchionesses, countesses, viscountesses and baronesses: The wives of dukes, marquises, earls, viscounts, and barons, respectively. The same terms apply to their widows, too, but that is certainly not what Celia has in mind. {The first *s* in *viscountess* is silent.}

Equity Draughtsman: *Equity* is a body of laws based largely on general principles of justice to correct flaws in common law. An *equity draughtsman* is a barrister skilled in drawing up complicated contracts, trusts, and wills (142), especially those involving the subtleties of equity law.

Beaux [two beaux to every string]: The plural of beau, an attentive male admirer. Switch the nouns and you have a first-class pun.

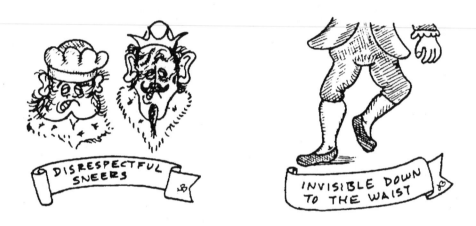

DISRESPECTFUL SNEERS

INVISIBLE DOWN TO THE WAIST

BLUSHING MISTRESS LALAGE

In casting about for a plot that would satisfy Sullivan, Gilbert turned to one of his earlier dramatic works: a play titled *The Princess*, a gently satiric work based on a narrative poem by Tennyson. (Gilbert described his version as "a respectful per-version.") The story deals with a princess who eschews men and establishes a girls' college — an innovation that was then still new in England, and not yet widely accepted. Gilbert reorganized his material, and *Princess Ida* was the outcome. Among the G&S operas, this one claims two distinctions: it is the only one written in blank verse, and it is the only one having three acts. (What is now the first act was originally a prologue followed by two acts.)

Princess Ida opened at the Savoy on January 5, 1884, and ran for 246 performances — a disappointingly short duration, and one that caught Gilbert and Sullivan unprepared with a replacement. Carte accordingly revived *Trial by Jury* and *The Sorcerer* to keep the theater and the Company occupied while he tried to maintain his artistic friends in double harness. In addition to his growing distaste for Gilbertian libretti, Sullivan was suffering from a kidney ailment that was to plague him continually through the rest of his life. Fortunately for us, Carte succeeded in his delicate task — as we shall later see.

Although *Princess Ida* ranks among the lesser known of the Savoy operas, it has a strong attraction for many Gilbert and Sullivan aficionados. Ida's three hulking brothers are among the funniest characters in all of comic opera; and musically, Ida's appeal to Minerva is as close as Sullivan ever came to setting Gilbert's words in grand operatic style. Ardent advocates of women's liberation may bridle at Gilbert's views, but his darts are gently tossed and draw little real blood.

CHARACTERS AND SETTING

Hildebrand: A name taken from a character in old German romances, the oldest and wisest of the chiefs and, like Merlin, a magician as well (55).

Adamant [Castle Adamant]: A legendary stone of impenetrable hardness. A derived meaning, which applies here, is "utterly unyielding in attitude or opinion in spite of all appeals, urgings, etc." (250).

Daughters of the Plough: Servant girls, presumably from farming families. Karr (170) suggests that these girls are assigned menial duties not because they are indigent or from the lower classes, but rather because their mental capacities and interests leave them unsuited to academic work. Remember Ida's strictures against "cruel distinctions, meant to draw a line 'twixt rich and poor." Many directors omit the daughters of the plough in actual production. They are not necessary in advancing the plot, nor are there any spare men in the show for them to wed in the end (although some of those "sons of the tillage" sneered at in *Ruddigore* would seem logical matches.)

Time and Place: Gilbert is delightfully vague about the time and country in which the opera is set. The armor worn by Gama's sons implies a wide range of medieval dates, and there are incidental references to Hungary, but that nation has had wide-ranging borders over the centuries. And no matter what century one suggests, the work is rife with anachronisms (211). Let's just say the opera is set once upon a time in Never-Never Land.

SEARCH THROUGHOUT the PANORAMA

Chapter VIII

ACT I

Pavilion: An open porch, probably under an elaborate tent-like cover. A royal pavilion would be expected to feature lots of colorful pennants, banners, and flags.

Panorama: An unobstructed view of the open countryside.

Plighted: Promised or pledged.

Liege [None, my liege]: A feudal lord.

Betrothed [To whom our son Hilarion was betrothed]: The term clearly means engaged, i.e., promised in marriage. Yet, later in the same act we find Hilarion singing about his "baby bride" and their wedding "twenty years ago." The logical explanation is that, although wed as infants, the marriage remained only tentative, and easily annulled, until consummated. There's an unbounded field of speculation on which I could discourse for hours. But, no; instead of that, see what is revealed about *Betrothed* in Chapter III.

Crumped [crumped it in fitful petulance]: Crunched. (In most editions the word is "crumpled," which seems correct.)

Adder [For, adder-like, his sting lay in his tongue.]: This reflects the old mistaken belief that an adder injects its poison through its forked tongue. It leads up to an overwrought pun, which you can figure out for yourself, in the next line of the libretto.

Corollary [From which I gather this corollary]: An additional proposition that logically follows a proven proposition.

Mustachios: A poetic way of saying "mustache." I can't resist mentioning that Kaiser Wilhelm II (the one who led Germany to defeat in WWI) took inordinate pride in his cocky mustache. In a state visit to Windsor he was accompanied by three valets, a hair dresser, and a hairdresser's assistant whose sole function was to titivate the royal mustache (201). There was an appointment that Pooh-Bah somehow overlooked.

En cavalier [And rides *en cavalier* in coat of steel]: Astride a horse (and wearing a knight's armor).

Trow {My dictionaries make it rhyme with crow, but Gilbert wants you to rhyme it with how.} [And his daughter, too, I trow!]: Believe, or at least suppose.

Quarter-day [As sure as quarter-day]: "One of the four days of the year when rents fall due" (75).

Transmutations [What transmutations have been conjured]: Changes from one form or species to another.

Conjured: Done by magic.

Alchemy: Brewer (56) says the word is taken from the Arabic and means the secret art. Its aims were threefold: the transmutation of baser metals into gold, the search for a universal solvent, and the search for the elixir of life. In broader terms, it can be taken to mean an agent of sweeping change. See also the entry for "Alchemist" in Chapter XI.

Baleful [baleful prophecies were rife]: Pertaining to sorrow, misery, and doom.

Rife: Abundant and widespread.

Forsworn [Ida has forsworn the world]: Renounced, meaning she has turned her back on worldly affairs.

Bib and tucker [All bib and tucker, frill and furbelow]: A tucker is an "ornamental frill of lace or muslin worn by women of the 17th and 18th centuries round the top of their dresses to cover the neck and shoulders. Hence, *with clean bib and tucker*, nicely dressed, looking fresh and spruce" (54). Stedman (274) says Louisa May Alcott's girls of the nineteenth century also wore tuckers.

Furbelow: A flounce or wide ruffle (or pleats) used to trim a dress.

Recumbent [recumbent in her foster mother's arms]: Lying on her back.

Foster-mother: Wet nurse; i.e., a woman other than the mother who breast-feeds a baby.

Hireling [the hireling mother-for-the-nonce]: One who serves for wages, in this case a wet nurse

For-the-nonce: For the moment; i.e., temporarily. See also Chapter XI.

Vestry: A room in a church in which ecclesiastical vestments are hung when not in use. In this case, a secluded retreat in which the wet nurse can feed her little charge with all due modesty. After the wedding ritual the register of marriage would be signed in the vestry (245).

Speak [For at that age I had not learnt to speak.] Hilarion is like the Old Testament prophet Jeremiah who said, "Ah, Lord God! behold I cannot speak; for I am a child."

Heralds [They are heralds evidently]: Official conveyors of important announcements or royal proclamations.

Sacred: Shielded by diplomatic immunity (but not for long, as it turns out).

Rex [Sons of Gama, Rex]: King.

Bent [They are not our bent]: An inclination or strong point.

Doughty {DOW-tee} [But with doughty heart]: Brave.

Philanthropist [I'm a genuine philanthropist]: One who does good deeds out of a love for mankind. A splendid example would be an enlightened person who buys bales of this lexicon to place in hotel rooms.

Erring {Rhymes with purring.} [In my erring fellow creatures]: Departing from the correct way.

Snub [little plans to snub the self-sufficient]: To treat scornfully, coldly, or with contempt. To bring up short with rudeness or indifference. Let me cite an example of snub and counter-snub. Back in 1707 the nations of Europe were concerned with the brash King Charles of Sweden, who had conquered Saxony and stood poised to upset the balance of power throughout the continent. England's most powerful leader was John Churchill, Duke of Marlborough. He requested an audience with Charles and was invited to meet the king in his temporary residence in central Germany. Since Churchill was not a monarch, diplomatic protocol demanded that his initial contact should be with Count Piper, Charles's de facto prime minister. When the duke in his carriage arrived at the palace, Piper sent word that he was busy and kept the duke waiting half an hour. Finally, as Piper came forward, the duke stepped out of his carriage, donned his hat, and walked right past the count without acknowledging his presence. Then, a few feet away, the duke calmly urinated against a wall, then turned and greeted Piper "in courtly fashion" (202). Next time someone snubs you, keep this riposte in mind.

Self-sufficient: Self-satisfied, conceited.

Mortify: To humiliate.

Interested motives: The hidden, usually selfish, reasons for taking a position that seems to be based on high principles.

Ascetic [I'm sure I'm no ascetic]: One who is sternly self-denying. The word derives from the Greek *asketes*, or hermit.

Snigger: A half-suppressed laugh.

Leer: A sly or furtive look expressive of malignity, lasciviousness, or triumph (75).

Prejudice [To everybody's prejudice]: Detracting from reputation.

Bandy [How dare you bandy words with me?]: To knock back and forth, or to wrangle. The word also means bent, as in bandy-legs (bow legs), to which Cyril alludes in his reply, "No need to bandy aught that appertains to you." The second meaning goes back to the seventeenth century, when a curved stick called a "bandy" was used in *bandy ball*, a game similar to hockey (12).

Aught: Anything.

Knave [as a traitor knave]: A dishonest person. The miserable, poorly educated sort who would write an unfavorable review of this book.

Chapter VIII

Snob: "Not a gentleman; one who arrogates to himself merits which he does not deserve" (56).

Safety matches: A comparative novelty at the time the opera was produced (178).

Knowledge box [they light only on the knowledge box]: The head (56).

Dr. Watts's hymns [She'll scarcely suffer Dr. Watts's hymns]: Isaac Watts (1674-1748) was an English theologian and prolific author of hymns, his total output reaching some 600, including "O God, Our Help in Ages Past." His works are available today in a reprint of his *Hymns and Spiritual Songs*, originally published in 1707.

Sue [humbly sue]: Entreat.

Sillery [And pops of Sillery]: "A high-class wine produced in and around the village of Sillery in Champagne" (228).

Bower [We'll storm their bowers]: The OED (229) offers several meanings including a dwelling, a poetic word for an idealized abode, a shady recess, or a lady's private apartment or boudoir. Any one of those would fit the context.

Triolet [Oh dainty triolet]: A poem of eight lines and a specific rhyming pattern, which starts out ab, aa, abab … Stedman (273) calls attention to the song "Expressive glances," in which the word occurs. The verses of the song are themselves close to being triolets.

Heigho-let [or gentle heigho-let]: *Heigh-ho* is an exclamation of weariness. "Heigho-let" is Gilbert's variation to rhyme with *triolet* and *violet* and, as he so thoughtfully goes on to say, means a little sigh.

Urbanity [On sweet urbanity]: Polished politeness.

Inanity: Pertaining to emptiness or silliness. In other words, sweet nothings for those shell-like ears.

Verbal fences: Oral thrusts and parries (as in fencing).

Amatory [With ballads amatory]: Pertaining to love.

Declamatory: Descriptive of a passionate appeal.

Wizen [Growing thin and wizen]: Short for wizened, or shriveled.

Requisitions [Of our requisitions]: Formal demands.

Bail [And bail they will not entertain]: Security (usually cash) pledged to a court to ensure that a person charged with a crime will show up at a later date to stand trial. The same term occurs in Chapters III, IX, and XIII.

Entertain: Consider.

Mandate [Should she his mandate disobey]: An official order.

ACT II

Empyrean: In classic literature, the highest heaven, or region of pure elemental fire (75).

Lore [Of every kind of lore]: Learning.

Classics: Study of the literature, art, and life of ancient Greece and Rome.

Helicon [If you'd climb the Helicon]: Elikón is a mountain in south-central Greece. In classical mythology it was the mountain of poetic inspiration, being regarded as the abode of Apollo and the muses.

Anacreon [You should read Anacreon]: "Famous lyric poet of Greece sixth century B.C. His poems ring the praise of wine and love" (75). The Walmisleys (299) note that Anacreon was "an amusing voluptuary and an elegant profligate." He lived to the age of 85, but died "from suffocation by swallowing a grapestone, while drinking." Cameron (66) assures us that all of the authors Psyche mentions are inclined to be bawdy. But be not shocked; a few lines later Psyche advises reading only cleaned-up versions: "Bowdlerized."

Metamorphoses [Ovid's Metamorphoses]: A long poem, considered Ovid's masterpiece.

The common thread is the mythological transformations by which inanimate objects receive human souls or humans are turned into something else. Daphne's metamorphosis into the laurel tree is an example. The epic contains many yarns about nymphs, goddesses, and mortal maidens who lose their virtue.

Aristophanes: Greek writer of comic plays such as *The Birds*, *The Frogs*, and *Lysistrata*. He lived around 450-380 B.C., and was distinguished for his keen satire and ribald jokes.

Juvenal: Roman satirical poet who inveighed against the social defects of his day. He lived around A.D. 55-135. Scholastic editions of Juvenal customarily omit the juicier parts.

Bowdlerized [You will get them Bowdlerized]: Expurgated. After Thomas Bowdler's cleaned-up, family edition of Shakespeare, 1818. As his friends may have declaimed, there's nothing bawdy about old Bowdly.

Not at all good form: Cricket players' expression meaning unfair or downright dishonest. A more general meaning is not in keeping with established conventions of good manners and behavior (54).

Ribald {RIB-eld} [Man's a ribald — Man's a rake]: A vulgar, scurrilous, bad-mouthed person — the kind who crinkles candy wrappers during Ida's first solo.

Rake: Among other things, an immoral rogue.

Mate [with whom you give each other mate.]: Refers to the winning position in chess in which one player has trapped the other's king. Asimov (11) says the pertinent term "checkmate" is from "a Persian expression meaning the king is dead."

Perambulator: A baby carriage, or pram.

Paragon [Paragon of common sense]: A model of perfection.

Erudition [Running fount of erudition]: Scholarship. Bierce (39) defines it as "dust shaken out of a book into an empty skull."

Minerva: The Roman version of Athena, the goddess of wisdom and patroness of the arts and trades. Rumor has it that she sprang, with a tremendous battle cry and fully armed, from the brain of Jupiter. Wow!

Unillumined [Their unillumined eyes]: Blind.

Neophytes: New converts, novices.

Rule of three [That's rule of three]: The routine for solving simple problems in arithmetical proportions. Given three terms in a proportion, you can find the fourth by multiplying the second and third and dividing by the first. Behold: 2 is to 4 as 6 is to X. To find X, multiply 4 times 6, then divide by 2. So X equals 12. Now try this: given that a man's brain is to an elephant's as a woman's brain is to a man's, who is smarter — a man, a woman, or an elephant?

Pedant [The narrow-minded pedant]: One meaning is an unimaginative, literal-minded person.

Swan, Edgar, Gask, et al.: These were all smart London shops with compound names. All are now defunct. A few details may be gleaned from Goodman (140) and Bradley (47).

Chaos [let Chaos come again!]: Everyone knows that chaos with a lower case c means utter confusion. With an upper case C, however, it refers to the state of the universe before the creation, when it was even more disorganized than it is today.

Abstract Philosophy [I, madam, on Abstract Philosophy]: Theoretical approaches to the search for truth.

Hypotheses [Given these three hypotheses]: Alternative assumptions or propositions.

Manet: The person named remains on stage. Latin for "He (or she) remains" (66). *Manent* applies to more than one person.

Coronal [Time weaves my coronal]: Crown.

Ween [Yet humble second shall be first, I ween]: I fancy.

Chapter VIII

Paling [Fence and paling]: Picket fence.

Bull-dogs [That bull-dogs feed on throttles]: Jumping ahead for a moment, throttle, as defined in the OED (229) means throat. This naturally leads one to interpret bulldogs as meaning pugnacious bowlegged dogs. Knight (177), however, believes that Gilbert meant horseflies. But, wait! There is another candidate. Brewer (54) says that at Oxford and Cambridge the official in charge of discipline was protected by two intimidating attendants called bulldogs. This leads Stone (283) to propose that as Gilbert's intent. Knight and Stone are welcome to their views, and so are you, but my vote is with the canines.

Throttles: As mentioned above: throats (targets most tempting to any self-respecting dog).

Broken bottles [broken bottles on a wall]: Refers to the practice of cementing pieces of broken glass on top of walls to discourage would-be intruders from climbing over.

Spring-guns [spring-guns breathe defiance]: These are guns that are fixed to fire when a person, or animal, comes in contact with a wire attached to the trigger.

Lay a crown: To wager a five-shilling coin. (Under the former British coinage system, the pound sterling was worth twenty shillings.) A crown, then, would be worth a quarter of a pound.

Wire [intend to send a wire]: Telegram. Alternatively, Dorsey (260) and Kravetz (181) suggest that they mean to extend a wire to the moon. Hilarion's source of information, being ambiguous, leaves the matter unsettled, alas.

Set the Thames on fire: This is an old expression for the impossible (115). Brewer (56) reveals that "He'll never set the Thames on Fire" was an old expression meaning he'll never amount to much. {Thames rhymes with hems, but don't ask why.}

Rigs [Then they learn to make silk purses with their rigs]: You wouldn't believe all the meanings conveyed by this word. Asimov (11) makes this reasonable surmise as to Gilbert's intent: "Among other things, a 'rig'

refers to a woman's outfit. [Perhaps Gilbert] is referring to a woman's sewing equipment, which is so much a part of her as to be considered an item of her total dress." Bradshaw (51), Karr (171), and Kesilman (174) all endorse this. Other equally valid interpretations are "devices" and "tricks." Brewer (56), for example defines "Run a Rig" as playing a trick.

Circe's {SIR-sees.} [Lady Circe's piggywigs]: Circe was the enchantress who turned the companions of Odysseus into swine.

Trepan [And weasels at their slumbers they trepan]: An obsolete meaning of the word is to entrap (115, 228), which seems more believable than boring holes in their sleepy little skulls. Brewer (54) explains the saying "to catch a weasel asleep" means to deceive a vigilant person or catch him napping.

Sunbeams from cucumbers: Brewer (54) reminds us of the grand academy at Lagoda (in *Gulliver's Travels*), where the scholars pursue research projects such as making pincushions out of soft stones and extracting sunbeams from cucumbers. The intent was to seal the sunbeams in phials and to release them later during inclement weather (177). And that reminds us of Samuel Johnson's advice about cucumbers: "A cucumber should be well sliced and dressed with pepper and vinegar, and then thrown out as good for nothing" (113).

Perpetual Motion: The continuous action of a machine apart from any new external supply of energy.

Phenomena [These are the phenomena]: The plural of *phenomenon*, meaning anything (or anybody) encountered, especially if marked by unusual attributes. As used later in reference to Lady Psyche, it means a prodigy.

Domina [That every pretty domina]: This is the feminine equivalent of the Oxford dons or doms, a contraction of the Latin *dominus*, fellows or tutors.

Circle [the circle— they will square it]: Refers to the insoluble problem of geometrically constructing a square with area equal to that of a given circle.

The little pigs, they're teaching for to fly: "When pigs fly" is a colloquial expression for "never" (115).

Flout [They mock at him and flout him]: To show contempt or scorn.

"Going to do without him": The phrase is in quotation marks because it was taken from a catch phrase (regarding doing without women) made popular in British music halls by Arthur Roberts in 1882 (237).

Matriculate: To enroll as a student.

Penitent [and penitent for deeds]: Repenting.

Askance [Looked at askance]: With suspicion.

Shades [Seek sanctuary in these classic shades!]: Sheltered academic retreats.

Innately [with a heart innately]: Pertaining to natural or inborn characteristics.

Roguery [Brimming with joyous roguery]: Playful mischief.

Hind [Timid am I as a startled hind]: Doe, or female deer.

Well-born [Three well-born maids of liberal estate]: From upper-class families.

Liberal estate: Favorable worldly circumstances.

Sizars {SIZE-ers} [You'll find no sizars here, or servitors]: Students who are charged reduced fees in exchange for waiting table, and so forth.

Servitors: Same as sizars. Stone (283) says this is the term of choice at Oxford, while *sizar* is preferred at Cambridge. Something to keep in mind when applying to either institution.

Tufts [You'll find no tufts to mark nobility]: This pertains to the gold tassels worn by peers' sons on their caps at Oxford (54).

Meretricious [False hair, and meretricious ornament]: Tawdry, cheap. Asimov (11)

informs us the word is from the Latin *meretrix*, meaning a prostitute.

Impertinence [To reckon Nature an impertinence]: Something uncalled for and out of place.

Willy-nilly: Whether we like it or not. The expression is derived from Anglo Saxon *willan*, to desire, and *nylan*, the opposite. Thus what one must do whether he wants to or not, he does *will he*, *nill he* or willy-nilly (266).

Unseemly [unseemly in their mirth]: Indecorous, unbecoming.

Ranunculus bulbosus: The bulbous, or European, buttercup, "having a bulb shaped root and bright yellow flowers" (250).

Hipparchus: The most famous astronomer of ancient Greece. He made an accurate assessment of the length of the year and originated the concept of latitude and longitude — among other contributions. No one knows for sure exactly when he lived. *The Encyclopædia Britannica* (104) says he "flourished" from about 146 to 127 B.C. His date of birth is given variously as 194 and 160 B.C., and he apparently died about 130-120 B.C. I'm telling you all this because some G&S references worry about whether he was yet born when he supposedly determined latitude in "B.C. one sixty-three!" Well, maybe Psyche was misquoted.

Docked [and he docked his tail]: Cut off short. Asimov (11), however, reminds us that apes have no tails. Kipling could have added to his Just-So Stories: "How the Ape Lost His Tail."

Tub [he took his tub]: Read: He learned to bathe.

Guinea {ginny} [and paid a guinea to a toilet club]: British monetary unit equal to £1.05, i.e., 21 shillings. In case you are not already in on the

HE TOOK HIS TUB

Chapter VIII

secret, there is no longer any such coin or paper money. For further details see Chapter VI.

> There was an old man from Kilkenny,
> Who never spent more than a penny
> At any one loo,
> But this could accrue
> On long walks to more than a guinea.

Toilet club: We are indebted to Hardwick (149) for explaining this recondite term: "An exclusive gentlemen's hairdressing establishment." Prestige (245) adds that it "could also be an exclusive Turkish bath establishment."

Darwinian Man: Alluding to Charles Darwin and his doctrine (published in 1859) "respecting the origin of species as derived from descent, with variation, from parent forms through the natural selection of those best adapted to survive in the struggle for existence" (290).

Étui {AY-twee} [Here is an *étui* dropped by one of them]: A small case suitable for carrying small articles such as sewing equipment or toiletries.

Minx: A saucy girl. See also Chapter III.

Rule the roast: Dominate and order others about. Often mistakenly transmuted into "rule the roost." Brewer (54) states that the expression was common in the fifteenth century. Shakespeare used the term, too.

Malice [Replete with malice spiteful]: Active ill-will, wishing to do harm.

Perversity: Unreasonable refusal to do what's right.

Hoity-toity [Sing, hoity-toity!]: A derisive reference to people who affect airs. Brewer (56) says it derives from the French *hoit-comme-toit*, meaning flightiness.

Marry come up: Brewer (54) gives this interpretation: "May Mary come up to my assistance, or to your discomfort!"

Plantagenet [although a born Plantagenet]: Family name of a long succession of English kings, from Henry II (1154) through Richard III (1485). Brewer (56) says the name derives "from planta genista (broom plant), the family cognisance first assumed by the Earl of Anjou, the first of his race, during a pilgrimage to the Holy Land, as a symbol of humility." Readers may note that the humility did not take root.

Worm will turn: Brewer (54) explains this is an old expression meaning that even "the most abject of creatures will turn upon its tormentors if driven to extremity."

"Are men" [but *"are men"* stuck in her throat]: A pun on Shakespeare's "amen stuck in my throat" (in *Macbeth* Act II, Scene 2). Better it should have stuck in Gilbert's throat.

Asphodel [Here in meadow of asphodel]: A collective term for lilies or daffodils. In Greek mythology, asphodel were the ever-blooming flowers that grew in the Elysian fields. Bunthorne found them attractive, too, if you'll recall.

Booby [And is the booby comely?]: Dunce. Ida isn't being personally insulting here. All men are dunces, at best, in her view.

Comely {Rhymes with dumbly.}: Good-looking.

Consisted [Consisted with my maiden modesty]: Harmonized.

Staid [downcast and staid]: Sober and sedate.

Demure: Grave, shy, or seemingly modest (75).

Flaunting [Flaunting it in brave array]: Impudently displaying.

Own [For his intrusion we must own]: Admit.

Doughty: Brave.

Desecration [Shame and desecration]: Violation of something sacred.

Execration [female execration]: Refers to the women's uttered curses.

Beard [To beard a maiden in her lair]: A take-off of "to beard a lion in his lair," meaning to settle an issue with an imposing person face-to-face on his or her own grounds. Ida, we fear, has mangled her metaphor, but she had all too little time to get her thoughts (or dripping hair) in order. See also Chapter VII.

Indisposed for parleying: In no mood for debate or discussion.

Chit [To fit the wit of a bit of a chit]: A youngster, usually a girl. Often used contemptuously — as in the present context.

To sulk in the blues: To act in a sullen, gloomy way.

Potentate [a peppery Potentate]: A ruler with great power. (That explains the capital P.)

Bate [Who's little inclined his claim to bate]: Abate, diminish, back down.

Wind [His menaces are idle as the wind]: Ida means wind, as in fast moving air, but clearly it should be pronounced the poetical way: winde. See also Chapter XII.

Fratricide [the guilt of fratricide]: The murder of one's own brother or brothers.

ACT III

Paynim [Struck his Paynim foe!]: An archaic term for an infidel, which to a Crusader usually meant a Muslim.

Martial [our martial thunder]: Warlike.

Paradox: A statement that seems ridiculous but is, in fact, true. Alas, poor Frederic!

The Needful [We find the Needful comprehended]: Lady Blanche's paradox becomes clear when you understand that "needful" is an old slang term for money (115).

Fusiliers [My fusiliers, advance!]: Soldiers bearing lightweight flint-lock muskets. The word *fusil* derives from an old French word meaning "steel for striking fire" (250).

Fulminating [We can dispense with fulminating grains]: Exploding. Bradley (47) explains that the term derives "from the Latin word *fulminare*, meaning to send forth thunder and lightning."

Saltpetre [We can dispense with villainous saltpetre]: Potassium nitrate, used in making gunpowder. Asimov (11) mentions a line in Shakespeare's *Henry IV*, Part I, in which occurs the phrase "villainous saltpetre," and that has become a standard coupling, much like "damn Yankee."

Blow them up: To scold.

Polemist {pah-LEM-ist} [That brutalize the practical polemist]: One who vigorously debates doctrines.

Dispensing chemist: What Americans call a pharmacist, the English call a dispensing chemist.

Cot [To Court and cot]: Cottage.

Bruisèd reed: The phrase comes from the Old Testament (2 Kings 18:21 and Isaiah 36:6) as a metaphor for something, or someone, treacherously unreliable (55).

Lath [My sword was but a lath]: A thin strip of wood of the sort used to form a rough base for plaster.

Rime [of frost and rime]: Frost and rime mean essentially the same thing: frozen condensation.

Unanneal [That fear can unanneal]: Weaken.

Loth {Rhymes with quoth.} [Is loth to war with women]: Same as loath: meaning strongly disinclined.

Popinjays [these popinjays, these tufted jack-a-dandy featherheads]: Vain, empty-headed fops, decked out in ornamental finery. The word is an old name for a parrot, related to the Greek *papagos*, which may put you in mind of Mozart's *Magic Flute*. See also Chapter XI.

Jack-a-dandy: "A little fop" (115).

Chapter VIII

Tufted: This pertains to the gold tassels worn by peers' sons, as already mentioned above.

Malignity [black malignity]: Extreme hate.

Wight: An archaic term for a person and not necessarily from the Isle of Wight. Frequently some element of commiseration or contempt may be implied (229).

Lank [Oh, don't the days seem lank and long]: Austere, thin, and unexciting.

German bands: Bradley (48) explains that "German musicians were a common sight on the streets of Victorian London. They tended to wear uniforms and play marches and other stirring oom-pah-pah numbers."

Music stands: Those German bands were apparently in the habit of erecting music stands right in the street (48).

Wagner {VOGG-ner}: The great German librettist and composer of interminable operas.

Bade {bad} [I bade them go]: Ordered.

Organ boys [The organ boys, they stopped their noise]: The reference is to a barrel organ, or what Americans call a grind organ

Hurdy-gurds [and grinning herds of hurdy-gurds]: This is Gilbert's abbreviated form of the word hurdy-gurdist. A hurdy gurdy is a mechanical, stringed musical device. The sounds are produced by turning a handle that rotates a rosined wheel across the strings, which are stopped by means of keys. The term has also come to mean a barrel organ.

Fads [they feed my fads]: Read: They pamper my whims.

Ring [ere you pitch your ring]: An area set aside for a conflict, e.g., a boxing ring.

Tittle-tattle: Idle chatter or gossip.

Arrant [It's an arrant molly-coddle]: Thoroughgoing.

Molly-coddle: An effeminate person (115).

Noddle [Fears a crack upon his noddle]: Head.

Swaddle [And he's only fit to swaddle]: To swaddle is to wrap a newborn baby. The meaning here is that he is only fit to be swaddled.

Cuirass {kwi-RASS} [This tight-fitting cuirass]: A breastplate of leather or metal — in this case, steel.

Brassets: Armor for the upper arms (Gilbert's misspelling of "brassart") (250).

Cribbage pegs: Little jiggers (Swahili for "pegs"), used in scoring cribbage games. Terry (286) explains that the items of armor Arac refers to are cuishe, knee-cop, greave or jamb, and sollert — providing protection from hip to toe, in that order. Isn't this impressive? We retail state secrets, too.

Shape suits: (This is what Gilbert says the brothers are wearing after removal of all that armor.) You will find below a copy of Gilbert's own sketch of a shape suit. It could best be described as tight-fitting pants and snug pullover tunic with decorative slashes. The colors are given as dark red except for the slashes, which are pink. For whatever psychological inferences you may care to draw, the fellow in the sketch looks like Gilbert himself.

[**Commentary:** History shows that real life warriors have on occasion doffed their armor before going into battle. Young David about to face Goliath is perhaps the first example, but see also Goldberg (138).]

Virago [Here's a virago!]: A shrewish woman. A second, archaic meaning is a masculine woman. Gama meant whichever interpretation would most infuriate the men. See also Chapter XIV. {The correct pronunciation is open to debate. Most dictionaries say vih-RAY-go, but most people seem to prefer vih-RAH-go. I suggest using whichever form is more popular in your environment.}

Termagant {TER-mah-gant}: A violent quarrelsome female. See Brewer (54) for derivation of the word.

[**Note:** Gama's insults are disappointingly flat, merely two-dimensional. While in Hildebrand's prison he should have studied such masters as Samuel Johnson. That worthy fellow once found it imperative to insult a total stranger, so he thus expressed himself (I paraphrase): "Sir, under pretence of operating a brothel, your wife is a receiver of stolen goods!" (45).]

Ejaculate [And piously ejaculate]: Blurt out.

Hungary [Oh, doughty sons of Hungary!]: Why has Gilbert dragged Hungary into the proceedings at this advanced point? Perhaps because Hungarians are traditionally known as fierce warriors. Berlioz's stirring and popular *Rákózy March* (written in 1846) exemplifies the martial association. Kravetz (181) says that Berlioz averred that the theme came from "an old Hungarian war song of unknown authorship." These characters may not be real Hungarians, but they are every bit as war-like. Bradley (48) shows a second verse that appeared in the American first edition. Here it is:

> But if our hearts assert their sway,
> (And hearts are all fantastical)
> We shall be more disposed to say
> These words enthusiastical:
> Hilarion!
> Hilarion!
> Oh prosper, Prince Hilarion!
> In mode complete
> May you defeat
> Each meddlesome Hungarian!

Chambers (72) suggests that Gilbert may have composed the second verse before composing the first. In the second verse he dragged in Hungarian simply to rhyme with Hilarion, leading him then in the first verse to drag in ironmongery to rhyme with Hungary. On the other hand, it is conceivable that Hungary was introduced simply to rhyme with ironmongery (48). Clearly, Gilbert was not at his most facile in these verses.

Ironmongery: Hardware; in this case weapons and armor.

Meet [it's meet that we consult the great Potential Mysteries]: Appropriate.

Chapter VIII

Subjunctive [The five Subjunctive Possibilities]: Pertaining to the mood (or mode) of a verb implying a condition, doubt, wish, or hypothesis. This served as the inspiration for Lady Blanche's song "Come, mighty Must!"

Abjure [abjure tyrannic Man!]: Renounce.

Staunch {Rhymes with launch.} [I alone am staunch!]: Firm, constant, loyal, and trustworthy. See also Chapter IV.

Experiments [Experiments are made on humble subjects]: Knight (178) suggests that this derives from *Fiat experimentum in corpore vile*, a saying that arose from the experience of Murat, a French humorist who, in a trance, narrowly escaped dissection.

Clay [try our grosser clay]: In the context, read "less precious raw material."

"We will walk this world ...": These noble lines are in quotation marks because Gilbert took them from Tennyson's poem *The Princess*.

Owning [The love I'm owning]: Admitting.

THE MIKADO

Chapter IX   The Mikado

All friction between Gilbert and Sullivan was dissolved — at least for a time — when Gilbert hit on the idea of setting the next opera in Japan, turning his back on topsy-turvydom and the magic lozenge — also at least for a time. Although the setting was Japanese, the butt of Gilbert's wit was very much English, albeit kimono-clad. Everything about *The Mikado* fell perfectly into place. The story line is clever, the characters are nicely drawn, the lines are witty, and the music is of enduring beauty and perfectly suited to the words.

The Mikado opened at the Savoy on March 14, 1885, and ran for a record-breaking 672 performances. It remains the most popular of all the Savoy operas and may well claim to be the most-often-performed theatrical work in world history (182).

CHARACTERS AND SETTING

Mikado: An honorific title for the emperor of Japan. The word is made up of the Japanese words *mi* (honorable) and *kado* (gate — of the imperial palace) (250). Knight (178) says the term is used in a spiritual, indirect sense, the spiritual emperor being held in such awe that a direct mention of his name would be impossible. More prosaically, we may mention that we have visited two towns that bear the name. One, in Michigan, was founded in 1885 but no official name was assigned until 1888, when the Assistant Postmaster General (apparently a noble G&S fan) chose to name it after the opera. The other, in Saskatchewan (Canada), was founded by expatriate Russian settlers. They chose that name as their way of thumbing their collective nose at the Tsar during the Russo-Japanese War (1904-05). In Michigan the natives pronounce it "muh KAY doe"; in Saskatchewan they call it "muh CAD oh."

Yum-Yum {As set to music, the name is best pronounced yum-YUM in some places and YUM-yum in others.}: In his children's version of the story (133) Gilbert gives this tongue-in-cheek translation of his heroine's name: "The full moon of delight which sheds her remarkable beams over a sea of infinite loveliness, thus indicating a glittering path by which she may be approached by those who

are willing to brave the perils which necessarily await the daring adventurers who seek to reach her by those means." As Gilbert goes on to remark, still tongue-in-cheek, the Japanese language is exceptionally compact.

Ko-Ko: Bradley (48) claims that the word has at least 37 meanings in Japanese, depending on how it is pronounced. MacPhail (194) and I, however, have independently concluded that Gilbert probably intended no meaning, but might well have taken inspiration from what was then a widely advertised hair tonic. Von Eckhardt (297) shows a photograph of a London horse-drawn wagon embellished with bold signs reading "Koko for the Hair." Contemporary advertising claimed the tonic would keep hair from turning gray or falling out. Stanley DeOrsey (260) adds that the tonic was made by the Koko-Maricopas Company of London. There are other suggested sources as well. Aurora (15) nominates the character Ko-ko-ri-ko in Offenbach's operetta *Ba-ta-clan*. Walters (303) suggests another candidate: Ko-kil-ko, a shopkeeper in Thompson and Hervé's *Aladdin*. The subject is now declared beaten to death.

Pooh-Bah: The name has come to be synonymous with any important personage (especially one who is all puffed up about it) and, indeed, you will find it entered in some dictionaries. In the Boundary Waters of Minnesota there happens to be a Poobah Lake, but that is supposedly an Indian name and has nothing whatsoever to do with the opera (304).

Pish-Tush: A name that marries two exclamations of contempt. Stone (284) mentions that Gilbert's Bab Ballad "King Borria Bungalee Boo" has a character referred to as "the haughty Pish-Tush-Pooh-Bah." This is but one example of how Gilbert used components of his ballads in the Savoy operas.

Go-To: This noble lord is listed in some editions of the libretto but not others. (He is a bass singer who is used in the madrigal in place of Pish-Tush if the latter cannot hit the low notes.) The expression is a bob-tailed version of "Go to _____" (fill in to suit your mood). Brewer (54) says it is an "exclamation, often of impatience or reproof, or as an exhortation like 'Come'." Shakespeare used it

Chapter IX

in *Julius Caesar*. More to the point, Gilbert has both Pooh-Bah and Katisha saying it in *The Mikado*. Prestige (245) says it is a mild reproof similar to "pish" or "tush."

Pitti-Sing: Victorian baby talk for "pretty thing."

Peep-Bo: This is not only the reverse of Bo-Peep, but is also what English parents may say instead of "Peekaboo!" (56).

Wards: These are minors under the court-appointed guardianship of an adult.

Katisha: {Burgess (60) recommends pronouncing it "catty sha," which seems appropriate.}

ACT I

Obi [He carries … a bundle of ballads in his *obi*]: A Japanese cummerbund. (In some editions no mention is made of Nanki-Poo's obi; the stage directions say he carries the bundle in his hand.)

Minstrel [A wandering minstrel I]: A musician, singer, or poet. In this case a struggling trombonist who is also an accomplished tenor who accompanies himself on a native guitar.

Shreds and patches: Scarecrows have been called "figures of shreds and patches." Brewer (54) notes that Vice used to be personified as a mimic king in motley garb. Shakespeare has Hamlet refer to his villainous uncle, the king, as "A vice of kings! A cutpurse of the empire and the rule … A king of shreds and patches." Well, Nanki-Poo is really a prince of shreds and patches, so it fits right in.

Ballads: Stories in verse set to music.

Snatches: Bits and fragments of song.

Cut and dried: Already prepared.

Serried [in serried ranks assembled]: Shoulder to shoulder.

Capstan [We'll heave the capstan round]: A manually operated reel for hauling in ropes aboard a ship. See the entry for "Handspike" in Chapter V.

A-trip [Her anchor's a-trip]: This means the anchor has been broken out of the mud and is ready to be hauled aboard so the ship can sail.

A-lee [her helm's a-lee]: This means that the rudder has been turned so as to swing the ship's bow into the wind and perhaps head her in another direction.

To lay aloft: To climb into the rigging, usually in order to raise or lower sails.

As the fiddler swings us round: The work of heaving up the anchor with a capstan was often given tempo by a man playing a fiddle. One more opportunity for you students of music.

And a rumbelow: The OED (229) tells us this is a meaningless set of syllables used as a refrain, originally by sailors when rowing. In some editions the word is mistakenly split into "rum below," which may have resulted from wishful thinking on the part of some thirsty typesetter. (But, see the entry for "Grog" in Chapter IV.) In his children's book *The Story of The Mikado* (133), Gilbert appends this footnote:

> I have no idea what a "rumbelow" may be. No doubt it is some nautical article that is extremely useful on-board ship, for it is so often alluded to in sea-songs. It seems to hold the same place in a sea-song that the "old plantation" does in negro minstrelsy.

Protestations [to listen to my protestations]: Assurances, in this case of undying affection.

Reprieved [reprieved at the last moment]: Given temporary suspension of a sentence, in this case, of death.

Succinct [in words succinct]: Brief and to the point.

Connubially [Unless connubially linked]: An adverb implying a state of being married.

Decapited: Gilbert's poetic license applied to decapitated, i.e., beheaded.

Pre-Adamite [of Pre-Adamite ancestral descent]: Brewer (26D) informs us that this was the name given by Isaac de la Peyrère to a race of men whom he thought to have existed before the days of the Garden of Eden. He thought that only Jews are descended from Adam and Eve and that Gentiles derive from Pre-Adamites.

Protoplasmal: Pertains to the substance from which all plant and animal life are formed. Bradley (48) reminds us that when the opera was written Darwin's theory of evolution was still relatively new and, whereas traditionalists argued that Darwin was demeaning mankind, Gilbert turns the debate around and shows that Pooh-Bah takes great pride in his family tree that extends back even beyond 1066.

Primordial: Original form of any matter.

Globule: A small sphere of matter.

Lord Chief Justice: "Title given to heads of the courts of King's Bench and Common Pleas. Now given to the President of the Queen's Bench Division of the High Court" (141). Note that the term "Chief" in the title implies the position of presiding officer in a court of several judges (75).

[**Note:** For authoritative explanations of all Gilbert's legal and political terms you cannot do better than refer to Goodman (141).]

THE YOUTH WHO WINKED A ROVING EYE

Commander-in-Chief: Top officer in the army.

Lord High Admiral: Top officer in the navy.

Master of the Buckhounds: Person in charge of the monarch's hunting dogs.

Groom of the Back Stairs: The term "groom" is not confined to a servant who takes care of horses. He may also be a household officer. Back stairs allow servants to go from floor to floor without disturbing the upper class inhabitants or their guests. A "Groom of the Back Stairs" is mentioned in *Vanity Fair* (287). Paget (230) says that until late in the eighteenth century English royal palaces had special "back stairs" guards. These discreet Yeomen of the Guard, on "back stairs duty," admitted private visitors to the monarch. The visitors, whether ministers or mistresses, entered the palace through an inconspicuous door and mounted the back stairs. This is the source of the phrase "back stairs influence." Isn't it delightful what titillating gems one can pick up in a lexicon? Incidentally, for what it's worth, a 1991 newspaper article (13) mentions a Page of the Back Stairs then currently employed in Buckingham Palace.

Archbishop of Titipu: The chief bishop in the region of Titipu. You may be sure that is an imaginary position.

Lord Mayor: The civic head of the town.

Minion [I a salaried minion!]: A common servant. See also Chapters I, X, and XVI.

Go to [Likewise go to]: Go-To the character has already been presented under "Characters and Setting." Here we find the expression in the form of an admonition to give up hope and depart.

Ablutioner [You very imperfect ablutioner]: Pooh-Bah seems to imply that Nanki-Poo needs a bath, which at first seems out of character for a G&S tenor. But remember that he has been traveling for a month, or nearly, and without so much as a pocket handkerchief to mop his brow or dust his sandals. Then, too, there are just so many words that rhyme with *executioner*.

Cut a dash: Put on a showy display (115).

Chapter IX

Toddle: A colloquialism for "stroll." See also Chapter XII.

Diminutioner: One who reduces something — or somebody. Another Gilbertian creation.

Defer: To yield, or bow, or both.

Recognizances [Liberated then on bail, on my own recognizances]: A contract entered into with a court by which a person pledges himself, without the posting of any bond, to appear at his trial when summoned (178).

Up in dates: This refers to little terrors who have memorized a bunch of historic dates and can't wait to prove they know more than you. Psyche, in *Princess Ida*, had been such an obnoxious little exhibitionist at an early age.

Pestilential: Noxious and vexing.

Tête-à-têtes {TET-ah-TETs}: French for "head-to-head," implying a confidential, perhaps romantic, conversation. See also Chapter XIII.

Piano-organist: One who earns a living by traveling around the streets of a city with a decibelious music-making contraption called a piano-organ. Some people toss coins in his hat hoping he will play more, others hoping he will go far away. The piano-organ takes its name from the barrel organ, which it resembles. Both are mechanical contrivances actuated like oversize music boxes; i.e., they have a large revolving cylinder, or barrel, studded with metal pins that trigger the tone-generating elements. The barrel-organist (a past master of that delicately modulated instrument) is required to turn the handle that turns the barrel. See entry for "Organ boys" in Chapter VIII.

Provinces [the lady from the provinces]: To a Londoner "the provinces" means anywhere in the United Kingdom outside Greater London.

Guy [who dresses like a guy]: This refers to the effigies of Guy Fawkes that are burned each November 5 in Britain to celebrate his lack of success in blowing up the Houses of Parliament in 1605 (54, 115, 257). Stedman (273) notes that the phrase "was also current

in Gilbert's day as meaning someone grotesque or ridiculously dressed — in this case the lady dresses inappropriately in attempting to look fashionable." Bradshaw (51) assures us the expression is still in use in England. Some observers think Gilbert had in mind the American slang term for a man. The term was in those days not well known in England (115), so I doubt the validity of the proposal.

Anomaly [That singular anomaly]: Something, or someone odd, strange, peculiar, abnormal, or downright weird. From Latin and Greek for "irregular."

Nisi Prius {Nigh-sigh PRY-us} [that *Nisi Prius* nuisance]: The literal meaning is "unless before," and was applied to cases that formerly were brought before local assize courts when, technically, they should have been heard in London. Actions such as these were entered for hearing at the Royal Courts of Justice unless heard before (48, 178). (Assizes were periodic courts held in the provinces and presided over by London judges on circuit) (75). McElroy (209) adds that Gilbert, knowing both law and wit, must have taken a wry view of certain judges who were wont to substitute poor wit for real law. Gilbert had had his share of being part of a captive audience

[**Note:** Latin teachers and other purists question the pronunciation shown above, but that is how it was traditionally sung by D'Oyly Carte performers, and is presumably how Gilbert wanted it (260).]

Lord Chamberlain: The manager of the officers and servants of the king's household. He was in Gilbert's day responsible for licensing stage performances and was, in effect, the official censor. Thus, a few minutes later when Ko-Ko wants to kiss Yum-Yum and she demurs, Ko-Ko appeals to Pooh-Bah (as Lord Chamberlain) for approval. Hyder (161) observes that Gilbert here is "stepping out of the proscenium and winking at the audience." See also Chapters XII and XIII.

Attorney-General: "The chief legal officer of the Crown in England" (75).

Chancellor of the Exchequer: British minister of finance.

Privy Purse: The Keeper of the Privy Purse is an officer of the British royal household who is in charge of the payment of the sovereign's expenses, including all the principal charities. Dunn (100) expresses doubt that Pooh-Bah could have held such a position because he was, after all, only a local official. Dunn forgets the all-too-apparent possibility that Pooh-Bah was also the Supreme Appointer to Exalted Stations.

Solicitor: In Britain solicitors are lawyers who can give legal advice, handle business transactions, and take cases before the lower courts. At the time of the opera, however, only barristers were allowed to plead cases in superior courts. If you were involved in a court case you had to retain a solicitor who would in turn "solicit" the services of a barrister. Keep this in mind next time you are arrested in Liverpool. For a more detailed exposition, see the entry for "Barrister" in Chapter II.

Cook the accounts: In colloquial English, "to cook" means to falsify (115). Need we say more?

Squared [I don't say that all these distinguished people couldn't be squared]: Bribed (115).

Abject [an abject grovel]: Degraded and contemptible.

Grovel {GRUV-el}: To abase oneself, face down in the dirt or whatever happens to be underfoot. The word is derived from Anglo Saxon *groof*, belly (266).

Trammels [From scholastic trammels free]: Constraints. (Those were in the good old days when students were expected to behave.)

Seminary [from a ladies' seminary]: "A school of secondary or higher level for young women" (250).

Genius tutelary [Freed from its genius tutelary]: The OED (229) says regarding *genius*: "With reference to classical pagan belief: The tutelary god or attendant spirit allotted to every person at his birth to govern his fortune and determine his character … ; also, the tutelary and controlling spirit similarly connected with a place, an institution, etc." To this we may add that *tutelary* pertains to guardianship.

Marine Parade: In seaside resort cities, a waterfront street or promenade, usually with the beach on one side and major hotels, shops, etc., on the other. Since few American audiences understand the term, Pitti-Sing might substitute some familiar words such as *board walk*. I admit this would spoil Yum-Yum's dumb reference to a musical instrument, but that's a badly strained joke that might well be left out anyhow

Tremendous swell: A person whose bearing and attire give every evidence of conspicuous consumption and self-esteem.

Prerogative [To our prerogative we cling]: A privilege appropriate to a person's rank or position. Pooh-Bah had a slew of 'em.

A marine parade

Chapter IX

Age [But I would wait until you were of age!]: Of full legal age.

Years of discretion: Same as *age of discretion*: "In law, the age at which a person becomes legally responsible for certain acts and competent to exercise certain powers" (250).

Lucius Junius Brutus: A Roman consul who lived about 500 B.C. He condemned his own two sons to death when they were caught in a plot to restore the villainous Tarquinius to the monarchy (55). Knight (178) adds that Lucius Junius Brutus's name has become synonymous with duty above all.

Capital [To flirt is capital]: "Capital" here means both wonderful and punishable by death. To pun may be capital, too.

Plighted [Were you not to Ko-Ko plighted]: Solemnly pledged, i.e., engaged to be married.

Con fuoco {KAHN foo-OH-ko} [To embrace you thus, *con fuoco*]: With fervor (Italian).

Gioco {JOE-ko} [Would distinctly be no *gioco*]: Italian for game, child's play, joke, fun, or jest. In some editions the word is spelled "giuoco. "

And for yam I should get toco: For today's audiences this is one of the most confusing expressions in the entire G&S canon. Let's start with *toco*. The OED (228) defines this as slang for chastisement or corporal punishment. There is good evidence that it was a common expression in Victorian England (115, 251). In some editions, incidentally, the word is spelled "toko." Partridge (234) has an entry: "*Toco for yam*. To be punished." It goes on to say that the expression, which dates back as far as 1860, is analogous to the Biblical stone for a loaf of bread. More explicitly, you can take it to mean "For doing something pleasant I should be punished." I think we can conclude that the term was generally understood in the vernacular of the day, but mystifies people today. Whoever is playing Yum-Yum can substitute "that" for "yam" and accompany "toko" with a finger drawn across her throat. If people still don't understand, it's their own fault for not owning a copy of this book.

Soliloquizing: Reciting to oneself (but letting the audience hear).

Apostrophe [You have interrupted an apostrophe, sir!]: A digression in speech to address some person or personification that may or may not be present.

Reserve [We might reserve that point]: To postpone a decision, particularly on a legal issue.

Earnest [an earnest of your desire]: Token or proof.

Adamant [but there I am adamant]: Absolutely unyielding. See also Chapter VIII.

Mortified: Disciplined and humiliated.

Condign [Of a hero fine, with grief condign]: Suitable.

Dock [in a dull, dark dock]: A small enclosed space, or cell. The original meaning was a rabbit hutch, fowl pen, or cage (229). This is not to be confused with the criminal court-room dock, which is an enclosure for the accused prisoner.

Pestilential [In a pestilential prison]: Extremely unhealthy.

Chippy [a cheap and chippy chopper]: "Unwell; seedy. Generally used to describe the results of overindulgence in eating and drinking, etc." (115). Alternatively, Walters (302) thinks "chopper" refers to the ax or sword and, being cheap, is unlikely to do the work neatly, but must chip away. Rees (254) proposes that *chippy* means the cutting edge of the instrument is ragged (chipped). See entry for "Awry" in Chapter XI. The following sketch is from one of Gilbert's Bab Ballads.

Respited [to be respited at the last moment]: Granted a temporary stay of execution.

Happy Dispatch: A euphemism for *Hara-Kiri*, from *hara* meaning "belly" and *kiri*, meaning "cut." It refers to suicide by disembowelment as formerly practiced, with due ceremony, by the highest classes in Japan when in disgrace. Knight (178) adds that the suicide's family was also required to die with him unless a special writ was obtained from the emperor. The practice went out in the late 1800s.

Fighting cock: [You'll live like a fighting cock] Brewer (56) says this means to "have a profusion of the best food" so as to increase endurance and pugnacity. (Cock fighting is still a popular activity in many rural communities throughout the world.)

Distracted [Yum-Yum distracted]: Frantically unhappy.

Line [If you can draw the line]: A firm and precise limit. The stage direction "Preparing rope" gives visual emphasis to the pun.

Hear, Hear, Hear!: English expression of approval. See also Chapters V, VII, and XVI.

Eventime [Life's eventime comes much too soon]: This is apparently Gilbert's made-up contraction of *evening time*. He could as well have used the established word *eventide*, which means the same thing. Metaphorically speaking, he is referring to late middle age.

Toast: A compliment or salute directed toward some person or cause. The word supposedly came from the ancient custom of floating a piece of toast in the drink hoisted during the speech (55).

Three times three: Brewer (56) has good deal to say about the number three. As a start it is associated with many pertinent matters in classical beliefs. The world was under the control of three gods: Jupiter (heavens), Neptune (sea) and Pluto (underworld). Jupiter is represented with three-pronged lightning, Neptune with a trident, and Pluto with a three-headed dog. There were three Fates, three Harpies, three Graces, and three Furies. In Christianity we find the Holy Trinity, and the three graces: faith, hope and charity. Going one step beyond, as Pooh-Bah has done, we multiply the potency of the number by multiplying it by itself, producing a trinity of trinities. Brewer lists many expressions using the number nine, ranging from cats with nine lives to the nine muses. He mentions that the cat-o'-nine tails was considered best for punishing evil-doers; being a trinity of trinities, it would be "both more sacred and more efficacious." Finally, he mentions that "We drink a Three-times-three to those most highly honored."

Blight [Rain blight on our festivities]: Ruin or frustration.

Perjured [I claim my perjured lover]: Guilty of violating an oath.

Cloy [delights that never cloy]: Grow tiresome.

Fleest {FLEE-est} [Oh fool, that fleest my hallowed joys]: Flees.

Hallowed: Archaic form of *hallow*, meaning sacred. "Hallowed joys" presumably means wedded bliss.

Equipoise [Oh blind, that seest no equipoise]: A counter-balancing factor, e.g., a fascinating right elbow to offset a caricature of a face. In his children's book (133) Gilbert adds this footnote: "I fancy that she meant by this that Nanki-Poo was so short-sighted as not to perceive that her moral and social qualities were an adequate compensation for the

Chapter IX

drawbacks of advanced age and damaged personal appearance. But when people lapse into poetry you never can be sure what they mean." Anyone who aspires to publish a G&S lexicon will particularly appreciate that last sentence.

Judgest, grudgest, etc.: Presumably pseudo-archaic forms of *judges* and *grudges* (or *begrudges*). The same for *rulest, foolest, scornest,* and *warnest* in Katisha's second verse.

Dole [Love's lightest dole]: An allocation.

Lore-laden years: Years spent in soaking up knowledge.

Smooth tongue: Glibness.

Knell [Thy knell is rung]: Slow tolling of a bell to signal a death. Katisha, we hope, does not mean this to be taken literally. Or does she? Prestige (245) thinks so.

Rue [this insult you shall rue!]: Regret.

Sue [on your knees you'll sue]: Make an appeal.

O ni! bikkuri shakkuri to!: This is the chorus's uproar for drowning out Katisha's exposé. Many authorities (21, 145, 147, 149, 157, 209, 210, 286) have proposed translations, but there emerges no consensus. As for Gilbert, he says only that it is a humorous song (133), and that ought to be good enough for us.

Gambado {Rhymes with Mikado.} [I'll spoil — your gay gambado]: The OED (229) defines this as, among other things, any sudden or fantastic action.

Oya! oya!: Meaningless filler words for the final repetition of O ni! bikkuri shakkuri to!

Owl [Ill-omened owl]: As one definition of the word, the OED (229) gives us: "Applied to a person in allusion to … figurative repugnance of light." In a single word, Karr (170) suggests "baleful." Walters (301) tells us "the owl was traditionally a bird of ill omen and its appearance was supposed to herald a great tragedy."

ACT II

Bridal toilet [seated at her bridal toilet]: The act of dressing and last-minute titivating in readiness for a wedding. (Perhaps you should know that the original meaning of "toilet" was a dressing table.)

Raven [Braid the raven hair]: Glossy black.

Deck [Deck the maiden fair]: Adorn.

Coral [Dye the coral lip]: Reddish-pink.

Roe [Like a frightened roe]: "A small, agile Old World deer" (250).

Marriage-tide [Modesty at marriage-tide]: Time of marriage.

Artless [in my artless Japanese way]: Natural, simple, uncontrived, and without guile.

Effulgent [He glories all effulgent!]: Giving off a flood of light.

Celestial [The moon's Celestial Highness]: Pertaining to the heavens.

Diffidence [Of diffidence or shyness]: Lack of self-confidence.

Take the top off it [It does seem to take the top off it]: To take the edge off it; to skim off the cream. Halton (147) says this is said colloquially of ale or beer that has gone stale.

Efface [Then we'll efface it]: Erase, expunge, delete.

Madrigal: An unaccompanied part-song for three or more singers. Madrigals as a form go back at least four centuries.

Tocsin [Though the tocsin sound, ere long]: A warning bell.

Master of the Rolls: The Master of the Rolls is the third most important judge in the English legal hierarchy, ranking below the Lord Chancellor and the Lord Chief Justice. He is also the chief custodian of official records (243). The position was introduced by George IV in 1838 to care for "all ancient state documents" (319). Goodman (141) expounds at some length on the historical developments affecting the office. He notes that the responsibilities in Gilbert's time were altogether different from those of today (to say nothing of those in Japan then or now).

Judge Ordinary: "The judge of the Court of Probate and Divorce, previous to 1876" (228).

Lord Chancellor: In Britain the Lord Chancellor is the highest judicial authority, about equivalent in rank to the Chief Justice of the United States. He is also the Speaker of the House of Lords. Goodman (142) says he is the only judge in England who is a politician, and has five separate functions (but I'll not burden you with the details). See also Chapter VII.

How-de-do [Here's a how-de-do!]: A colloquialism, short for "How do you do?" (115). Today we might say, somewhat less delicately, "Here's a can of worms!" MacPhail (194) says that Sullivan in his autograph full score invariably writes "How d'ye do."

Ignominiously: In public disgrace.

Blue-bottle [I never even killed a blue-bottle]: A large fly about equivalent to a horsefly.

Nominal [the duties were purely nominal]: Literally "in name only." In short, Ko-Ko thought that as Lord High Executioner his duties were to attend to the superficial formalities but not the actual dirty work.

Affidavit [when making an affidavit]: A "statement in writing made on oath, sworn before someone who has authority to administer it" (141).

Secretary of State for the Home Department: "Minister of the home office responsible amongst other things for the role of the police at a national level" (141).

Perjure [are required to perjure ourselves]: To involve oneself in violating an oath; e.g., to falsify an affidavit. Tush.

Commissionaire: A uniformed messenger, doorman, or porter. For further details see entry for same term in Chapter I.

Miya sama: The start of the chorus at the entry of the Mikado. The words are an authentic Japanese marching song of Gilbert's day. The meaning is approximately as follows: "Oh, Prince, what is that fluttering in front of your horse?" A second verse, which Gilbert omits, gives this reply: "It is the imperial standard given to us to carry with us as we go to punish enemies of the Imperial Government" (197). Bradley (48) offers further details.

Sect [I govern each tribe and sect]: "Any group, party, or faction united by a specific doctrine or under a doctrinal leader" (250).

Own [All cheerfully own my sway]: Admit.

Sway: Rule.

Philanthropist [a true philanthropist]: One who does good deeds inspired by a love of mankind; just the sort of person who organizes amateur G&S performing groups.

Pent [each prisoner pent]: Locked up in durance vile.

Prosy [All prosy dull society sinners]: Prosaic, unimaginative, and probably long-winded.

Mystical Germans: Halton (147) explains that these were Lutheran evangelists who traveled around England delivering long, and often tiresome, sermons.

Madame Tussaud's waxwork {Tussaud's: too-SOZE}: A London museum exhibiting lifelike wax effigies of famous people. A native of Switzerland, Madame Tussaud learned modeling in Paris, and started a museum exhibiting figures of famous and infamous people. Bradley (48) claims that she was compelled to make wax casts of the heads of victims of the guillotine. She moved her exhibit to London in 1802, one hopes without those replicated heads.

Puce [or stains her grey hair puce]: A dark or purplish brown. The word is derived from the French for "flea," puce being the color of the little rascals, if you look carefully and closely. Or perhaps you'd be willing to take our word for it.

Chapter IX

Permanent walnut juice: In case you didn't know it, walnut juice leaves brown stains on your skin that may last for days or weeks depending on how often and with what vigor you wash. As pointed out in Chapter I, a dark complexion was considered a distinguishing mark of the lower classes.

Buffer [We only suffer to ride on a buffer]: One of those big shock absorbers you see on the ends of British railroad cars. If you've never seen one, you may rest assured they are not meant for riding.

Parliamentary trains: In 1844 the British Parliament decreed that each workday every railroad company had to run at least one train in each direction, with stops at every station, and run at least twelve miles an hour. The law was changed in 1883, but those minimum-fare parliamentary trains were still slow and uncomfortable (48, 178).

Music-hall [The music-hall singer]: Music halls were a unique feature of Victorian England. They were in effect glorified saloons. Food and drink were served along with musical entertainment. Catering to a working class audience, the performers were not necessarily top-rate, nor were their selections of the highest order (or least Gilbert didn't seem to think much of them).

Masses [Of masses and fugues and "ops"]: A mass is a composition for mixed choir, generally with instrumental accompaniment. The text is in Latin and follows a set pattern of the Roman Catholic liturgy. Originally intended for worship services, masses may also be performed in secular settings.

Fugues: Musical compositions in a strict style involving counter-play between various voices or groups of instruments. See also Chapter V.

"Ops": This is presumably meant to be the plural of the contraction of *opus* (meaning a musical work) (164). The audience would surely be familiar with it as the standard abbreviation seen in their concert programs. Gilbert might also have meant it as an abbreviated form of *opera* (294). Either interpretation fits the context.

Bach: Johann Sebastian Bach (1685-1750): The great German organist and composer. Bradley (48) points out that Sullivan inserts at this point the first twelve notes of Bach's Fugue in G Minor, to be played by clarinet and bassoon.

Spohr: This is Ludwig (or Louis) Spohr, a German composer (1784-1859) who produced a goodly number of oratorios, symphonies, chamber works, and operas. There was a time when many musicians considered him to outrank Beethoven (8).

Beethoven: Ludwig van Beethoven (1770-1827): Another great (perhaps the greatest) composer, also a German.

Monday Pops: Popular concerts. Jacobs (163) explains the term as being short for "Classical Monday Popular Concerts." They were established in 1858 by the music publishing house of Chappell and were held in St. James's Hall, on the site of the present-day Piccadilly Hotel. See Goodman (140) for many more details.

Sharp [The billiard sharp]: Among the many meanings of sharp are "artful" and "dealing cleverly but unfairly." A billiard sharp, like a card sharp, reflects these characteristics while wakefully working his wonderful wiles to win wrongful wagers from witless wretches. The modern term is "hustler."

Barred [On a spot that's always barred]: I interpret this as meaning behind bars. On the other hand, Bradley (48), Halton (147), Terry (286), and Walmisley (299) propose that the term refers to a rule of billiards. Terry puts it thus: "… after the red ball has been 'potted' (= pocketed) a number of times, that stroke is barred. The balls, on being taken from the pockets, are placed on spots on the table: hence the term." I invite them to rethink the context: "He's made to dwell in a dungeon cell on a spot that's always barred. And there he plays extravagant matches … " In Rees's view, Gilbert may have intended the second meaning to be taken as a pun (251). Karr (171) and Kesilman (174) concur. Perhaps we can all accept that compromise, which gives double value to the term.

Finger stalls: The OED (229) says a finger stall is a protective covering for an injured finger. Several other sources (56, 171, 181, 302, and 320) support this. Halton (147) says it is a cue bridge, i.e., one of those scalloped fittings on the end of a stick for guiding the cue when you are too portly to bend over the table. Knight (177) endorses this. The fact remains, however, that none of my English friends professes to having heard the term used in that sense. MacPhail (194) has uncovered a reference to a tailor-made device that Gilbert purportedly used on the fingers of his left hand to act as a cue guide. MacPhail believes that is what Gilbert meant by a finger stall. Be that as it may, I have yet to see any evidence that Gilbert or anyone else ever called the device by that name. My vote is with the OED.

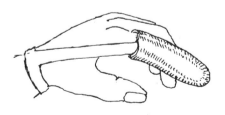

Cloth untrue: An imperfectly stretched green baize cover on the playing surface of a billiard table, possibly wrinkled.

Elliptical [elliptical billiard balls]: Oval-shaped. As Goldberg (210) points out, *elliptical* pertains to two-dimensional shapes. Gilbert might better have said "ellipsoidal."

Coroner: A legal officer responsible for investigating deaths, particularly ones that are violent, sudden, or suspicious.

House [Very good house]: The expression is a theatrical term for a well-filled auditorium.

Gurgled and guggled: They both mean he made a bubbling, choking noise.

Snickersnee: An old, jocular word for a long knife or small sword; the term is from the Dutch *snik and snee*, a sailor's knife (115). It has also been ascribed to the musical chord emitted by a well-swung vorpal blade (67).

I DREW MY SNICKER-SNEE

True [the sabre true]: Well suited to the purpose, or well aimed, or both.

Cervical vertebrae: {Make it rhyme with "did he"}: Neck bones.

Deference [the deference due]: Respect.

Bolted [bolted from our Imperial Court]: Rushed away and escaped.

Visiting card [on presentation of visiting card]: Something akin to our modern business cards but without details pertaining to employment or e-mail address.

Circulation [As for my circulation, it is the largest in the world]: Katisha is referring here to the blood supply for her generous proportions. Hyder (161) adds a second, less

Chapter IX

obvious meaning: the large number of admirers who come to view her charms, as one would refer to a newspaper's circulation. MacPhail (194) recalls that *Lloyd's Weekly Newspaper* (published in London 1849-1902) boasted in a line beneath its mast-head: "Largest Circulation in the World."

Knightsbridge: A prominent street in London, which gave its name to the section of town in which there was a Japanese exhibition at the time Gilbert wrote the libretto. Goodman (140) gives a detailed description of the street and the exhibition. Any gag location may be substituted. MacPhail (194) observes that Gilbert gave express written permission for changing the locale. As far as we know that is the only example of Gilbert putting such a general sanction into writing.

Tiresome [this is very tiresome]: Tedious.

Compassing {COME-pess-ing} [I forget the punishment for compassing the death of the Heir Apparent]: Contriving, bringing about, or becoming involved in any way.

Slovenly [That's the slovenly way]: Careless, negligent, sloppy.

Fates [See how the Fates their gifts allot]: In classical mythology the three goddesses who were supposed to preside over the course of human life. One held the distaff and fibers, from which the second spun the thread of life, and the third cut the thread when life ended.

Chaffing: Teasing in a good-natured way.

Nectar [Nectar quaffing]: In classical mythology the life-giving drink of the gods.

Quaffing: To drink heartily, copiously, and without reserve. Urp!

Fortune [If I were Fortune]: Fortuna, the ancient Roman goddess of luck.

Corroborative [Merely corroborative detail]: Confirming or certifying.

Verisimilitude [artistic verisimilitude]: The appearance of truth.

Cock-and-a-bull stories: Unbelievable boastful fictions. The origin of the term is uncertain, but Knight (178) cites a tale by one L. Fisher from 1660 in which is mentioned a tale as strange as a cock and a bull transformed into a single animal. For more details see the entry for "Cock and bull" in Chapter XI.

Put in your oar: To meddle or interfere in other people's business. The expression dates back at least to the sixteenth century (115).

Reprieved [you're reprieved]: Legally cleared and out of trouble.

Honeymoon: Surely you all know what this means; but there's a nice story that goes with its derivation. It means literally "honey-month." It seems the ancient Teutons had the custom of drinking honey wine for thirty days after their marriage. Moreover, you may also be interested to learn that Attila the Hun drank so much of the stuff at his wedding feast that he died. Let that be a lesson to you.

Persiflage [Is this a time for airy persiflage?]: Banter. Shipley (266) says the word derives from the French *persifler*, to whistle.

Connoisseurs: Expert judges, especially in the fine arts.

Pin my heart: The allusion is to the chivalric custom of pinning to one's sleeve some token given by one's lady love. This was indicative of a pledge to do or die (55).

Caricature {CARE-ik-ahchir suits the score.} [with a caricature of a face]: Cartoon.

Sepulchre: A tomb, a grave, or burial vault.

Miscreant: Originally the word meant "false believer." Now we apply it to any vile and unprincipled wretch; one who sneers at the Savoy operas.

Suppliant [behold a suppliant at your feet!]: A humble petitioner.

Palate [only the educated palate]: Literally the roof of the mouth. The meaning here is in the figurative sense of intellectual taste or liking.

Tom-tit: A bird of the tit family, all being cute little chickadee-like rascals. Brewer (56) and the noted ornithologist Michael Walters (302) both agree that *Tom* implies not male, but small, as in Tom Thumb. This being so, was Gilbert careless when referring to "a little tom-tit"? In any event, the context clearly implies a small male bird.

Willow [Willow, titwillow, titwillow]: The willow tree has long been associated with sadness. Remember "I'll hang my harp on a weeping willow tree"? Then in *Othello*, Desdemona sings a song that ends thus: "Her salt tears fell from her, and soften'd the stones; Sing willow, willow, willow" (54). Sullivan also set her words to music (163). See also Chapter VI.

Dicky-bird: Any small bird.

Callous [if you remain callous and obdurate]: Unfeeling.

Obdurate: Unyielding.

Congo [From the Congo or the Niger]: The general region of central and west Africa (now largely the nation calling itself the Democratic Republic of Congo) drained by what was then called the Congo River.

Niger: The general region of northwest Africa drained by the Niger River. Many critics have complained that tigers are not native to the Congo, Niger, or any other regions of Africa. Not only that, but *Niger* does not rhyme with *tiger*. Ko-Ko's education (a drop-out Ph.D. in tailoring) obviously was not of the highest order. Gilbert, presumably, was only kidding.

Derry down derry: A meaningless expression often used as a filler line in folk songs.

Registrar: An official whose duty it is to keep a record of official transactions. He is also licensed to perform civil marriages (245).

Told off [told off to be killed]: Hyder (161) points out that the expression means *counted off*, "as one would pick a man out of a rank of soldiers for some unpleasant duty." I suppose that would be used in place of the less dignified "Eeny meeny miny mo … " The roots of the term also explain why bank clerks are called "tellers." I knew you'd like to know.

ADOPTING THE DISGUISE OF A SECOND TROMBONE

AN ACQUIRED TASTE

RUDDIGORE

127

BASINGSTOKE
IT IS!

A CAREER OF
UNLICENSED
PLEASURE

FAIR IS ROSE
AS THE BRIGHT
MAY DAY

WE ONLY CUT RESPECTABLE
CAPERS

Owing perhaps to *The Mikado's* great success, Sullivan became more amenable to continuing his collaboration with Gilbert. *The Mikado's* long run gave the composer time to engage in what he considered his real forte: oratorios and other serious compositions. He also engaged in a good deal of travel and socializing with the upper crust. Gilbert found time to develop a non-lozengian libretto, a parody of old-time blood-and-thunder melodramas, which he titled *Ruddygore*. Melodramas have been defined as serious plays intended for undiscriminating audiences. In such works conflicts and calamities are more interesting than the characters, who tend to be stereotyped as either good or bad. Much like modern TV shows, one finds in melodramas passion, excitement and action in plenitude, but seldom much in way of motivation (214).

The new opera opened at the Savoy on January 22, 1887. Almost anything following *The Mikado* would suffer by comparison, and *Ruddygore* most certainly did. Audiences and critics were less than enthusiastic. Gilbert and Sullivan quickly effected some revisions, among which was to change the spelling of the title to *Ruddigore* — considered less offensive to genteel English tastes. The opera then ran for 288 performances, which was not a bad record — except in contrast to *The Mikado's* 672.

Ruddigore's place in the hearts of Gilbert and Sullivan devotees is akin to *Princess Ida's*. Although the opera is among the less well known, it bears repetition and will seemingly always be popular among more experienced Savoyards.

CHARACTERS AND SETTING

Gilbert gives the time as "Early in the nineteenth century." For reasons to be explained later we can infer that the time should have been no later than 1805.

Ruthven [Sir Ruthven Murgatroyd]: This is an old Scottish family name that should be pronounced "Rivven," except as noted at the start of the second act. The name has dark overtones. In 1566 William, fourth baron Ruthven, was involved in the murder of David Rizzio, Mary, Queen of Scots's secretary and suspected lover. Worse yet, in 1600 the Earl of Gowrie, whose family name was Ruthven, kidnapped James VI of Scotland. In retribution, the Scottish Parliament passed an act stating "that the surname of Ruthven sall now and in all tyme cumming be extinguischit and aboleissit for euir." The law was subsequently relaxed for one branch of the clan. For further details see "Gowrie Conspiracy" in *The Encyclopædia Britannica* (103).

Ruthven was also the name of the vampire in Polidori's novel *The Vampyre* (1819) and two derivatives: Planché and Nodier's play *The Vampire* (1820), and Marschner's opera *Der Vampyr* (1828). Gilbert used that same name for the villain in one of his own early plays: *A Sensation Novel* (277).

Oakapple: An oak apple is a gall or swelling on oak leaves. May 29 is designated as Oak Apple Day in England, celebrating the Restoration (1660), that being the birthday of Charles II, who, after losing the Battle of Worcester, hid from Cromwell's Roundheads in an oak tree (140). That happens also to be the date of Gilbert's death (in 1911).

Richard Dauntless: His name identifies him as a stock melodramatic seafaring character, brave, honest and forthright.

Foster brother: Foster brothers are unrelated boys raised by the same family.

Sir Despard Murgatroyd: There are those who note that nearly all the characters in this opus have names of particular interest. What about Despard? Conceivably, Gilbert could have had in mind Edward Despard (1751-1803), a renegade British Army officer who was hanged for conspiracy against the Crown. On the other hand, it seems more likely that Gilbert simply thought the name resonated with visions of desperately despicably dastardly deeds.

Baronet: The title means in effect a "little baron" (17, 43, 165, 229, 266). Quoting J.C.G. George Esq. FSA (Scot), Garioch Pursuivant of Arms (123): "In the United Kingdom a baronet ranks above a knight and below a baron. Unlike a knight his title is hereditary but although he is of the nobility he has no seat in the House of Lords. The rank was officially instituted in 1611 when …

Chapter X

thirteen knights and five esquires were created Baronets."

Some students of the Savoy operas have noted that Sir Roderic Murgatroyd was the 21st Baronet of Ruddigore. That made Robin the 22nd and Sir Despard the 23rd. Since the time frame from first to last baronet could not have exceeded 194 years (i.e., 1611, when the rank was established, until 1805), the average incumbency works out to be less than a decade. That seems unrealistically short to some persnickety critics. George (123) defends Gilbert. He observes that there were 22 Popes during the period 1605-1830, much like the period in question. He adds, "Nor is it a question of generations. Brothers and/or cousins of the same generation can, and not infrequently do, succeed to titles held by senior members of the same generation." To this I can add the further observation that the travails of the Murgatroyd Baronetcy were enough to drive any man to an early grave — or to an escape like that of Robin's. If you are willing to believe that ancestors can step out of picture frames, you can easily believe there were 23 baronets in 200 years.

Adam [Old Adam Goodheart]: Brewer (26A) and Bradley (47) believe the name and character are modeled on Adam, the faithful old servant in Shakespeare's *As You Like It*. The expression "Old Adam" is sometimes taken as a theologian's figure of speech denoting man in his unredeemed state (52, 250). There is little evidence, however, to suggest that Gilbert meant Robin's elderly servant to be anything but a mellow old man who had difficulty in switching character for the changed conditions of the second act.

Mad Margaret: Perhaps the name Margaret comes from Faust's innocent prey, Marguerite, who goes mad from the guilt of bearing and murdering Faust's illegitimate offspring. As traditionally portrayed in the Savoy opera, however, she is a parody of such madwomen as Ophelia and Lucia di Lammermoor. Munich (220) proposes that Margaret's nickname (Mad Meg) may have been inspired by Bruegel's "terrifying" painting *Dulle Griet* (meaning Mad Meg), which shows "a huge figure of a sword and skillet-wielding housewife [who] seeking mastery breaks through the boundaries of the kitchen. Even in hell she is a menace. Mad Meg may

be understood as archetypal of all women … who defy propriety."

Dame [Dame Hannah]: Here is a term with many implications. It might be applied to a noble lady or simply the mistress of a respectable household. Our Hannah was probably addressed as "Dame" simply because she was a well-liked and well-regarded middle-aged woman. Gilbert identifies her parenthetically as Rose's aunt; but if Rose was what she claimed to be, namely a foundling, Hannah must be her aunt by adoption.

Rederring: Imaginary fishing village in Cornwall; generally taken as a pun on red herring.

Cornwall: A county on the southwest coast of England, chiefly known for Penzance and its Pirates. Goodman (142) informs us that "although administered as a county, Cornwall is proud of being an independent duchy belonging to the Prince of Wales in his alternative title of Duke of Cornwall."

ACT I

Endowed [an endowed corps of professional bridesmaids]: Financially supported by some kind of formally established investment.

Duck [duck them in his lake]: One form of testing if a woman was a witch was to tie her to a pole and plunge her into the water. If she were a witch her witchcraft would prevent submergence. Otherwise she would merely drown and the authorities would be obliged to apologize to her bereaved family. Towns with civic pride set up permanent ducking stools for this vital research.

Village green: A communal grass-covered plot typically centered in an English village.

Palsied [A palsied hag]: Afflicted with palsy; trembling.

Ween [what took place, I ween]: Think, fancy, imagine, or believe— one by one, or all at once.

O'erplied [until, with guilt o'erplied]: Short for "overplied." One meaning of *ply* is to take some form of persistent action. Sir Rupert, in short, was overcome by his guilty conscience arising from his many crimes.

Cloyed [with sinning cloyed]: Surfeited—which is a funny way of saying fed up.

Wont [as is thy wont]: An archaic term for *habit*.

Lo [Lo, here is some peppermint rock]: Look, see, or behold!

Peppermint rock: Peppermint flavored hard candy. It usually comes in cylindrical form, perhaps an inch in diameter and a foot long. You find them for sale as souvenirs at seaside resorts.

Gaffer: A nice old rustic fellow, generally in need of false teeth. Supposedly derived from *grandfather* or *godfather*. It was a common prefix to the name of elderly men in rural communities. Walters (302) says it is the male counterpart of *Dame*.

Hereaway [Is there none hereaway whom thou couldst love?]: In these parts.

Verily [verily it would ill become]: Archaic for *truly*, or *in truth*.

Sorely [thy words pain me sorely]: Archaic for *grievously*.

Dish-cover [Hung in a plated dish-cover to the knocker of the workhouse door]: Stell (278) explained that a dish-cover is one of those dome-shaped metal covers placed over plates or platters to keep the food hot and steaming until ready to serve. Rose Maybud's dish-cover was presumably silver-plated. That would lead us to infer that her mother might have been an unmarried servant in some manor house. Who knows? Rose might even be the unwanted result of one of those daily crimes, hence a close relative of Robin's; so there is the germ of yet another Gothic plot. Perhaps you may recall that the eponymous hero of Melville's *Billy Budd* explains that, "I heard that I was found in a pretty silk-lined basket hanging one morning from the knocker of a good man's door in Bristol"

(212). And Jack Worthing, in *The Importance of Being Earnest*, was found in a valise in London's Victoria Station (313).

Workhouse: A place where poor people were lodged and given work. Workhouses were little better than jails. Residents were in social disgrace. See also "Work'us" in Chapter I.

Baby-linen: Infant attire.

Monitor [my guide and monitor]: "Something that serves to remind or give warning" (250).

Precepts [By its solemn precepts]: Instructions intended as rules of conduct, especially moral behavior.

Bites his bread: In those days a refined person would not be caught picking up a slice of bread and biting off a chunk. No. One was expected to break off a wee bit and pop it into one's mouth in an inconspicuous manner.

Marquis {MAR-kwis} [He combines the manners of a Marquis with the morals of a Methodist.]: In Britain, a marquis is a nobleman ranking next below a duke. This assessment of Robin is something of a switch from what Samuel Johnson (45) had to say about Lord Chesterfield's *Letters* to his natural son: "They teach the morals of a whore and the manners of a dancing master."

Hallowed [the hallowed name of Robin]: Past participle of *hallow*, meaning sacred.

Chapter X

Passing [It is passing fine]: The term is ambiguous. It can mean passably (i.e., moderately), or surpassingly. Take your pick. See also entry for "Passing fair" in Chapter II.

Fain [I would fain consult you]: Like to.

Ban [the ban that compels all who succeed to the baronetcy]: Curse.

Tom-Tit [his ship the *Tom-Tit*]: A small bird of the tit family, possibly a blue tit (something like a chickadee). As in *H.M.S. Pinafore*, Gilbert is deriving fun from the British Navy's inclination toward giving their fighting ships awe-inspiring names. Nelson's fleet at the battle of the Nile, for example, included ships named *Goliath*, *Audacious*, *Minotaur*, *Theseus*, and *Majestic*. More fun is derived from the reminder of Ko-Ko's pathetic little bird.

Welkin [Let the welkin ring]: Heavens.

Shipped [I shipped, d'ye see, in a Revenue sloop]: Sailed as a member of the crew.

Revenue sloop: A patrol boat that cruises along the coast to discourage smugglers who are intent upon evading customs and excise duties (taxes).

Cape Finistere: There is a Cape Finisterre at the northwest corner of Spain, and that is probably what Gilbert had in mind (11, 147, 48). McElroy (209) has argued that it seems more likely that Richard is referring to Finistère, the westernmost department (political division) of France's Breton peninsula. One would think that to be a more logical place for a British revenue sloop to be cruising and for a French frigate to be encountered. In fact, however, around 1800 the area off the Spanish headland was frequently patrolled by British warships, both

large and small. They were there to defend against French and Spanish privateers lying in wait for British merchant ships trading to nearby Porto, a busy port in Portugal to which British ships carried fish and grain from North America and carried away wine for England (36, 85).

Going free [A Frenchman going free]: Sailing downwind.

Mounseer [the bold Mounseer]: A colloquial term for a Frenchman, derived from a poor pronunciation of *monsieur* (mister). Derrick McClure (260) says, "Dick [Dauntless], by his speech seems to combine a lack of education with a superabundance of native wit! And the result is a comic character out of Gilbert's very top drawer." Well spoke, messmate!

Frigate [But she proved to be a Frigate]: A relatively fast naval craft of the late eighteenth and early nineteenth centuries, ship-rigged and armed on one or two decks. By "ship-rigged" we mean that the ship had three masts all fitted with square sails. Frigates were generally faster than ships of the line, but more lightly armed. One could easily overwhelm a revenue sloop.

Ports [and she up with her ports]: The expression means that the other ship opened the hinged covers over the gun ports — those being the little square apertures in the ship's side out of which they poked the cannon. See page 49, Item No. 12.

Thirty-two [And fires with a thirty-two]: A cannon that fires a 32-pound cannon ball.

Parley-voo: A slang term for a Frenchman, derived from the early French lesson's *Parlez-vous français?* (Do you speak French?)

Sartin [She is sartin for to strike]: Certain.

Strike: Strike her colors, i.e., haul down her flag, i.e., surrender.

Fal-lal [to fight a French fal-lal]: A derisive term implying affectation in dress and manner (177).

Lubberly [It's a lubberly thing for to do]: *Lubber* is seagoing parlance for a clumsy or inexperienced sailor. Here it means something unworthy of gallant seamen. Relates to *landlubber*, and looby, a heavy, clumsy fellow.

Helm [So we up with our helm]: When you "up the helm" you move the tiller up wind, which turns the bow of the ship away from the wind so she scuds. See next entry.

Scuds [we scuds before the breeze]: Sail down wind — usually at a good speed.

Froggee [Froggee answers with a shout]: Derisive term for a Frenchman, derived from the popular impression of the Gallic fondness for frogs' legs. Brewer (55) offers another explanation, which is that an ancient French heraldic device consisted of three frogs or toads, which eventually developed into the now-familiar fleur-de-lis. Quite an improvement.

Hornpipe: A vigorous solo dance once popular among sailors.

Jawin' tackle [I'll just stow my jawin' tackle and belay]: This means he will stop talking. {As expounded upon in our chapter for *H.M.S. Pinafore*, a sailor would probably pronounce the second word as TAY-kill; but there is less reason for it in this context, and the meaning might be more obvious if it were spoken in the usual lubberly way: TACK-ill.}

Belay: Make fast or stop.

'Vast heavin' [But 'vast heavin', messmate]: Stop sighing. 'Vast is short for "avast," which is a seaman's way of saying "Stop!" The word is thought to come from the Dutch *houd vast*: hold fast (290).

Messmate: Strictly speaking a messmate is another sailor who eats alongside the speaker. In this case, however, it simply implies close friendship. See also Chapter IV.

A-cockbill [What's brought you all a-cockbill?]: Out of sorts. There are two explanations of this term. One relates to the condition of an old fashioned stock anchor when it turns on its side and does not dig into the mud as it should. The other relates to the old custom of tipping a ship's yard (i.e., a spar at the top of a sail) out of its usual horizontal position as a sign of sorrow, particularly when the ship was about to be scrapped.

To'-gall'n'm'st {tah-GAL-en-mist} [strong as a to'-gall'n'm'st]: Topgallant mast: the third (usually uppermost) segment of a mast above the deck. See page 49, Item No. 13.

Fore-stay [taut as a fore-stay]: Part of the standing (i.e., non-moving) rigging of a ship, which prevents a mast from falling back. See page 49, Item No. 2.

Barrowknight: Dialectal for "baronet."

Diffident [I'm timid, Dick; shy — nervous — modest — retiring — diffident]: There! Gilbert has defined it for you.

Binnacle light: Compass light.

Bowline {BO-len} [sail ten knots on a bowline]: To make good progress even when beating up wind. Sailing on a bowline means sailing close-hauled. Ten knots would be a

Chapter X

little over eleven statute miles per hour, not bad for a sailing ship.

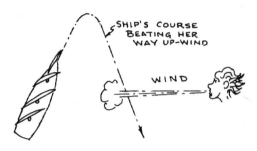

SHIP'S COURSE
BEATING HER
WAY UP-WIND

WIND

Becalmed under my lee [when she's becalmed under my lee]: Read when I'm in a position to speak to her.

Fish [fish you two together]: To splice or join, i.e., marry.

Bumptious: Rude, pushy, quarrelsome, and overly self-oriented. Not at all like you, dear reader.

Bos'n's mate {BO-sun's mate}: A sailor's way of saying "boatswain's mate." A *boatswain* is a non-commissioned officer who supervises work, usually as ordered by a higher ranking officer. A boatswain's mate is his assistant. But, how does Robin happen to know Richard's rank? This suggests that one of his sleeves should carry some sort of distinguishing emblem.

Addled [And hampered and addled]: Confused. If my dictionary (250) is telling the truth, the word derives from a cognate with an old German word meaning liquid manure. Isn't that romantic! See also Chapter VII.

Crichton {CRY-tun} [A Crichton of early romance]: James Crichton ("the Admirable Crichton"), a Scottish scholar, adventurer, and linguist of the sixteenth century. A true genius and a gentleman. A more complete sketch is to be found in Chapter VII.

Stump [You must stir it and stump it]: To boast or swagger, also to make stump speeches (115).

Blow your own trumpet: Alludes to the heralds who used to announce with a flourish of trumpets a knight entering a list (55).

Ovid {AH-vid} [From Ovid and Horace to Swinburne and Morris]: A Roman poet who lived from 43 B.C. to about A.D. 18. For details turn to Chapter VII under the heading "Ovidius Naso."

Horace: Quintus Horatius Flaccus (65-8 B.C.): Another famous Roman poet.

Swinburne: Algernon Charles Swinburne (1837-1909): English poet and critic. One of the aesthetes whose mindless followers were lampooned in *Patience*.

Morris: William Morris (1834-1896): Another well-known Pre-Raphaelite. Although best remembered for his designs of furnishings, wall paper, and furniture, he was a poet as well. He and Swinburne both lived long after the time of the supposed setting for the opera: "Early in the nineteenth century." But, no matter.

Port Admiral: The naval officer in charge of managing a naval fleet stationed in a given harbor. He would assign mooring locations, arrange for supplying water and stores, and oversee necessary maintenance and repairs.

Tight [she's a tight little craft]: Carefully built, i.e., neat and shapely; in no way resembling a sack full of old shoes.

Lord Nelson [she's fit to marry Lord Nelson]: Viscount Horatio Nelson (1758-1805): England's greatest naval hero, killed in the Battle of Trafalgar. Gilbert specifies that the action takes place early in the nineteenth century. This reference to Nelson pins the time down to the first few years of that century.

Aback [took flat aback]: The term means greatly astonished (56). The expression comes from the condition of a square-rigged ship when a change in relative wind direction causes it to act on the wrong side of the sail and so slow or stop the ship's forward motion. (The ship shown on page 49 is square-rigged.)

Parbuckle [Parbuckle me]: To parbuckle an object, you raise or lower it with ropes that are looped around it. This is rather rough treatment. In modern lingo read, "Fry my hide."

Meet [Is it meet … ?]: Fitting and proper.

Chartered [I was chartered by another]: The phrase means that he was acting on behalf of another.

False colours [never sail under false colours]: Don't be hypocritical. The allusion is to the underhanded way in which pirates would fly some respectable flag (rather than the Jolly Roger) so they could approach another ship and take her by surprise.

Blue jacket [the happiest blue jacket in England]: Popular term for a naval seaman, named from the color of their jackets (54).

Admiral of the Fleet [I wouldn't change places with the Admiral of the Fleet, no matter who he's a-huggin' of]: This may be a sly dig at Nelson's shockingly open liaison with Lady Hamilton.

Salute [might I be permitted to salute the flag]: Euphemism for kiss, and the "flag" would be Rose Maybud's cherry lips.

Welter [from tempest's welter]: Related to being tossed about in waves.

Engender [A life-love can engender]: To cause to exist, to create.

Nuptial knot: Wedding.

Spoke [I have— so to speak — spoke her]: When Dick says he "spoke" Rose, he is using good nautical parlance to say he has communicated with her (92, 250).

Skulk [don't skulk under false colours]: To lurk out of sight in a furtive way.

Oil [and much corn and oil]: This refers to vegetable (probably olive) oil. Stedman (274) reminds us that "corn and oil" is a Biblical reference to agricultural wealth. There are literally dozens of references to oil in the Good Book. The First Book of Kings, for example, relates how Solomon gave Hiram corn and oil in exchange for cedars from Lebanon. (And keep in mind that Rose Maybud is addicted to expressing herself in the King James vernacular.)

Strong waters [he drinketh strong waters which do bemuse a man]: A euphemism for alcoholic beverages.

Bemuse: Befuddle.

Wild beasts of the desert: I have heard doubts expressed that any wild beasts could live in a desert. But here's an authentic list: antelopes, elephants, gemsboks, giraffes, lions, suricates, and zebras (30).

Lothario [a regular out-and-out Lothario]: A charming seducer and deceiver. The name is derived from a character in Nicholas Rowe's tragic play *The Fair Penitent* (1703).

LITTLE PRONE TO LEAD SERIOUS AND THOUGHTFUL LIVES

Dead-eye [a better hand at turning-in a dead-eye]: A dead-eye is a round block of wood with, usually, three holes drilled through the flat face. They are used in pairs as a crude block-and-tackle to apply tension to the shrouds of a mast. For a picture see Chapter IV. "Turning-in" refers to the art of wrapping a rope around the dead-eye and

Chapter X

binding it with lighter cord. Fortunately, the plot line is in no way dependent upon your understanding all this esoteric nautical lore. Read on.

Settle [You mean to settle all you've got]: Prestige (245) explains: "This refers to a marriage settlement, wherein the husband will give his wife a life interest in his property when she becomes a widow."

Tack [Hearts often tack]: Change direction. To tack means to zigzag upwind. See entry for "Bowline" on page 133.

Strain [its latest strain]: You may interpret this as "its latest order."

Cot [Cheerily carols the lark over the cot]: Cottage.

Whisht!: Hush!

Bowers [he wanders through its bowers]: Arbors or shady recesses.

Wanton: Straying from moral rectitude.

Cytherean {sith-er-EE-en} [Cytherean posies]: Related to Cythera, the ancient name for the Greek island of Cerigo, famous for a temple of Aphrodite (Venus). Thus Cytherean posies are flowers gathered to advance an affair of the heart.

Fisht! [But that's all gone. Fisht!]: An otherwise meaningless word but said in a sibilant way expressive of rapid motion, like *w h o o s h!* (257).

Italian glance [He gave me an Italian glance — thus]: Halton (147) claims the "expression originated in the person of Machiavelli, an Italian, noted for being unscrupulous, crafty and cynical." Stedman (273) says that a character in Mrs Radcliffe's novel *The Italian* sparked a line of Gothic villains with mesmeric eyes. This became a stock character in Gilbert's time. Indeed, he used it in at least two of his plays. Wilson (320) proposes "a suggestive, melodramatic look." Hyder (161) believes "it refers to an emotional, melodramatic, mesmeric, and even romantic look." Kesilman (174) and Knight (177) hold similar views. Asimov (11)

supposes it to be a romantic look. The old D'Oyly Carte Opera troupe underscored the term with a dramatic flourish, holding cape in front of face with one arm and pointing melodramatically with the other. The term *glance* implies a fleeting look, but that need not be taken too literally. In truth, of course, Margaret tends to babble incoherently, so directors are free to interpret the expression any way they choose, and so are you.

AN ITALIAN GLANCE

Land-agent [I would treat you as the auctioneer and land-agent treated the lady-bird]: A person retained by a landowner to manage an estate, collect rents, and so forth. (257).

Lady-bird: The little beetle Americans call a ladybug. Are these lines intended to make sense? I doubt it. So does Asimov (11). Kravetz (181) believes Gilbert is parodying Ophelia's lines in *Hamlet*.

Commissioner [Come to a Commissioner and let me have it on affidavit]: Evans (111) explains that a Commissioner is a solicitor "especially empowered by the Lord Chancellor to administer an oath to an affidavit." Goodman (142) adds that court officers and notary publics can also fulfill the function. The full title is Commissioner of Oaths.

Affidavit: A written statement signed under oath.

Bucks and Blades: One definition of a *buck* is "a man of spirit or gaiety of conduct." As for a *blade*, well he is "a roysterer; a gallant; a sharp keen fellow; a free and easy, good fellow. (Probably from BLADE, a sword, a soldier ...)" (115).

Gentry [Welcome, gentry]: Men of respectable families and good breeding. In its broadest sense the term applies to ladies as well as gentlemen.

Sated [With flattery sated]: Filled to capacity, stuffed to saturation,

Intramural [From charms intramural!]: Indoors, or within city walls. "Charms intramural," then, would refer to the enticements of refined city ladies, as distinct from the unsophisticated attractions of the young country women of Rederring.

Elysian [Is simply Elysian]: Pertaining to the part of the classical Greek underworld reserved for the blessed (66).

Amaryllis [Come, Amaryllis, come, Chloe and Phyllis]: Amaryllis is a classical name for a rustic sweetheart.

Chloe: Chloe was the shepherdess beloved by Daphnis, "and hence a generic name in literature for a rustic maiden — not always of the artless variety" (54).

Phyllis: Phyllis is another name associated with an Arcadian setting. The word comes from the Greek for "green bough."

Tillage [The sons of the tillage]: Farm land. The sons of the tillage are young farmers, the masculine equivalents of the Daughters of the Plough mentioned in *Princess Ida*.

Clodhoppers: Rustic boors.

Drovers: Those who drive sheep or cattle to market. Also those who sell the animals.

Hedgers: Those who cultivate and trim hedges. Hedges are often used in place of fences. The aim is to make them, as the old expression goes, "horse high, bull strong, and pig tight."

Carters: Those who drive carts.

Keepers: Those who care for flocks, i.e., shepherds.

Trice: One meaning of the word is a rope-and-pulley arrangement. Since one form of catapult was powered by twisting heavy ropes, I suppose Gilbert was justified in stretching *trice* to mean *catapult*.

Steeped [steeped in infamy]: Soaked, saturated.

Infamy: Public disgrace, ill fame.

Bishopric [endowed a bishopric]: The diocese or office of a bishop (250).

Nation [I will give them all to the Nation, and nobody shall ever look upon their faces again]: Probably refers to the National Portrait Gallery in London. Walters (302) says museums and galleries have a reputation of keeping large stocks of paintings in storage. Goodman (142) says portraits are sometimes given to the Crown as equivalent payment for death duties. Such acquisitions may end up gracing the dimly-lit corridors of civil service buildings. Shepherd (263) reports having heard "Smithsonian" substituted for "Nation" in some productions. That may seem out of place, but at least American audiences would understand the joke. Turnbull (294) mentions that after the Art Council of England refused the D'Oyly Carte Opera Company a grant, Kenneth Sandford, playing Despard, changed the line to: "I will give them all to the Arts Council "— a well-deserved jab that received enthusiastic audience acclaim.

Ax [Ax your honour's pardon]: Asking.

Doldrums {DOLE-drums, or DOLL-drums} [becalmed in the doldrums]: A belt of calms astride the equator. Colloquially a state of mental depression.

Quarter-deck orders: Orders from a naval officer and not to be debated. The quarter-deck of a ship was the area of the upper deck generally reserved for officers. See Item No. 4, page 49.

Stand off and on [Ought you to stand off and on]: To vacillate or dither. In nautical parlance, to tack in and out along the shore.

Bring her to: Stop her advance. Figuratively, to warn her.

Thraldom [the hideous thraldom]: Serfdom.

Fiddle-de-dee [To shirk the task were fiddle-de-dee]: Foolish, not open to serious consideration. Shipley (266) says the word derives from the Italian *Fedidio, Fe di Dio* (by the faith of God) and is used as an ironic equivalent of "you don't say so!" Brewer (56) on the other hand says it "is meant to express the sound of a fiddle-string vocalized. Hence 'sound signifying nothing'." Readers who wish to delve further into this profound matter might gain some clue from what Lewis Carroll's Alice had to say on the subject: "If you'll tell me what language 'fiddle-de-dee' is, I'll tell you the French for it!" (67).

Teem [teem with glee]: Overflow.

Cloy: Become tiresome.

Gavotte: An old French dance somewhat like a minuet but less stately (250). Knight (178) says it originated with the Gavots, the inhabitants of the district of Gav in the Province of Dauphiné. Hyder (162) says a gavotte has four beats to the measure, a minuet three.

Enjoyed [His rightful title I have long enjoyed]: One meaning of enjoy is "to have the use of." That fits the context far better than the usual meaning of the word.

Rated [But when completely rated]: Established.

Bart [When I'm a bad Bart]: Baronet. One of the standard abbreviations for baronet that

would be appended to the full name, thus: "Sir Ruthven Murgatroyd, Bart." An alternative abbreviation is "Bt." Next time you write to a baronet be sure to keep this in mind. "Dear Bart" won't do.

Taradiddles: Fibs or yarns. Relatively innocuous little lies (115).

Falsest of fiddles: Splendaciously mendacious (with a tip of the hat to Rudyard Kipling).

Sententious [my morals sententious]: Expressed as maxims. Stuffy.

Gainsaid: Contradicted.

Filly [happy the filly]: A young female horse.

Pound [A pound to a penny]: Refers to the unit of British currency, the pound sterling. A pound in those days was worth 240 pennies (pence). Thus Rose and Richard are implying that lovers, when embracing, are 240 times happier than anyone (or anything) else in the world.

Boon: A favor granted. See also Chapters XI, XIII, and XIV.

Man of descent: Someone of noble, or at least notable, family.

Lea [that bloom on the lea]: Meadow.

Deed [Who's signing a deed]: A legal document. "The reference here is to a mortgage deed, or deed of assignment, signed by a debtor in favour of a creditor" (245).

ACT II

[**Note:** The next two entries are from Gilbert's description of the scene.]

James I [from the time of James I]: His name is familiar to us as the royal sponsor of the best known version of the Bible. He was the only child of Mary Stuart and reigned as king of Scotland (as James VI) from 1567 until his death in 1625. In 1603, upon the death of Elizabeth I, he took the English

Ruddigore

throne as well. He was once aptly described as "the wisest fool in Christendom." He was one of the targets of the Gunpowder Plot, with which the name of Guy Fawkes is closely tied.

Roué [Sir Ruthven, wearing the haggard aspect of a guilty roué]: A dissolute person. (Some texts substitute "Robin" for "Sir Ruthven.")

Elision [With greater precision — without the elision]: This could be described as the telescoped version of a word, i.e., shortened by omitting one or more syllables. Thus, Ruthven becomes "Rivven." But, perhaps it would be good to repeat the entire stanza:

I once was as meek as a new-born lamb,
    I'm now Sir Murgatroyd — ha! ha!
    With greater precision
    (Without the elision),
Sir Ruthven Murgatroyd — ha! ha!

In only this one place the name Ruthven is pronounced as spelled rather than as "Rivven." Reference to "Sir Murgatroyd" is a grammatical error because to be correct the "Sir" should be prefixed to a nobleman's Christian (i.e., first) name, not his family name. Thus "With greater precision" means "more correctly." In short, he might have said, "To speak more correctly, I'll apply the 'Sir' to my first name, which in this one instance I'll pronounce exactly the way it's spelled."

Valley-de-sham: *Valet-de-chambre*, i.e., personal servant. Only in comic operas do we find a pure and blameless peasant who can afford one of these.

Steward [As steward I'm now employed]: Estate manager.

Dickens [The dickens may take him]: A euphemism for the devil. Shakespeare used the word in *The Merry Wives of Windsor* (115).

Paramount [a ... man's oath is paramount]: Of supreme importance.

Creep under my lee: Come under my protection.

Immure [would immure ye in an uncomfortable dungeon]: Imprison. Did you need to be told that the dungeon would be uncomfortable?

Union Jack: The national flag of the United Kingdom, comprising the superimposed crosses of St. George, St. Andrew, and St. Patrick. "Jack" has many meanings, one of which is a flag flown on a ship to show her nationality.

Solicitous [we're solicitous very]: Eager and concerned.

Subterfuge: A slippery way of wiggling out of a difficult situation.

Cloying [from your cloying guiltiness]: Satiated, perhaps even disgustingly so.

Poltroon: A wretched coward. It may be derived from the French *poltron* or the Italian *poltro*, both meaning lazy (75).

Squeamer: Gilbert's creative word meaning a person who is squeamish, i.e., easily shocked or sickened.

Grisly [set on thee his grisly hand]: Gruesome, inspiring horror.

Hearsèd [Dead and hearsèd, all accursèd!]: Carried off in a hearse. This is from one of the first-night choruses no longer used (3).

Spectre: A ghost or apparition.

Alas, poor ghost!: Here Robin, in speaking to his uncle's ghost, echoes a remark made by Hamlet to his father's ghost. Hyder (162) labels this "a bit of Gilbertian whimsy."

Chimney cowls: Hooded tops for chimneys.

Funeral shrouds: Winding sheets for corpses, and popular every-night attire for ghosts.

Footpads [when the footpads quail]: Robbers who travel the highways on foot. One meaning of "pad" is a highwayman, i.e., a highway robber (250).

Fen [the mists lie low on the fen]: Low marshy land or bog.

Chapter X

Mop and a mow [Away they go, with a mop and a mow]: "Gestures and grimaces" (75). Brewer (54) adds that "mop" comes from the Dutch *mopken* to pout. Farmer and Henley (115) agree that a *mop* is a grimace and they quote Shakespeare (from *The Tempest*) "Each one tripping on his toe,/ Will be here with mop and mow." Bosdêt (43) says "mow" derives from mouth, and is used for distortion, such as sticking out one's tongue.

Ladye-toast: One meaning of *toast* is "a lady whose popularity is acknowledged by frequent toasts in her honour" (75). Why the appended *e* in *ladye*? Sir Roderic confesses later that he is foggy and that is the only excuse that I can produce. Some observers (254, 274, 302) think Gilbert wanted to make it look archaic, while Stone (284) suggests that Gilbert was perhaps unconsciously influenced by his Bab Ballad "The Ghost to His Ladye Love." See also Chapter XI.

Lantern chaps [With a kiss, perhaps, on her lantern chaps]: "Long thin jaws, giving a hollow appearance to the cheek" (228), or "Cheeks so thin that one may see daylight through them, as light shows through the horn of a lantern" (56).

Bank Holiday [Monday was a Bank Holiday]: A British civil holiday, then recently instituted by Parliament (142). See also Chapter VI.

Fox [On Thursday I shot a fox]: We all know what a fox is. What Americans may not appreciate is the seriousness with which English landed gentry are likely to take their fox hunting. As Burleigh (61) explains, the hunters, on horseback, gallop along after the hounds, who in turn chase a fox with the intent of catching it and tearing it to pieces. Shooting a fox, in the eyes of such huntsmen, is little less than criminal. Fox hunting, it might be added, is no longer politically correct.

Forged his banker [I didn't say I forged his banker — I said I forged his cheque.]: In those days the only place you could cash a check — or do anything else with it — was at the bank where you had an account. It was, in short, like a withdrawal slip. Therefore, forging a check for a fellow who had no bank account was about as innocuous a deed as one could imagine. Robin is merely sidestepping the issue by saying he didn't forge his banker (meaning, of course, his banker's signature). Boswell (45) tells of a clergyman who was hanged for forgery, so apparently that was looked upon as no petty crime.

Syllogistic form: A formal line of reasoning comprising two premises, major and minor, and a conclusion.

Hold water [they wouldn't hold water]: They wouldn't bear inspection. Picture a ship's hull that is tight and so holds water out or, if you prefer, a pot that holds water in (56).

Gideon Crawle [Gideon Crawle, it won't do]: This name is found in place of Old Adam in some older editions of the libretto. Allen (3) explains that on opening night Gilbert had Old Adam change his name in the second act to go with his altered character. Shortly after that, however, Gilbert changed his mind and scratched out all references to Gideon Crawle, including a verse explaining the switch in the duet that opens the second act. He missed this one entry, however, and some editors and publishers slavishly kept it in until at least 1959, thus mystifying whole generations of Savoyards (129). Chambers (72) reports that some producing groups have chosen to reintroduce the second verse, and so have revived poor old Gideon Crawle. Bradley (48) shows the words for that second verse.

Compunction [Away, Remorse! Compunction, hence!]: Pity or scruple.

Hence: Go away, begone!

Petrified [a petrified heart]: Turned to stone.

Confidence tricking: "A method of professional swindling, in which the victim is induced to hand over money or other valuables as a token of 'confidence' in the sharper" (229).

[**Note:** The next five entries are from a first-night song (3) now long deleted. It comes between the time Old Adam is sent to carry off a maiden and the entry of Despard and Margaret, mad-woman, retired.]

Lemon squashes [I played on the flute and drank lemon squashes]: "A drink made from the juice of a lemon, with soda-water, ice, and sometimes sugar" (229).

Macintoshes: Waterproof garments made of two layers of cloth glued together with something like rubber cement. Named after the inventor, Charles Macintosh (1766-1843). See also Chapters XIV and XV.

Satyr {SAY-ter, to rhyme with first-rater.} [My ways must be those of a regular satyr]: In this context, a lecher.

Cropper [If I now go a cropper]: Experience a downfall.

Tip-topper [he who was once an abandoned tip-topper]: An abandoned tip-topper is a member of the upper crust who is given over to vice.

[**Another note:** The next eleven entries are from another version of the same song found in many of the newer versions of the libretto (129, 131) but seldom sung in performance.]

Old Bailey [On a regular course of Old Bailey]: Refers to London's Central Criminal Court, taking its nickname from the street on which it is located. Consult Goodman (140) for some significant historical details. See also Chapter II.

Prigging [There's postage-stamp prigging]: Petty thievery. Taking home stamps from the office.

Thimble-rigging: The old shell game, a swindle using three or four thimbles and a pea. A swindler places a pea on a table, covers it with one of the thimbles, then after shuffling them about asks his victim to bet which thimble covers the pea, and the victim always guesses wrong and so forfeits his money. Brewer (56) explains that the sharper conceals the pea under his finger nail. Now that you know the secret, you may become a sharper as well and be grateful to this book forevermore.

Three-card delusion at races: The OED (228) defines three-card trick as "a trick popular with race-course sharpers, in which a queen and two other cards are spread out face downward, and bystanders invited to bet which is queen." The game is called "Three-Card Monte" in America. As in England, the bystander has no chance of winning. Now you know; don't try it.

Squires [Ye well-to-do squires, who live in the shires]: Country gentlemen, landed proprietors ranking just below knighthood.

Shires: Counties, such as Hampshire, Berkshire, Lancashire, and Yorkshire. Also defined as "the counties in the Midlands in which [fox] hunting is especially popular" (250). Joseph (167) associates the term with any rural areas in the provinces.

Athenaeums [Who found Athenaeums and local museums]: Scientific or literary clubs.

Tradey [all things that are tradey]: A presumably made-up word pertaining to shopkeepers.

M.P.s [Ye supple M.P.s]: Members of Parliament.

Indite [as your leaders indite]: Write or say.

Snuff [You don't care the snuff of a candle]: One definition of snuff is "the charred or partly consumed portion of a candlewick" (250), i.e., a thing of no value. An alternative interpretation could be "You are unwilling to do even such a trivial thing as snuffing out a candle."

Abandoned person: Someone who yields to unrestrained impulses.

Romances [Even in all the old romances]: The word carries a wide range of meanings, from a narrative of knight errantry in the Middle Ages to a highly colored falsehood. (75)

Blameless dances: In Victorian England some extreme social reformers condemned all dancing as improper. Despard and Margaret know they are skating on thin ice.

Spleen and vapours [Suffering much from spleen and vapours]: Melancholy and nervous weakness.

Chapter X

Linen-drapers [She didn't spend much upon linen-drapers]: Retailers who deal in fabrics and other dressmaking supplies. Stedman (274) and Goodman (142) say they also used to sell ladies' underwear, or "body linen." There are two reasonable inferences. One is that Margaret went around in rags. The other is that she was scantily clad. Maybe both interpretations are valid. Kravetz (181) notes that Jessie Bond, who created the role of Mad Margaret, came on stage dressed in rags. Moreover, with arms and feet bare, she would have been considered scantily clothed in those days.

Dab [Now I'm a dab at penny readings]: Expert. Supposedly a corruption of *adept* (115). Often found in the form of "a dab-hand" (54, 294).

Penny readings: Quoting Jessie Bond (193): "At that time what were called 'Penny Readings' and 'Sixpenny Readings' — mixed entertainments of music, recitations, and readings — were popular institutions in almost every town and village of England, and excellent were the programmes provided for those small sums." (She explains all that because she herself gained early performing experience in a sixpenny reading.) Goldberg (139) tells us that George Grossmith was a highly successful penny reader with the YMCA until Gilbert induced him to create the role of John Wellington Wells. For our new initiates, Jessie Bond was a leading soubrette at the Savoy for many years, creating the roles of Hebe, Edith, Lady Angela, Iolanthe, Melissa, Pitti-Sing, Mad Margaret, Phoebe, and Tessa. George Grossmith created the comic leads from John Wellington Wells to Jack Point, inclusive. Those are still referred to as the "Grossmith roles."

National School [In fact we rule a National School]: A school for the poor, one of a group founded in 1811 for education in the principles of the Established Church (166). On the first night, the expression was "Sunday School" (3). Directors of American productions might want to revert to that.

District visitor: A church worker who helps a clergyman in pastoral visits (75).

Eschew [eschew melodrama]: Abstain from.

Barley-water [and give them tea and barley-water]: Thin barley soup. One recipe of the day called for two ounces of pearl barley boiled in a quart of water. After that it was strained and a small piece of lemon peel added. Knight (177) says it was used to soothe fevers. It was also credited "as a medicament in the treatment of diarrhea in infants" (250). The OED (229) says it is "a drink made by the decoction of pearl barley, used as a demulcent." (*Decoction:* an extract from boiling down. *Demulcent:* a soothing substance.) Don't mistake it for the modern concoction, a fruit cordial of stronger constituency.

Deadly nightshade: A kind of poisonous plant.

Latticed [latticed casement]: A lattice is a net-like framework made up of bars crossing one another diagonally.

Casement: A hinged window.

Basingstoke: A prosaic town southwest of London. Goodman (142) describes it as "horribly modern and faceless." Bosdêt (44) explains that at about the time Gilbert was writing the libretto the summer was so hot, "the newly laid macadam road surfaces in Westminster and Mayfair sizzled and ran off into the sewers, clogging them up. [Prime Minister] Gladstone and the cabinet were trying to get several bills through Parliament, e.g., Home Rule for Ireland. What with the heat, the smell from the drains, and the party's unpopularity with *hoi polloi*, the chief ministers spent long periods out of town at [a] Basingstoke mansion, and were jeered at in many journals and newspapers. The government fell in the autumn but 'Basingstoke' was still good for a giggle, if not a guffaw, the following year." That was probably true at the time, and Stedman (276) concurs. If Bosdêt's hypothesis leaves you unconvinced, an earlier one by Wilson (321) was apparently endorsed by the D'Oyly Carte Opera Company, and is repeated by Bradley (48). In any event, humor now arises from the singular unsingularity of the town of Basingstoke. Margaret is simply daft.

Profligacy {PROFF-lig-ah-see} [your horrible profligacy]: Shamelessly immoral behavior, like failing to pay your G&S society dues.

Ratepayer [a pure and blameless ratepayer]: One who pays his local taxes.

Zenith [the very zenith of their fullness]: The highest point.

Behests [I will refuse to obey their behests]: Commands.

Oration [and make him an oration]: A formal speech.

Twopence-halfpenny {TUPP-ence-HAY-pinny}: You know what it is, but did you know how to pronounce it?

Willy-nilly: Whether desired or not. See also Chapter VIII.

Mad as any hatter: This expression was made popular by Lewis Carroll's *Alice in Wonderland* (1865). Although it dates back at least thirty years before that (113). It presumably has its roots in a former felt hat-making process. (The mercurous oxide that was used often led to Sydenham's chorea, also known as St. Vitus's dance.) There are other possible origins, but Gilbert was probably thinking of Alice's Mad Hatter. See Brewer (54) for further elucidation.

Idyll {Rhymes with either bridle or fiddle.} [a rather interesting idyll]: Two definitions from Collins (75): "a narrative or descriptive passage written in an elevated and highly finished style; a picture of simple perfection and loveliness." The usually preferred pronunciation is like "idle," but in this context the alternative should be used.

Indiwiddle: A humorous way of mispronouncing "individual" so that it rhymes with idyll. Walters (302) suggests it would have been a Victorian's affected way of saying the word.

Patter [this particularly rapid, unintelligible patter]: All G&S fans know that a patter song is one that is learned so well that it can be sung at top speed without pausing to think. The origins of the word, however, are unknown. It has been interpreted as a term

for muttering or chattering in a monotone with the brain in neutral (115). It may also have theological roots as explained in Chapter III (in the note just below the entry for "Unified"). Brewer (56) suggests that it may come from the pitter-patter of falling rain drops.

Minion: A servant or any subordinate, often used in the sense of being a henchman. See also Chapters I, IX, and XVI.

Stiles [over stiles]: Steps over a fence or wall.

Poniard: A slender dagger.

Miscreant: A vile, unprincipled wretch. Someone who borrows this book and never returns it.

Lower {Rhymes with sour.} [When the tempest 'gan to lower]: Threaten.

Lackaday!: Derived from *lackadaisical*, which Brewer (56) defines as "Affected, pensive, sentimental [or] artificially tender." Bushland (64) observes that the root "alackaday" is a contraction of "alas the day." See also Chapter XI.

Mickle [But his gallantries were mickle]: This is an archaic term that suffers under the burden of meaning much (or many) in some instances, and small (or few) in others. The OED (229), Samuel Johnson (165), and then-contemporary dictionaries (77, 250, 290) all focus on the former meaning alone. Nevertheless, in current usage the second meaning seems more likely to apply. That is presumably Gilbert's intent here (48, 294). See Chapter XI for another example of the same interpretation.

Sickle: A crescent-shaped reaping blade with a short handle. Gilbert really means a *scythe*, which is akin to a sickle but is bigger and swinging requires two arms rather than one. The scythe is the traditional implement shown in pictures of the Grim Reaper.

Tantamount [tantamount to suicide]: Equivalent in significance, i.e., "amounts to."

[**Note:** The final entries are found in some, but not all, versions of the libretto.]

Chapter X

Mousie in the fable: Knight (177) explains that this refers to one of Aesop's fables. In it a mouse disturbed a sleeping lion. The lion was about to eat the mouse but laughed and let him go when the mouse offered to aid him in the future. Later, when the lion was captured and bound up, the mouse gnawed the ropes and freed him.

Pipe … eye [why I do not pipe my eye]: Cry (54, 115, 229, 250). You can imagine fitting one's eyes with pipes to bring in a goodly supply of tears. See also Chapter VII.

Bread and cheese and kisses: An early edition of Brewer (56) defines this as a bachelor's fare. That seems an unsatisfactory definition within the context of Dick Dauntless saying: "… with Zorah for my missis, there'll be bread and cheese and kisses …" A later edition of Brewer (54) defines "Bread and cheese" as the barest necessities of life. So let's say Dick is aware he'll never be rich, but he and Zorah will nevertheless live happily ever after.

The Yeomen of the Guard

WERE I THY BRIDE

Chapter XI The Yeomen of the Guard

Ruddigore's disappointing reception accentuated Sullivan's distaste for further collaboration with Gilbert. Hailed as the Mendelssohn of his day (for his serious compositions), Sir Arthur found greater attractions in hobnobbing with the nobility at soirees, racetracks, and gambling casinos. Always the driving force behind the pair, Gilbert tried in vain to reintroduce the lozenge plot. Sullivan refused, his back stiffened by Queen Victoria's offhand suggestion that he write a grand opera. Carte, meanwhile, refloated *H.M.S. Pinafore* at the Savoy as he strained to hold his partners together. Then Gilbert hit on the idea of an opera set in the Tower of London during the reign of Henry VIII (1509-1547). Gilbert conceived a romantic, adventuresome plot and an interesting cast of characters. Sullivan was pleased, and the two collaborators stepped back into harness. Carte kept the Company together with other revivals until October 3, 1888, when the Savoy's curtain went up on *The Yeomen of the Guard*. Although the new opera was initially well received and ran for 423 performances, Gilbert, and more particularly Sullivan, were disappointed that it was not another *Mikado* in the public's esteem.

The Yeomen of the Guard holds a special place in the Savoy canon, being unique in its mixture of comedy and pathos. The jester, Jack Point, contains a good deal of Gilbertian self-portraiture, and several of the other characters are recognizably human — in contrast to so many of Gilbert's farcical portraits. In their later years, both Gilbert and Sullivan counted *Yeomen* as their favorite collaboration (163, 318).

CHARACTERS AND SETTING

Tower: The Tower of London is a fortress dating back in part to William the Conqueror. Located on the north bank of the Thames, it occupies about eighteen acres and includes more than a dozen individual towers. Rich in history and bloodshed, the Tower is a centerpiece of British history (107).

Yeomen: In England a yeoman was originally a man who owned and farmed his own land. The term later came to be applied to archers and cavalry soldiers recruited from among the nation's farmers and countrymen.

The Yeomen of the Guard was originated in 1485 as a bodyguard for the monarch. Until 1548 their duties included service at the Tower of London. Ever since that date a similar group, called the Corps of Yeomen Warders, has had that specific duty. The Tudor uniforms worn by the two corps are almost identical and this causes the two to be confused. There are those who think Gilbert made that mistake. Goodman (140), however, notes that Gilbert specifies that the opera is set in the sixteenth century. If we assume that the action takes place before 1548, then Gilbert cannot be accused of mis-naming the opus. For a complete exposition on the history of the actual Yeomen of the Guard, see Paget (230).

HR: If you see the letters HR on the front of the uniforms, that would be Henry VIII's insignia, standing for *Henricus Rex* (King Henry).

Sir Richard Cholmondeley: The most important thing to know about Sir Richard is that his family name is pronounced "Chumley." You may also want to know that there really was such a person in command of the Tower during the time of Henry VIII (319). Extensive wrangles have developed over Gilbert's intent in using the name. Was he using the character or just the name? No one knows; nor need we be much concerned. Let us press on.

Lieutenant of the Tower: The lieutenant served under the constable of the Tower. The constable was Henry VIII's chief security officer throughout the greater London area. The lieutenant of the Tower was in charge of day-to-day operation of the Tower itself, the most important stronghold in the nation. As a royal appointment, it was an exceedingly important and prestigious post (319).

Tower Green: An open square within the Tower of London. Most public executions took place on Tower Hill, just outside the walls of the Tower. Especially important prisoners, however, were executed in the relative privacy of Tower Green. Anne Boleyn and Catherine Howard were accorded that privilege (319). Why should Colonel Fairfax be so honored? To simplify staging, I presume.

Chapter XI

ACT I

Heigho [With a sad heigho!]: Applegate (8) raises a question about how this should be pronounced. The favored American way is "hi-ho," and that is the way the old D'Oyly Carte Opera Company sang it for a time. Then they changed to "hay-ho." The switch is staunchly defended by Williams (316) in a letter to *The Gilbert and Sullivan Journal*. But, let it be noted that in *Princess Ida* "heigho-let" must rhyme with violet. In any event, Webster (307) says the expression is "used typically to express boredom, weariness or sadness and sometimes to serve as a cry of encouragement." (That last must have been what those seven dwarfs had in mind.) The dictionaries all seem to split *heigho* with a hyphen (heigh-ho), but perhaps they will change now that we point out how Gilbert spelled it.

Littered [The wild beasts all littered down?]: Phoebe is asking Wilfred if he has provided straw for all the prisoners' beds. On a more literate plane, Knight (178) finds that before 1828 one of the functions of the Tower, for several centuries, was to keep wild animals. In the context, however, it would seem more likely that Phoebe had the prisoners in mind.

Little Ease [Is the Little Ease sufficiently uncomfortable]: A narrow place of confinement; specifically, the name of a dungeon cell in the White Tower (286). The cell is reportedly so small that the prisoner can neither stand up nor lie down. Guy Fawkes is thought to have spent fifty days there after trying to blow up the Houses of Parliament (47). Wilson (319), however, avers that no one has ever proven that such a cell actually existed within the Tower.

Racks [racks, pincers, and thumbscrews all ready for work?]: A rack was an instrument of torture in which the victim's arm-and leg bones could be pulled out of their sockets.

Pincers: Hinged, plier-like tools with sharp points.

Thumbscrews: Torture instruments used to compress a thumb until the joint was crushed. But, let's move on to pleasanter things.

Sorcerers [We can't all be sorcerers]: Magicians who foretell the future with the help of evil spirits. See also Chapter III

Alchemist: Alchemists sought to convert base metals into gold. Wilson (319) says that in 1605 Henry Percy, a son of the earl of Northumberland, was imprisoned in the Tower for his role in the Gunpowder Plot. He practiced alchemy, astrology, and philosophy. He also spent much time in concocting medicines and potions. All this esoteric activity led to his being dubbed "The Wizard Earl." Perhaps he was in part the inspiration for Colonel Fairfax. (See the definition of "Alchemy" in the Chapter VIII.)

Beauchamp Tower {BEE-chum}: One of the main towers in the Tower of London. Goodman (140) tells us it was built around 1300 and remained nameless until 1397, when Thomas Beauchamp, Earl of Warwick, was imprisoned there and his name thereby became associated with it. It was used as a place of confinement for high ranking prisoners. Rudolph Hess, Hitler's henchman, spent time there, too.

Jade [You are a heartless jade]: A word of many meanings. Here it means a cruel woman.

Warders [Tower Warders]: Warders are guards, watchmen, caretakers, or officers in charge of prisoners.

Pikemen [gallant pikemen]: Soldiers armed with spears (of the jabbing, not throwing, variety). Johnson

(165) says a pike is "a long lance used by the foot soldiers to keep off the horse, to which bayonets have succeeded."

Bearing [Brave in bearing]: Manner of acting or behaving.

Autumn [In the autumn of our life]: Referring to post-middle age years. Members of the corps were selected from among recently retired warrant (i.e., low-level) military officers.

Ample clover: Economic security.

Repining [We recall without repining all the heat of bygone noon]: The phrase means that they recall their bygone passions but are just as happy to have outgrown them. See also Chapter XIV.

Richard Colfax, et al.: These are all imaginary names, of which only Colonel Fairfax is heard from again.

Cold Harbour: Another tower in the Tower of London. Wilkes (315) calls attention to an apparent slip on Gilbert's part. The two words should be joined, thus: "Coldharbour." Wilson (319) says it was used as the queen's residence during the time of Henry VII. Goodman (140) adds that the tower was demolished in about 1670.

Blunderbore [or it's not good enough for the old Blunderbore]: This was "the cruel giant in *Jack the Giant Killer* cycle of folk tales, who imprisoned Jack" (223). Stedman (273) adds, "I think the point here is that Blunderbore was a carnivorous giant, who ground men's bones to make his bread — just as the Tower grinds and devours living men … The tower is personified as the giant."

Keep [I was born in the old keep]: A keep is the strong, innermost structure in a fort or castle. In this case the reference is probably to the White Tower (315).

Norman [our gallant Norman foes]: Here we had better review a bit of English history. William, the Duke of Normandy (ca. 1027-87), claimed that his cousin, the late King Edward the Confessor, had bequeathed to him the crown of England. To enforce his claim he led his army across the English Channel and invaded England. He was opposed by the Saxon King Harold II, whom he defeated at the Battle of Hastings in 1066. William subsequently appended a well-justified "the Conqueror" to his name and built the first part of the Tower of London, the White Tower.

Saxon: During the fifth century A.D. England was overrun by waves of Teutonic invaders: the Jutes, the Angles, and the Saxons. Those three tribes came to rule over most of England. By A.D. 800 the Saxons, centered in Wessex (West Saxony), predominated, and it was their self-proclaimed king, Harold, who was the target of William the Conqueror's invasion in 1066 (43).

The Conqueror: The aforementioned William.

Panoply [In its panoply of stone]: Complete protective covering.

Trow [Insensible, I trow]: Suppose (archaic). {My dictionary (250) says it should rhyme with toe, but Gilbert asks you to rhyme it with brow. Do as the Master says.}

A queen to save her head: Bradley (47) suggests two likely candidates for this reference: Anne Boleyn in 1536 and Catherine Howard in 1542. Each had the misfortune to be a wife of Henry VIII. Walters (302) nominates Lady Jane Grey, who ran afoul of

Chapter XI

"Bloody Queen Mary" and lost her head in 1554. Ossa once triggered a flurry of messages on the SavoyNet (260) by observing that none of the ladies mentioned above came to the Tower to save her head, but each was dragged there with beheading likely to follow. Ossa proposes that a more appropriate candidate would be Queen Eleanor of Provence, wife of Henry III, who did indeed take refuge in the Tower during the rebellion of Simon de Montfort (ca. 1265), and it appears likely that by so doing she literally saved her head from an unruly mob of local citizens. The ensuing internet exchange of views suggested other queens as well, but the majority opinion was that Gilbert probably had Ann Boleyn in mind, she being the one best known to his audience. The question is still alive, however, and freely available to anyone who wants to make it the subject of a Ph.D. thesis.

A-suing: Seeking justice (something not easily found in those days).

Golden hoard [O'er London town and its golden hoard]: The wealth of London. The term may also apply to the royal jewels under safeguard in the Tower.

Watch and ward: Quoting Brewer (54): "Continuous vigilance; watch and ward being the terms formerly used to denote guard by night and by day respectively." The King James version of the Bible also makes the same distinction.

Block [From the dungeon to the block]: The chopping block used in beheading.

Scaffold [From the scaffold to the grave]: A platform for executions. The grisly act was done at an elevation to allow the public a better view of the proceedings (64).

Fortalice: Collins (75) defines this as "a small fort or outwork." It has also been defined as a fortress (obsolete) (250). The latter fits the context better than the former.

Reprieve [Has no reprieve arrived]: A document delaying a punishment, or possibly canceling it.

Standard [as a reward for his valour in saving his standard]: A consecrated battle flag "carried at the head of troops in battle as a rallying point and intended to inspire" (178). Terry (286) says a standard would be carried by a cavalry regiment. What the infantry carried would be called the colors. Neither is carried any longer except in parades.

Court [from Windsor, where the court is]: This would imply the court of Henry VIII.

Windsor: A town on the Thames about 25 miles upstream from London. The site of the royal residence, Windsor Castle .

Circumspection [a very dragon of virtue and circumspection]: Prudence, discretion and vigilance (directed toward his little sister's reputation).

Pursed [my lips pursed up]: Closed tight, like a miser's purse.

Foster-brother: Foster-brothers are unrelated boys raised by the same family. (There are plenty of details in the libretto that make it hard to believe that Leonard and Fairfax were really foster-brothers. But then it might as well be confessed that this opera is shot full of inconsistencies, if you want to be picky.)

Advent [due notice of his advent]: Imminent arrival.

Boon [no light boon]: Benefit or favor. See also Chapters X, XIII, and XIV.

Grim old king: Death.

Sooth [for, in sooth, I have tried both]: Truth.

Another moon: Another month.

Plaint: Short for complaint.

Whit [Then count it not a whit]: A little, or jot.

Essay [He should all means essay]: Attempt.

Sir Clarence Poltwhistle: A villainous character who never appears on stage, but who would be hissed off if he so dared.

The Yeomen of the Guard

Secretaries of State: Among the king's chief ministers (245). Each was given responsibility over some aspect of government (64).

Devolves [which devolves to him]: Transfers or passes down.

Grace [by your worship's grace]: Kind assistance.

Dower: "A widow's share of her husband's property" (75).

Crowns [a hundred crowns to boot]: The crown was a British coin worth five shillings or one quarter of a pound sterling. One hundred crowns would be worth £25 — a lot of money in those days. For example, ancient records show that the lieutenant of the Tower was then paid £100 per year (plus luxurious lodging), putting him in a class with London's wealthier burgesses (319). Goodman (142) says £5 would represent three or four months' wages for a laborer. Knight (178) says the coins were first struck in 1526.

Warranted: Legally justified.

Follify [Come, fool, follify!]: A Gilbertian word demanding of Jack Point some instant examples of his wit.

Vapour [If you vapour vapidly]: As a verb: to pass off as a gas — from which we derive, figuratively, to talk idly or to brag (75).

Vapidly {Rhymes with rapidly}: Without animation, flavor, or underlying content (64).

Quip [Give us quip and quiddity]: A witty remark.

Quiddity: A trifling nicety of speech, perhaps revealing the essential nature of something. Aurora (19) reminds us that Falstaff uses the expression "quip and quiddity" in Shakespeare's *Henry IV*.

Philosophy [the truest philosophy]: The literal meaning is "the love of wisdom," but it has acquired other meanings, such as one's view of the meaning of life and how to live it.

Couplet [We can rhyme you couplet, triolet, quatrain, sonnet, rondolet, ballade]: "A pair of lines of verse, especially if rhyming and of equal length" (75).

Triolet: A poem of eight lines and a specific rhyming pattern about which I shall not worry you here.

Quatrain: A stanza of four lines, often rhyming alternately.

Sonnet: "A poem of fourteen lines of iambic pentameter, with a definite rhyme scheme …" (75). A proper sonnet expresses but a single theme, idea, or sentiment (250).

Rondolet: A short song in which the main theme is frequently repeated.

Ballade {b'LAHD}: "A short poem of one to three triplet stanzas of eight lines, each with the same rhymes and refrain, and an envoi of four or five lines" (75). An envoi is a little postscript or epilogue. Isn't it amazing how ignorant you were until you read this?

Saraband [Or we can dance you saraband, gondolet, carole, pimpernel, or Jumping Joan]: "A slow and stately Spanish dance in triple time" (228).

Gondolet: Hyder (161) has uncovered evidence that there is a Basque folk dance called the gondolet. We can assume that is what Gilbert had in mind.

Carole: A ring of men and women holding hands and singing while moving around in a dance step. Knight (177) says it originated in France; Terry (286) says Saxony. *The Encyclopedia Americana* says it originated in the Middle Ages as a folk dance, but later became an aristocratic dance, often associated with a song (105).

Pimpernel: This seems to be original with Gilbert. Some editions of the libretto, incidentally, show it spelled with a capital P, others do not. For the version with the capital P, see the picture of Gilbert giving a personal demonstration opposite page 128 in Pearson (240).

Jumping Joan: "A country dance" (108).

151

Chapter XI

Farce [the singing farce]: A light-hearted style of comedy in which the humor derives from the situation rather than from any character development.

Loon [a love-lorn loon]: A simpleton (corruption of *lunatic*).

Heighdy {HAY-dee} [Heighdy! Misery me, lackadaydee!]: Heighdy is presumably a variation on heigh-ho, implying weariness (75). Bushland (64) says it is "an attempt to spell what a sigh sounds like."

Misery me: Simply means the singer is feeling miserable.

Lackadaydee: Derived from *lackadaisical,* which Brewer (56) defines as "Affected, pensive, sentimental [or] artificially tender." Bushland (64) observes that the root "alackaday" is a contraction of "alas the day." See also Chapter X.

Peerly [peerly proud]: An obsolete word meaning "in the manner of a peer or equal" (229). A peer would be a nobleman.

Ladye [for the love of a ladye]: Lady. Perhaps Gilbert spelled it this way to make sure you would pronounce it to rhyme with HAY-dee. Rees (254) says it is probably just an attempt to make it look early English. See also Chapter X.

Knell: Ringing of a funeral bell.

Dirge [a doleful dirge]: Funeral music, from the Latin *dirige,* the first word of the prescribed service for the dead. See also Chapter XV.

Popinjay [It's a song of a popinjay, bravely born]: Vain, empty-headed fop, decked out in ornamental finery (115). Not the sort you'll find reading this book. The word is taken from the dummy bird formerly used in target practice (2). See also Chapter VIII.

Bravely [bravely born]: Referring to *brave* in the sense of being noble.

Pother [What is this pother?]: Confusion, bustle, disturbance.

Strolling players: Small troupes of performers who rove the countryside seeking appreciative audiences willing to toss a few coins.

Interludes [playing brief interludes]: Among other possibilities: "any intermediate performance or entertainment, as between acts of a play" (158). These would presumably be comedies or farces (178). Are Jack and Elsie at the Tower of London to keep the boorish bourgeoisie from becoming beastly bored between beheadings?

Bridget Maynard: Like Secretary Poltwhistle, Elsie's mother never appears on stage. She is introduced to head off any inference that Elsie and Jack Point are traveling without benefit of chaperone. Furthermore, Elsie's marrying for money to save her dying mother is a noble deed well suited to a Victorian heroine (64).

Electuary: "A medicine compounded with honey, syrup, or conserves to disguise the taste" (75). Brewer (54) says it comes from a Greek word meaning to lick up, and applies to any sweetened medicine.

Out of place [like some of my jests, out of place]: Inappropriate. A second meaning is unemployed — as Jack Point happens to be at the moment.

Marry [Marry, sir, I have a pretty wit]: Indeed, or why, to be sure. Stedman (273)

A PRETTY WIT!

notes that the word is an abbreviated derivative of an oath involving the Virgin Mary, and is often thrown in to add gentle emphasis.

Extempore [I can rhyme you extempore]: Without previous thought or preparation.

Conundrum: "A riddle, the answer to which involves a pun or play on words" (250). See also Chapter I.

Sardonic: Bitter, scornful, mocking, and so forth.

Jibe: A sneering comment.

Crank [and quip and crank]: A twist of language of the sort Frederic loved to hear until he found the joke was on him. Milton used the expression "Quips, and cranks, and wanton wiles" (266).

Aim my shaft: Select my figurative target.

Winnow [winnow all my folly]: Sift through to separate the valuable from the useless parts.

Whim [I can wither with a whim]: This could be interpreted as a flippant rejoinder.

Gild [always gild the philosophic pill]: Brewer (54) claims that pills used to be gilded, i.e., lightly covered with a layer of sugar, to make swallowing less unpleasant. The expression is now taken to mean "to make a disagreeable task less offensive."

Archbishop of Canterbury: The primate (chief dignitary under the monarch) of the Church of England. Prestige (245) mentions that the Archbishop of Canterbury is "Primate of All England," while the Archbishop of York is "Primate of England." Gilbertian, what?

Stocks [and set me in the stocks]: An instrument of punishment consisting of a wooden framework with holes for clamping the ankles (and perhaps wrists), so as to expose the offender to public ridicule and abuse.

Scurril [a scurril rogue]: Johnson (165) offers several definitions. Among these the

one most likely to put a jester in the stocks is "lewdly jocose."

Lief [I had as lief not take post again]: Gladly. In other words, he would rather not take post again.

Dignified clergy: Bradley (47) explains that the "dignified clergy" were those occupying senior positions within the hierarchy of the Church of England. That left the term "undignified clergy" to be applied to parish priests and curates. We trust they did not take the words too literally. Stedman (274) thinks Point merely wants to avoid stuffy clergymen who have underdeveloped senses of humor.

Expunged [anything objectionable is expunged]: Eliminated.

Helped [what is underdone cannot be helped]: Served. As the lieutenant observes, that manner of thing would be somewhat irritating.

Do you take me?: Catch on? (An elbow in the listener's ribs is the proper accompanying gesture.)

Brain-pan [a cook's brain-pan]: Skull. Halton (147) claims that he once asked Gilbert for the answer to the riddle involved here. Gilbert's reply was, "Fred, your guess is as good as mine!" Well, let's not give up. How about this, as ascribed to David Eden by Stephen Turnbull (294): One is under a meal-making brain; the other under a wheel-breaking strain.

Odd freak: An unexpected occurrence.

Chapter XI

Fain [I would fain have espied them]: Willingly, gladly.

Espied them: Spied on them.

A live ass [a live ass is better than a dead lion]: Phoebe has her sayings mixed up. The Bible has it (Eccles. IX:4) that a living dog is better than a dead lion; whereas the Italians assure us that a live ass is worth more than a dead doctor (54). No matter; she has a good point.

Implication: An idea conveyed, but not directly in so many words.

Inference [by inference and by innuendo]: A conclusion or deduction.

Innuendo: An indirect hint (usually derogatory).

Slyboots: "A seemingly simple but really clever and designing fellow" (115). The term dates back to at least 1680.

Ruff [this ruff is too high]: A pleated collar.

Unbosoming [a torrent of impulsive unbosoming]: Revealing innermost thoughts.

Wag [I am a mad wag]: Johnson (165) defines this as anyone who is "ludicrously mischievous; a merry droll."

For the nonce [suppose it for the nonce]: For the occasion only. See also Chapter VIII.

Turtle dove [The tender turtle dove]: A kind of old-world pigeon, noted for soft cooing and devoted attachment to its mate The "turtle" is derived from the Latin *turtur*, which Shipley (266) says is echoic of the dove's cooing call. See also Chapters XIII and XIV.

Lute: A musical instrument somewhat like a guitar with six or more pairs of strings. Said to be popular in the fourteenth and fifteenth centuries. See also Chapter XIII.

Carrion [Were as a carrion's cry]: Short for carrion crow, a European species of crow.

Halbert: A medieval weapon combining an ax blade and spear on a long handle. You can still see them carried by the Swiss Guards at the Vatican. The word is more commonly spelled "halberd."

Orders [The welcome news we read in orders]: The written directions for the guards' activities for the day: the orders of the day.

Debarred [And debarred from all escape]: Cut off.

Derring-do: Reckless daring (75). The expression derives from Middle English "dorryng don," meaning daring [to] do (229).

Boltered [Boltered with the blood you shed]: "Blood-boltered:

clotted or clogged with blood, especially having the hair matted with blood" (228). The line is from a verse that is usually cut (3).

Deuce [Who the deuce may *she* be?]: A euphemism for the devil.

Forsooth [Thyself, forsooth?]: In truth.

Fraternal: Brotherly.

Fell [The consequences fell]: Dire.

Plight [I'll repeat my plight]: Promise.

The bell of St. Peter's: This refers to the garrison church of St. Peter ad Vincula, which was within the Tower, adjacent to Tower Green. Goodman (140) and Bradley (47) both assert that this particular bell was always tolled during processions to executions. Wilson (319) says the original church was built by Henry II in about 1185 in penance for the murder of Thomas à Becket. It was rebuilt in 1306 and again (after a fire) in 1512.

Headsman: The executioner, whose mode of operation is decapitation administered, if all goes well, with a short, sharp shock.

THE HEADSMAN

Immured: Imprisoned, walled in.

Double gratings [The double gratings open were]: Inner and outer metal gates to the cell.

Troth {Can rhyme with either broth or both} [by my troth]: Word of honor (archaic).

Forfeit [Thy life shall forfeit be instead!]: Given up as punishment.

Misbegotten [Who is the misbegotten knave]: Of illegitimate birth. We might term it "S.O.B."

Knave: A dishonest person or villain.

Vindictive: Revengeful.

Marks [A thousand marks to him]: A medieval English coin worth 13.33 shillings or two-thirds of a pound sterling (75). That reward would have amounted to more than six years of the lieutenant's salary (319).

ACT II

Pall [Night has spread her pall]: A black cloak or cover.

Yoke [has shaken off his yoke]: Figuratively: constraints or burdens.

Shackle: A U-shaped metal link with a heavy pin closing the free ends, used for joining lengths of chain (75).

Fetter [fetter and chain]: Leg irons.

Hugh Ambrose [The Merrie Jestes of Hugh Ambrose]: Like Richard Colfax and Warren the preacher-poet, Hugh Ambrose is apparently a fictitious name.

Councillor: One who gives official counsel. In this case perhaps a member of some civic governing body.

An-hungered: Hungry (an expression found in both Shakespeare and the Bible).

Mumming [Ah! 'tis but melancholy mumming]: Acting in a dumb show, usually wearing a mask.

Chapter XI

Jerry [jerry-jailing]: "Jerry" is used as a prefix to denote poor workmanship or shoddy material (229). Although of uncertain origin, some think the word may come from Jericho, whose "walls came tumbling down" at the sound of Joshua's trumpets (43, 54). Alternatively, Stone (284) thinks it more likely to derive from "jury mast," a corruption of *joury* mast, being a spar used temporarily when the mast has been carried away. This is from the French *jour*, meaning a day. Thus something jerry-built is not intended to last.

A JESTER'S CALLING WOULD SUIT ME TO A HAIR!

Butt [a big butt of humour]: A cask, or barrel.

Gimlet: A hand tool for boring small holes.

Jibe: Tease.

Wrack: Cause you to distress your brain excessively, perhaps over some riddle like those involving cooks' brain-pans and over-wound clocks. Although the word is sometimes spelled "rack," it shares roots with *wracu* (misery) rather than the torture rack.

Buffoon [a private buffoon]: Here is a word of many meanings, one of which is a fool or jester.

Loon [a light-hearted loon]: A stupid person, perhaps "tetched in the head."

Death's head and cross-bones: The standard sign for poison. Also the pirate flag.

Auricular [each person's auricular]: The literal meaning pertains to the ear. Gilbert refers here to the figurative meaning of a person's reaction to what you tell him, based on his attitudes and prejudices. See also Chapter XIII.

F sharp: Perhaps this is more than the musical note F#. Brewer (56) would have us believe that the expression is a slang term for flea: F standing for flea, and sharp to describe his bite.

Carp: To complain of small faults petulantly and without reason, a common characteristic of certain theater critics whose names shall generously go unmentioned here.

Flout: To mock or treat with contempt.

D.D. [Comes a Bishop, maybe, or a solemn D.D.]: A Doctor of Divinity, i.e., a cleric with an advanced degree in theology.

Orthodox smack: A flavor, or characteristic, aligned with accepted religious tenants.

Imported from France: Risqué.

Rack [Though your head it may rack]: A variation of "wrack": to cause pain and distress.

Bilious [with a bilious attack]: Pertaining to bile: the bitter greenish fluid secreted by the liver. See also Chapters VI and XIV.

Perpend [So hold thy peace and perpend]: To think or ponder (about what is going to be proposed).

Arquebus {ARE-kew-bus}: An early form of firearm. Because of its size and weight it was usually fired from a supporting crutch.

Paradoxes: Seemingly impossible statements that may indeed be true. The most famous example threatened Frederic's courtship.

Cock and bull: A cock and bull tale is an unbelievable, boastful bit of fiction as exemplified by Pitti-Sing's story about catching the beheadee's eye and inspiring him to whistle an air. But that's another opera and another land. Brewer (54) believes that the expression hearkens back to "old fables in which cocks, bulls, and other animals discoursed in human language." The phrase dates back to at least 1692. Another edition of Brewer (57) suggests two other possible sources for the expression (both ancient) : (1) a combination of *concocted* and *bully*, Danish for "exaggerated" and (2) related to fables about Persian and Egyptian idols. One suspects Brewer was trying too hard. We may conclude that the etymology is unknown; but see Chapter IX.

Conjugal fetters: Figurative marriage chains.

Gyves {jives} [Gyves that no smith can weld]: These are usually leg irons but in this case Fairfax is referring to the figurative marriage chains, which were lots sturdier in those olden times than they are today.

E'en [I'll e'en go]: Contraction for *even*. We might say "I'll just be going."

Tush [Tush, old lady]: English people might instead say "pshaw," while Yanks would more likely say "baloney," or even worse.

In thy teeth: Right back at you!

Kirtle [or I'll swallow my kirtle]: "A kind of short gown or jacket: an outer petticoat" (75). The expression is equivalent to "I'll eat my hat."

Trolling [Strange adventure that we're trolling]: Singing.

Winsome [this winsome Elsie]: This word abounds in pleasant meanings: attractive, charming, cheerful, agreeable, winning, engaging, and all those other happy adjectives that go to describe the young women in a G&S show.

Lucky bag [Fortune's lucky bag]: A grab bag containing prizes, much in use at bazaars and children's parties (54).

Wrought [I was highly wrought]: Frenzied, in a tizzy.

Parlous [I am consumed with a parlous jealousy]: Extremely bad, perilously so!

Epitaph [his epitaph is set up!]: An inscription on a tomb. Bierce (39) defines it as showing that virtues acquired by death have a retroactive effect. Mark Twain noted a remarkable attribute of a toppled tombstone: it could lie on its front and its back at the same time.

Fig [a fig for this Fairfax!]: Equivalent to a snap of the fingers. The expression supposedly has its roots in the twelfth century. It seems that the Milanese, in revolting against Frederick Barbarossa (emperor of the Holy Roman Empire), had the temerity to drive his queen out of town riding backwards on a mule. The Mikado would have applauded Frederick's revenge. Upon recapturing the city he "compelled all his prisoners, on pain of death, to extract with his (or her) teeth a fig from the fundament of a mule, and the thing being done, to say in announcement 'ecco la fica' [behold! the fig]. Thus *far la fica* became an universal mode of derision" (115). How little one knows of the finer things of life until one reads a G&S lexicon!

Portent [What can the portent mean?]: "An omen, especially of evil" (75).

Forbear [to rashly judge forbear]: Abstain. See also Chapter XVI.

Draperies [To his draperies I hung]: Clothing.

Dint [by dint of stronger muscle]: Violence, force, or power (165).

Infernal juggle: A devilish maneuver.

Dispatch [with what dispatch ye may!]: To get under way in haste.

Chapter XI

By my head: Truly (64).

Unchidden [my tears may flow unchidden]: Without rebuke.

Gainsay [that none may gainsay]: Contradict.

Plaguey [a plaguey ill-favoured face]: A colloquialism for troublesome or annoying (115).

Ill-favoured: Ugly, deformed, or villainous (75).

Hang-dog [A very hang-dog face]: "A pitiful rascal, only fit for the rope or the hanging of superfluous curs" (115). Walters (302) describes such a face as miserable or obsequious. Goodman (142) thinks Gilbert meant a sad face, the expression coming from the bloodhound's sagging cheeks.

Awry [make him strike awry]: In the wrong direction, off target. At his own execution Sir Thomas More "cautioned the executioner not to be afraid to do his work. His neck was short, More said; if the executioner cared for his reputation as a headsman, he should not strike awry" (199). See entry for "Chippy" in Chapter IX.

Sophistries [threadbare sophistries]: Subtle but unsound logic.

Engage [If he will, I'll engage]: Promise.

A MAN WHO WOULD WOO

'Prentice: Short for "apprentice" (as a verb). To place oneself under contract to serve a master craftsman and learn the trade. Remember Frederic?

Jack ... Jill [But every Jack, he must study the knack if he wants to make sure of his Jill!]: Brewer (54) cites the old phrase, "Every Jack must have his Jill," and quotes Shakespeare to lend an air of authenticity.

Lime [His twig he'll so carefully lime]: The act of smearing a sticky substance on twigs to catch and entangle the wings of birds (165).

Clime [Whatever its plumage or clime]: Natural habitat.

Ods bodikins: An oath; literally "God's little body" (115).

Cloy [sweets that never cloy]: Become too much of a good thing. To induce loathing through overindulgence.

Mickle ['Tis but mickle Sister reaps!]: This old Scottish word means either large or small depending on the context. Its more correct interpretation is big or many; but it has been misused so often that you never know what to expect. In this case Gilbert certainly means to say "little." See also Chapter X.

Undoing: Bringing to ruin.

Plague [What a plague art thou grizzling for now?]: Let's interpret this as meaning, "Why the dickens are you grizzling?"

Grizzling: Complaining or whimpering.

Craven: Cowardly.

Cock-on-a-hill: A colloquialism for one who struts about.

An [what he'd do an he dared]: This is an archaic form of "if," which appears regularly in old English literature, including Shakespeare (302).

Fallible [We are but fallible mortals]: Liable to error.

Ods bobs [Ods bobs, death o' my life!]: "Reduction of and corruption of: *ods bodkins*, a jocular exclamation, is a late C. 19-20 perversion of *ods bodikins*, lit. God's little body, a C. 17-19 oath" (233).

Cockatrice [thou kissing, clinging cockatrice]: "A fabulous animal represented as a cock with a dragon's tail; a fabulous serpent imagined to possess the powers of the basilisk, whose glance deals death" (75). That's not Phoebe. Try this: "A name of reproach for a woman" (228).

Chine [I'll cleave thee to the chine]: The OED (228) defines the expression as meaning "I'll break thy back." Most of my knowing friends (none of whom is really bloodthirsty) are inclined to associate "cleave" with "meat cleaver" and so conjure up visions of gory work with a broadsword or battle-ax. Stedman (273) and Zavon (326) visualize the victim dropping in two pieces — left and right — from one mighty vertical blow, head to crotch. Prestige (243), Rees (251), and Knight (179) imagine Wilfred threatening a frontal slash, opening up the torso all the way to the backbone. Asimov (10), however, makes what I think is the best proposal: "To cleave to the chine is to cleave to the beginning of the backbone — in other words to split the skull from top to bottom." Any one of these definitions would produce the same end result: no long lingering death for the real Leonard Meryll, certainly nothing with either boiling oil or melted lead. "Cleave," incidentally, also means to stick together — as used in wedding ceremonies. We are sure that is not what Wilfred had in mind.

Chuck: "A term of endearment" (75).

SNUG LOVE IN THAT MIDDLE-AGED BOSOM

Votary [When love's votary]: Devotee or worshiper.

Notary [Seeks the notary]: A notary public, usually a solicitor authorized to take affidavits, certify deeds, etc. In this case we suspect a marriage contract is implied. See also Chapters III and XIV.

Polity [Joy and jollity then is polity]: Reigning.

Satanity: Conduct or character befitting the devil (229).

Privity [Courting privity]: Privacy, seclusion, single bliss.

Declivity: Downward slope.

Bowery [Bright and bowery]: Bower-like, sheltered and secure.

Harrying [Yields to harrying]: Harassing, i.e., proving a nuisance by repeated attacks.

Elegiacs: "Pertaining to elegies, a set of verses in alternate hexameters and pentameters…" (177).

Tender [Tender his due to him]: Offer.

Suppliant [A suppliant at thy feet]: One who asks humbly. See also Chapter VII.

Unalloyed: Not debased, pure; like a well performed Savoy opera.

A MAN WHO-
WOULD WOO
A FAIR MAID

NIGHT HAS SPREAD
HER PALL ONCE MORE

A GLANCE OF
DESPAIR IS
NO GUIDE

SIR CLARENCE
POLTWHISTLE

THE PINK AND FLOWER
OF ALL THE GONDOLIERI

Chapter XII The Gondoliers

The period between *The Yeomen of the Guard* and its eventual successor, *The Gondoliers*, was an extremely trying one for the triumvirate. The Queen's perhaps offhand remark about grand opera was taken to heart by Sullivan and Carte. Gilbert wisely declined their invitation to join in such a venture, but Carte was convinced that English opera would appeal to English audiences. He therefore planned and started building a large opera house and urged Sullivan to write a serious opera that would assure the venture's success. While this was going on, Gilbert started work on a new comic opera. Sullivan was in Venice, and he, Gilbert, and Carte were burdening the mails with a series of increasingly troublesome letters. Sullivan clearly felt himself imposed upon and complained to Carte that "excepting during the vocal rehearsals and the two orchestral rehearsals I am a cipher in the theatre." Carte was brave (or foolish) enough to show the letter to Gilbert, who thereupon stopped work on the new libretto and wrote a blistering yet flattering letter to Sullivan, which perhaps helped clear the air. Eventually Carte brought the two back together and Sullivan found himself composing serious opera and comic opera simultaneously. The new comic opera was *The Gondoliers*; it opened at the Savoy on December 7, 1889, and ran for 554 performances.

The Gondoliers reflects the reconciliation between the two artists. Sensitive to Sullivan's desire for more emphasis on music, Gilbert provided a cornucopia of opportunities for musical invention, and Sullivan responded with some of the most joyous melodies in all of musical theater. Further reflection on their relationship is seen in the two kings who reign jointly "as one individual." *The Gondoliers* will surely long remain a solid favorite with music lovers everywhere.

CHARACTERS AND SETTING

Barataria [The King of Barataria]: This is an imaginary island kingdom and the locale of the second act. The name is also well known as Sancho Panza's island in *Don Quixote*, as well as from the real Barataria Bay in Louisiana, which was the mini-kingdom of the infamous pirate Jean Lafitte in the early 1800s. There is also a town of that name in Trinidad. The word comes from Spanish: *barato*: cheap.

Plaza-Toro [The Duke of Plaza-Toro]: Spanish for "Place of the Bulls," i.e., the bull-ring.

Grandee [a Grandee of Spain]: A nobleman of the highest rank, one of whose distinguishing characteristics was the privilege of wearing head gear in the presence of royalty (48).

Grand Inquisitor: "The presiding officer of a court of inquisition" (250). The famous Spanish Inquisition was formed by Ferdinand and Isabella at the request of the Pope. Although dedicated to strengthening the Catholic faith, it was under the control of the state rather than of the Pope, whose influence was limited to naming the presiding officer (called the "Grand Inquisitor" in some countries, the "Inquisitor General" in others). The tribunal had a permanent staff of state employees with its head office at the capital; its influence was felt and dreaded until well into the nineteenth century (54, 77, 105, 229, 250).

Here the Grand Inquisitor takes one name, "Alhambra," from the Moorish palace at Granada. and the other, "Bolero," from a Spanish dance in triple time. He may well be modeled after Tomás de Torqemada (1420-1498), the Spanish Inquisition's infamous first Grand Inquisitor (34). The fact that he was selected by the Pope may explain why Don Alhambra was residing in Venice rather than somewhere in Spain. More to the point, however, is the fact that when Gilbert set out to write the words Sullivan was vacationing in Venice and both realized that there was a perfect setting for a comic opera (27).

Contadine: Country girls or peasant girls.

Foster-mother [the King's Foster-mother]: A woman who raises one or more children not her own.

Piazzetta [The Piazzetta, Venice]: The small open square next to the Doge's Palace in Venice. As originally conceived by Gilbert, the Doge's Palace should be on stage right

Chapter XII

with the lagoon and island of San Gorgio Maggiore in the background. The Piazetta features two famous pillars, one surmounted by a winged lion, the heraldic emblem of the Venetian Republic; the other by a statue of Theodore, the city's patron saint (48).

ACT I

The Ducal Palace: The ancient residence and office of the Doge, the chief magistrate of the Venetian republic.

Posies [we bind you into posies]: A posy is defined as a flower, bouquet, or nosegay (a bunch of sweet-smelling flowers).

Bloom [Ere your morning bloom has fled]: State of perfection and greatest beauty.

Peerless [Two so peerless in their beauty]: Unequaled.

Pink [the pink and flower]: Finest.

Tacitly [we tacitly ignore you]: By implication, but not in so many words. (Here's a how-de-do! How can you tacitly ignore the men if you tell them that's what you're doing?)

[**Note:** With expert guidance I have tried to show how to pronounce the Italian words that follow. If you are involved in a production you may want to get further help from someone proficient in the language.]

Dolce far niente {DOLE-cheh far nee-ENN-teh} [enjoy your *dolce far niente*]: Italian for "sweet idleness."

Contradicente! {CONE-trah-dee-CHEN-teh} [nobody *contradicente*!]: Italian for "contradicting."

Jealousy yellow: Green is more often associated with jealousy, but yellow is sometimes called upon to serve the same purpose (54). Phoebe, in *The Yeomen of the Guard* mentions "yellow, bilious jaundiced jealousy." Moreover, since the gondoliers go on to say they will drown "Jealousy yellow" in the shimmering blue, might not the combination of yellow and blue produce green? (Rhetorical question.)

Ben venuti! {ben veh-NOOT-ee!}: Welcome!

Buon' giorno, signorine! {bwon DJORNO, SEEN-yore-een-eh!}: Good morning, ladies!

Gondolieri, carissimi! {gohn-dole-YEH-ree, cah-REES-ee-mee!}: Dearest gondoliers!

Siamo contadine! {see-AH-moe cohn-tah-DEEN-eh!}: We are only peasant girls!

Servitori umilissimi! {sair-vee-TORE-ee oom-ee-LEES-ee-me!}: We are your most humble servants!

Per chi questi fiori — Questi fiori bellissimi? {pair KEE qwes-tee fee-OH-ree bell-EES-ee-me?}: For whom are these really lovely flowers?

Per voi, bei signori, O eccellentissimi! {pair voy, bay seen-YORE-ee, oh etch-ell-enn-TEE-see-me!}: For you, O gracious and charming gentlemen!

O ciel'! {oh TSCHEL!}: Oh Heaven!

Buon' giorno, cavalieri! {cah-vahl-YEHR-ee!}: Good morning, gentlemen!

Siamo gondolieri: We are only gondoliers.

Signorina, io t' amo! {seen-yore-EEN-ah, EE-oh TOM-oh!}: Young lady, I love you!

Contadine siamo: We are only peasant girls.

The Gondoliers

Signorine!: Ladies.

Contadine!: Peasant girls! (Remember, the girls are speaking here — demurely coy.)

Cavalieri: Gentlemen.

Gondolieri! Poveri gondolieri! {POE-very}: Gondoliers! Just poor gondoliers! (Now it's the men's turn to be modest.)

Vagary [But that's a vagary]: A caprice.

Honorary [It's quite honorary]: Without reference to pay. In their opening duet Marco and Gieuseppe are saying in effect, "Ostensibly we earn our living as gondoliers, but truth to tell we do it just for amusement, and the resulting income is strictly incidental."

Short-coated [Since we were short-coated]: The OED (229) and Collins (75) associate *short coating* with infant attire. Chambers (72), on the other hand, notes that gondoliers wear short coats; so the expression may refer to their becoming gondoliers. That seems a more likely interpretation, given that in their next line they refer to being devoted to [feminine] beauty.

Nooning [At summer's day nooning]: The OED (229) offers three alternative meanings, any one of which would fit the context: (a) noontide, (b) a noonday meal, (c) a mid-day interval for rest or food.

Weary lagooning [When weary lagooning]: This is short for "when weary of lagooning," which is short for "when weary of propelling our gondolas on the lagoon." (The lagoon is the sheltered water surrounding Venice.)

Thrum [We lazily thrum]: "To play on a stringed instrument, as a guitar, by plucking the strings, particularly in an idle … manner" (250).

Vespers: Church bells announcing the evening service of the Roman Catholic Church.

Fate [let impartial Fate]: The mythological irresistible power controlling human destiny.

Viva! {vee-VAH!}: Three cheers!

Three horses [My papa he keeps three horses]: This expression doesn't need to be defined, but a few comments would seem in order. First, a question: Why would any Venetian want to keep even one horse? Second, since these are peasant girls, those horses are probably used to work the farm, so there is no hint of snobbery such as that associated with keeping one's carriage. I think we can conclude that the girls are simply singing a nursery rhyme originally sung to city children. (See the entry for "Carriage" in Chapter VI.) Hyder (162) adds that he finds it amusing that Sullivan's tide of Italian-flavored music suddenly descends to the very English, very childlike tune that accompanies the words.

Dapple grey: A horse with a coat marked with different shades of gray in irregular pattern.

Take your courses: Set off in the direction of your choice.

Conjugal [Conjugal and monetary]: Pertaining to married life.

Monetary: Pertaining to money. Apparently the brides are promising to find ways to generate income in their spare time.

Venetia's {Veh-NEE-shahs} [To Venetia's shores have come]: The Roman or Latin word for Venice.

Drum [own particular drum]: An archaic meaning of the word, as you might guess, is one who drums (250).

Chapter XII

HIS GRACE'S PRIVATE DRUM

Castilian [As a Castilian hidalgo of ninety-five quarterings]: A native of the Spanish province of Castile, a region noted for the haughtiness of its nobility. There are those who aver that members of Castilian noble families affect a lisp in their speech. This leads some directors to ask members of the ducal party to do likewise. I suspect Gilbert would not approve. Authenticity is admirable, but not if it gets in the way of clear enunciation.

Hidalgo {ee-DOLL-go}: "A Spanish nobleman of the lowest rank" (75, 250). (Gilbert has slipped up here, having already told us that the duke was a grandee.)

Quarterings: The number of families included in one's coat of arms. You would need a magnifying glass to appreciate the full extent of the duke's family connections. In the second act he stumbles and almost lets drop that he is ninety five quarters behind in his payments.

Equestrian [equestrian exercise is impracticable]: On horseback.

Suite [Where is our suite?]: The train of attendants of a distinguished person. Sir Joseph Porter, K.C.B. had his lovely bevy of sisters, cousins, and aunts. Reginald Bunthorne had twenty love-sick maidens. The Duke of Plaza Toro, in straitened cir-cumstances, can afford only one: the drummer, Luiz, who is probably pleased to work for a niggardly wage for reasons soon to be revealed.

Menial: The humblest sort of servant, one assigned to the most degrading duties. See also Chapters III and IV.

Plebeian [his plebeian position]: Related to the common herd. See also Chapter XIV.

Halberdiers: Guardsmen armed with halberds: those combination spears and axes one sees in romantic movies or in the hands of the Swiss Guards at the Vatican.

Mercenary: Sordid, interested only in money.

Stipulated for a trifle on account: They wanted a down payment.

Band [And the band who were to have had the honour of escorting us?]: Our English friends call a small orchestra a band, but the duke probably had a military band in mind, with plenty of brass and percussive complement.

Cornet-à-piston {core-nay tah pees-TONE}: This is just a fancy way of referring to a cornet, the poor man's trumpet.

Graziers [We are not a parcel of graziers]: Herdsmen. Or should we say herdspersons?

Count [Count Matadoro]: On the European continent a rank of nobility about equal to an English earl.

Matadoro: Mock-Spanish for "matador," the fellow who finally finishes off the bull in a bullfight. Olé!

Baron [Baron Picadoro]: A relatively low ranking member of the nobility.

Picadoro: Mock-Spanish for "picador," the mounted man who torments the bull with little lances.

Prattling [a prattling babe]: Uttering unintelligible (except to grandparents) sounds.

Married by proxy: With someone else acting on your behalf (because you aren't even there).

Wesleyan Methodist: A member of the Protestant denomination founded by John Wesley shortly before the time of the opera, which Gilbert gives as 1750. For further commentary see Knight (178).

A WESLEYAN METHODIST OF THE MOST BIGOTED & PERSECUTING TYPE

Fortnight [a fortnight since]: Two-week period.

Straitened [straitened circumstances]: Financially embarrassed. Broke.

Limited [a Company, to be called the Duke of Plaza-Toro, Limited]: A limited company is equivalent to an American corporation in that the shareholders cannot lose more than their investments if the enterprise fails. See also Chapter XIII.

Work [a Company … is in course of formation to work me]: To exploit, as one "works" a gold mine.

Allotment [I shall myself join the Board after allotment]: When a limited company is newly formed, it issues a sales brochure, or prospectus, and invites investors to apply. When the applications are all in hand, the company allots shares to the various investors. As for the duke not joining the board until after allotment, Walmisley (299) explains that the duke was the principal salesman for the shares, and it was the custom for such salesmen and the company to maintain a

semblance of independence until after the initial sale of shares.

Liquidation [in process of liquidation]: When a company is liquidated its physical assets are sold and it closes its doors. The process, called "liquidation," is usually associated with bankruptcy and that is the implication here.

Wind him up [If your father should stop, it will, of course, be necessary to wind him up]: The expression has double meaning. When a company goes out of business it is "wound up" in the sense of winding up its affairs. The duchess also means that the duke will be wound up again like a mechanical toy. This reflects Gilbert's complaint about limited companies: the entrepreneurs could sell stock to trusting investors, mismanage a company into bankruptcy, then step aside — without any personal financial loss — and start a new enterprise. Gilbert's views on this practice are all too well aired in *Utopia Limited.*

Martial [In enterprise of martial kind]: Military.

Paladin: The term dates back to Charlemagne's twelve heroic peers, typified by the gallant Roland. The word itself is derived from the Latin *palatinus*, an imperial functionary (250). The Duke of Plaza-Toro's deficient personal characteristics are of course in marked contrast to those of the chivalrous knights of legendary fame.

Grosser clay: "Clay" refers to one's body, as distinct from one's soul. A person of grosser clay is simply one of less noble blood.

Tether [May join in temporary tether]: A means of keeping together.

Feigning {FAYning} [a course of feigning]: Pretending.

Arraign [So much the bitterer their arraign]: This is from a second verse of Luiz and Casilda's duet used on opening night (3), but since cut. The term is short for "arraignment" and can be taken to mean the threat of punishment.

Chapter XII

Inquisition: This is explained under the entry "Grand Inquisitor" above.

Retrospectively [to act retrospectively]: In the past.

Thrall [Each in the other's thrall]: Literally, serfdom. Let us interpret it as their being completely devoted to one another.

Requiem: Funeral music, from the Latin *Requiem aeternam dona eis* (Grant them, O Lord, eternal rest).

Abstracted [so thoughtfully abstracted]: Separated. (The Grand Inquisitor shortly applies the less euphemistic "stole" to his action.)

Jimp: Slender and elegant. The term is of Scottish origin (229).

Access of dignity: Elevation to exalted position. See also Chapter XIV.

Timoneer: From the French *timonier*: a helmsman or steersman, and by poetic license, a gondolier.

Bratling: A small brat, or child (contemptuous).

Tippling [his terrible taste for tippling]: In Gilbert's day this simply meant drinking alcoholic beverages to excess (115, 229). Today it more often means taking small, but frequent, intoxicating drinks (75, 250). "He sometimes drinks a little — if that's all that's left in the bottle."

A TASTE FOR DRINK, COMBINED WITH GOUT

Stripling [the Royal stripling!]: A teenager. A boy on the verge of becoming a man. (The clear implication of the narrative is that the prince was still a baby at the time, but let's consider the exigence of rhyme and be forgiving.)

Bier: A portable frame or stand for carrying a body to a grave.

Gout [combined with gout]: An arthritic affliction associated with acute swelling and painful inflammation of the smaller joints, especially of the big toe. Baptisto Palmieri's

They call it "gout", + I can't g' out !

taste for drink may be in part to blame for his affliction (106). Gilbert himself suffered from gout. He presumably realized that, though the disease is not fatal, its torment can drive a man to ruin his liver through excessive resort to the bottle. We show Gilbert's self-portrait while enduring gout in both feet. The note says "They call it 'gout', and I can't g'out." (From the Gilbert and Sullivan Collection, Pierpont Morgan Library, courtesy F.W. Wilson.)

Doubled him up: A slang term meaning to punish or cause to collapse (115). (Picture a hearty blow to the solar plexus.) Adding "forever" implies killing.

Modulated [that delicately modulated instrument]: Regulated. In musical terms, "to modulate" means to pass from one key to another. (The Grand Inquisitor can't resist a little sarcasm.)

Brigand: A highwayman, or thief, or both. Most often found in mountains or forests.

Cordova {CORE-d'-vah}: Also known as Cordobá, a name shared by a province in southern Spain and its capital city. The mountains referred to are the Sierra Morena.

Emissaries: Agents charged with a secret mission.

Skein [life's tangled skein]: A skein is a coil of yarn or thread. The image here is of a somewhat snarled coil, and the allusion is to "the thread of life spun and eventually cut off by the Fates" (273).

Canker [Care's a canker that benumbs]: A spreading sore. (Can such an affliction benumb?)

Wherefore [Wherefore waste our elocution]: For what purpose? Why?

Elocution: Oratory employing careful enunciation and effective gestures, exactly what Gilbert wanted from his performers.

Enigma: A puzzling fact or riddle.

Stigma: Mark of disgrace.

Lyre [String the lyre]: An ancient musical instrument resembling a small harp.

Fancy [Hop and skip to Fancy's fiddle]: The personification of whimsical thought.

Shrink [That we shrink from giving up]: The word has two meanings: (a) to hesitate, and (b) to reduce in size, as happens to a newly deceased body. Another nifty pun.

Voluble [Voices all voluble]: Fluent, flowing, and rapid.

Goose [Every goose becomes a swan]: "All his geese are swans" is an old expression signifying over-optimism (54).

Chrysalis: "An insect … in the quiescent stage before it becomes a butterfly" (75). In short, a pupa.

Vain-glory: Excessive pride or boastfulness.

Abdicate: Give up power of office, in this case the throne.

Grand Canal: The main waterway that weaves its way in a giant *S*-shape through Venice.

Scramble money [scramble money on the Rialto]: Scatter coins on the pavement, usually resulting in a mad competition between all those who happen to be on hand.

Rialto {ree-AHL-toe}: The famous bridge over the Grand Canal at about mid-length.

Insuperable: Impossible to overcome.

Stem [Before our flowing hopes you stem]: Dam up or stop.

Chapter XII

SOME SOURCE OF UNEXPLAINED DELIGHT

Ween: Fancy, or believe.

Carriage and pair: A carriage drawn by a pair of horses. In those days only people of wealth would be so equipped. See also Chapter VI.

With the King on her left-hand side: This would place the queen at the king's right hand, the traditional place of honor. There are dozens of Biblical references to that being the place of honor, and this custom carried through to Victoria's day (287) and even modern times. See Knight (178) for details on the exceptional cases where the king and queen would switch sides. This will give you some idea about how seriously the royal family takes such grave matters. Napoleon, too, paid attention. Castelot (69) tells about an incident that occurred shortly before Napoleon crowned himself emperor. As the Pope approached Paris to attend the magnificent coronation, Napoleon met him and insisted that the Pope join him in Napoleon's carriage. As the two walked to the vehicle, Napoleon carefully contrived to enter it by the right hand door, leaving the Holy Father to ride into the city seated on his left. Oneupsmanship at its best.

Bear away the bell: Take first prize, or otherwise win the competition. Brewer (56) says the expression dates back to earlier days, before cups were given to winners of horse races, when little gold or silver bells were awarded.

Ebullition {EBB-ah-LISH-en} [This sudden ebullition of unmitigated jollity]: Outburst of feeling, a welling-up and bubbling over.

Unmitigated: Unconstrained.

Pavilions [to pavilions and palaces]: Open porches, often with tent-like covers, possibly decorated with banners. The word can also mean tents, or small ornamental buildings in gardens. See also Chapter VIII.

Chancellor [The Chancellor in his peruke]: A high official of state, probably the Lord Chancellor.

Peruke: A periwig; one of those tailored wigs that were fashionable in the seventeenth and eighteenth centuries.

Earl [The Earl, the Marquis, and the Dook]: In England a nobleman ranking above a viscount and below a marquis. See also entry for "Duchesses" in Chapter VII.

Marquis {MAR-kwiss}: A nobleman ranking above an earl but below a duke.

Dook: Dialectical pronunciation of "duke," the highest order of nobility in the British peerage.

Coutts {Rhymes with suits} [The Aristocrat who banks with Coutts]: This refers to Thomas Coutts (1735-1822) who, with his brother, James, formed the London banking house of Coutts and Company. Its origins, however, date back to 1692 and a company founded by one Thomas Campbell (112, 224). The bank is still in business and prides itself on being bankers to the royal family and privy purse. An article in the *New York Times* (153) shows a picture of the Queen's messenger arriving at the bank. It seems he is conveyed there each day in a horse-drawn carriage. Tradition is just as strong within the walls; all male employees must be clean-shaven and wear frock coats.

Plate [The Noble Lord who cleans the plate]: Tableware or ornaments of silver or gold. See also Chapter V.

Grate [who scrubs the grate]: Frame of iron bars to hold fuel in a fireplace.

Orthodox [The Lord High Bishop orthodox]: Holding established views.

Box [The Lord High Coachman on the box]: "The driver's seat on a carriage" (75).

Stocks [The Lord High Vagabond in the stocks]: A frame in which a guilty person is clamped for public ridicule and abuse. See also Chapter XI.

Wind {winde} [As tell the wind]: Use the poetic pronunciation to make it rhyme with kind. See also Chapter VIII.

'Xebeque' {ZEE-beek}: A three-masted Mediterranean sailing ship.

Quay {KEY}: A landing place for ships built along the bank of a body of water.

ACT II

Cup and ball [some ... playing cup and ball, "morra," etc.]: "A toy consisting of a cup at the end of a stem to which a ball is attached by a string, the object being to toss the ball and catch it in the cup ... Also the game played with this" (228).

Morra: A game for two players requiring not even so much as an old deck of cards. In one version, starting with a clenched fist, the challenger holds up a number of fingers of his hand in an attempt to match the number simultaneously held up by the defender. The two players alternate in the roles of defender and challenger. The one who first succeeds in matching the defender a given number of times wins the contest. Versions of the game have been traced back to the ancient Romans and Egyptians.

Pith [Of happiness the very pith]: The most essential part, or essence.

Beau-ideal [The beau-ideal of its kind]: Model of excellence, e.g., a Savoy opera.

Bereft [of undue pride bereft]: Deprived.

Bread-and-cheese: The barest necessities of life (54). See also Chapter XIV.

Ventilate [one little grievance that we should like to ventilate]: To air or bring up for discussion.

Legal fiction: Something assumed under the law even though it is obviously untrue in any literal sense. See also Chapter XIV.

Full Court [for argument before the Full Court]: The formal assembly of a sovereign's councilors and ministers.

Interim order: An order of court, such as an injunction, permitting or forbidding some action pending the outcome of the case before the court (178).

Indemnify [to indemnify in the event of an adverse decision]: Pay back.

Subscription lists [heading the subscription lists to all the principal charities]: The implication is that they must contribute generously to all those charitable causes. Prestige (245) says that in Victorian times, when charitable appeals were made, newspapers published the names of the donors and the amounts contributed.

Chapter XII

Levée [We may hold a Royal *levée*]: One reference (250) gives three definitions, paraphrased as follows: (i) historically, a reception of visitors upon rising from bed; (ii) in Great Britain, a court gathering held in early afternoon for men only; and (iii) a reception, usually in someone's honor. In the context, we could expect only men to be on hand, but the timing could hardly have been either upon rising from bed or early afternoon. I therefore vote for the third definition, but you are welcome to reach your own conclusion.

"Shalloo humps!" and "Shalloo hoops!": Transcription of a drill sergeant's barked orders. Kravetz (181) thinks these are probably the way the drill sergeant barks, "Shoulder arms!"

Potentate: Someone who holds great power, usually a sovereign.

Valet {VAL-ee, to rhyme with "generally."} [dress our private valet]: A personal manservant.

Regalia [we polish the regalia and the coronation plate]: The symbols of royalty such as crown, scepter, and orb.

WE ARE ALLOWED TO BUY OURSELVES MAGNIFICENT CLOTHES

Coronation Plate: Although each word is easily defined, the combination turns out to be somewhat controversial. *Coronation* pertains to the ceremony of crowning a sovereign. *Plate* has many meanings, the most appropriate of which is "utensils for table and domestic use, ornaments, etc., originally of silver or gold" (228). Contrary to popular opinion, plate does not imply plated. So what is meant by "coronation plate"? Here is a list of proposals: (i) State regalia such as the orb and scepter (142). (ii) Ceremonial plate or plates used in communion service during the coronation in Westminster Abbey (257). (iii) Tableware used during the coronation banquet (242). (iv) The service plates (the oversize metal plates that are removed after the soup course) used during the coronation banquet (271). Take whichever suits your royal fancy. See also Chapter V.

Titivating [Spend an hour in titivating all our Gentlemen-in-Waiting]: Putting the finishing touches on one's personal appearance. Hair combed? Sash straight? Medals all in place? Spats buttoned? Monocle screwed in place? Pants buttoned?

Gentlemen-in-Waiting: The OED (228) defines a gentleman-in-waiting as "A man of gentle birth attached to the household of the sovereign or other person of high rank." The term "of gentle birth" means that he comes from a family of good social position.

Deputation [Or receive a deputation]: A small group of representatives from a commercial, charitable, or social body, commissioned to place a view before the sovereign, or to present a loyal address (245).

Peer [we possibly create a peer or two]: In England a nobleman of the rank of duke, marquis, earl, viscount, or baron—all hereditary positions. See also Chapters IV, VII, XIII, and XVI.

Garter [With the Garter or the Thistle or the Bath]: "Badge of the highest order of knighthood in Great Britain" (75). The commonly held belief is that the order dates back to 1344, when Edward II was dancing with a lady, and her garter slipped to the floor. Seeing her embarrassment, the king gallantly put the garter on his own leg and said (in translation), "Shame on anyone who thinks ill of this" (266). See also Chapter XVI.

Thistle: The highest order of Scottish knighthood, taking its name from the royal emblem of Scottish kings (56).

Bath: "An order of knighthood, the second in rank in Great Britain, so named from the former ceremony of purification at the inauguration of a knight" (75). There are those who doubt this etymology, but they offer no alternative (142).

Toddle: A colloquialism for "stroll." See also Chapter IX.

Semi-State [toddle off in semi-State]: Attire suitable for ordinary ceremonial occasions (but never mind the crowns or ermine-trimmed robes).

Fête {Rhymes with state}: A festival or celebration.

Ever and anon: From time to time (55).

Merciful eclipse: Lowered eyelids.

Having passed the Rubicon: Having gone too far to turn back. This is based on Julius Caesar's march on Rome in 49 B.C. The Rubicon was the river marking the boundary of Caesar's assigned authority. When he crossed it he was, in effect, in mutiny.

Fingerettes: Gilbert's baroque word for fingers of the most refined, delicate, and feminine variety.

Cot [Take a pretty little cot]: A cottage.

Dainty [a dainty man to please]: Overly fastidious.

Main [we've crossed the main]: Any wide expanse of ocean. In this case, more likely the Mediterranean Sea.

Livery [Ain't the livery becoming]: The special (and usually fancy) clothing provided by a lord to his household servants.

Cachucha: An Andalusian dance in three-quarter time, usually with castanets accompaniment. It is of uncertain origin, but was made popular in the United States by Fanny Elssler (1810-84), a Viennese who became the lead ballerina at the Paris Opera. One evening while crossing the ocean she found her cabin invaded by a knife-wielding member of the ship's crew intent on stealing her jewelry. Fanny had other ideas, so she "took a preparation and did a turn during which she hit him with her extended leg with such force that he fell to the floor" — and died a few days later (75, 83, 84, 159).

The authentic Spanish pronunciation {kah-CHOO-cha} is something like a sneeze; but Gilbert, Sullivan, and the D'Oyly Carte Opera Company all pronounced it {kah-CHOO-kah}. Perhaps they thought it was more easily understood that way.

(You should know that in some parts of the Spanish-speaking world "cachucha" has become an obscene vulgarism.)

DANCE A CACHUCHA

Fandango: A lively dance in triple time performed by one or more couples with castanets. Bradley (48) gives complete descriptions of these dances and the bolero, in case you are interested.

Xeres {SHAY-res, although the Cartes pronounced it ZER-es} [Xeres we'll drink — Manzanilla, Montero]: This is sherry. The OED (229) assures us that sherry is: "Originally the still white wine made near Xeres (now *Jerez de la Frontera*, a town in Andalusia, near Cadiz); in modern use extended to a class of white wines of similar character." Walmsley (299) explains further that the English used to refer to the wine as Jerez-wine, pronounced Sherez-wine — and that led to the term "sherry." {The Spanish pronounce it HEH-res, but an Anglicized SHAY-ress is more appropriate on the stage.}

Manzanilla {mahn-zah-NEE-yah}: "Light-brown dry sherry" (75).

Chapter XII

Montero: The context leads to the inference that this must be some kind of wine, but pinning it down has proven difficult. Kesilman (174), Walmisley (299) and Asimov (11) call it a sherry. Green (145) is "reasonably certain" it is a sherry. Dunn (100), Halton (147), Hardwicke (149), and Bradley (46) all define it simply as a Spanish wine. Walters (301) suggests that Gilbert may have meant *Montilla*, "a fairly 'fresh-tasting' sherry, somewhere between a true sherry and manzanilla." Knight (177) thinks Gilbert invented the name to rhyme with bolero. Stone (283) has this suggestion: "There are two Italian wine-country villages, Monterosso and Monteroberto, both of which have given their names to wines, and either of which Gilbert may have had in mind and shortened to *Montero* to make it rhyme with *bolero*." There is a "Montero" wine from near San Severo in Italy, but it has been produced for no more than the past forty years. My tentative guess is that Walters is right: Gilbert had Montilla in mind. The Spanish would pronounce it mon-TEE-yah, and shifting to "Montero" to rhyme with bolero seems eminently logical. Montilla wine is a Cordoban variant on Elizabethan Sack. It takes its name from a region of Spain in the Sierra Nevadas midway between Cordoba and Granada. (I dare say Gilbert would have enjoyed a nice chuckle over all the inconvenience this single word has caused.)

Groom [I saw a groom dancing, and a footman]: A servant. See also Chapter IX.

Footman: A male servant, often decked out in livery, and performing such menial chores as waiting at table or helping his lord and lady in and out of carriages. The position has been traced back to ancient Rome. Romans associated the left side with bad luck and so stationed a servant at the entry door to the house to make sure visitors entered with right foot first (12). That is as specialized a job as street sweeper in a one-horse town.

Gentry: People of gentle birth and breeding; the class immediately below the nobility (229). (I suspect Don Alhambra is being sarcastic and pulling a full-fledged sneer.) See also Chapter X.

Lord Chamberlain: In England, a peer of the realm who conducts the business affairs of the royal household (75). To this, Knight (178) adds that the Lord Chamberlain "keeps on file all the officers under the crown and would know that the titles bestowed by Marco and Giuseppe on members of their court are not possible." See also Chapters IX and XIII.

Rusk [A plate of macaroni and a rusk]: Stedman (273) cites a Victorian cookbook to the effect that Italian rusk is made by baking small slices of stale Savoy or lemon cake until brown and hard. Prestige (245) describes it as "a kind of hard biscuit."

Lord High Chancellor: In England the Lord Chancellor is roughly equivalent to the Chief Justice of the United States, and is about as likely to be seen playing leapfrog with his own cook.

Tuppenny [Of being told to tuck in his tuppenny]: Brewer (54) explains that the expression means "mind your head!" It is a schoolboy's warning to the child over whose back the leap is being made in playing leapfrog. "Tuppenny" is a slang word for the head (108), and that is the common way of pronouncing "two-penny."

Rhenish {WREN-ish}: From the vineyards of the Rhine Valley. Barker (27) suggests that Gilbert's audiences probably recognized lines from *Hamlet* that involved Rhenish wine (and the trumpet's bray as well). Knight (178) comments that German wines were popular in England, and all were likely to be referred to as "Rhenish" even though they might have come from other regions of Germany. He adds that Hochheim on Rhine was a major exporting port and in more recent years the term "Rhenish" has been replaced by "Hock," a contraction of "Hochheim."

Junket [That some, at junket or at jink, must be content with toddy]: Merrymaking, a feast, or picnic.

Jink: Short for high jinks: boisterous fun; merry capers.

Toddy: A drink of whisky or brandy, sugar, and hot water.

Lord Chancellors [Lord Chancellors were cheap as sprats]: See the entry for "Lord High Chancellor" above.

Sprats: A small fish related to the herring and pilchard. The term is associated with anything of little consequence.

Shovel hats: Those clerical hats with broad brims rolled up at the sides but sticking out flat in front and back like a shovel.

Prime Ministers [Prime Ministers and such as they]: In England the prime minister is the elected leader of the party holding the most seats in the House of Commons. He (or she) and his (or her) cabinet are charged with governing the nation. The position is roughly equivalent to the presidency of the United States.

Small beer [Small beer were Lords-Lieutenant deemed]: Trivial or petty (115). Persons or things of small consequence (54).

Lords-Lieutenant {lords lef-TEN-ent}: These are high officials appointed directly by a sovereign to represent the sovereign in each county (245). In some instances in former years they served as head of magistrates of the county (75). Their principal duty today would be to accompany any member of the Royal Family passing through their territory. Gilbert was a Deputy-Lieutenant for the County of Middlesex (142).

Cloth of gold: "A heavy rich brocade woven from materials which include gold wire" (285).

Shoddy: Cheap, inferior fabric made of reclaimed wool. See also Chapter XIV.

Illustrated papers: Illustrated newspapers were still relatively new in England when the opera was written, but were still far in the future when the opera was set (1750).

Mount Vesuvius: The volcano near Naples that buried Pompei in A.D. 79.

Vulgar fraction [one can't marry a vulgar fraction]: Also called a "common fraction," is one with a numerator above and denominator below a horizontal or diagonal line. Both numerator and denominator are integers. Such fractions are called "vulgar" because they are in the form commonly used by most people. (The Latin word for people is *vulgus*.)

Dunder-headed: Foolish, cabbage-headed (115).

Duck [distinctly he's a duck]: A colloquial term used in admiration or endearment (115).

Trice [I can prove it in a trice]: An instant. One definition in the OED (229) is a sudden action.

Flea in her ear: Brewer (54) says this means she is sent off discomfited by a reproof or repulse; as a dog with a flea in his ear runs off in terror and distress. The expression dates back at least five hundred years in English and even earlier in French (55).

Messer [If she married Messer Marco]: A variation of the Italian *Messere*, an archaic word meaning sir or master (151).

Spinster: An unmarried woman, usually taken to be one of advanced years.

Know her again [If I can get at her I doubt if her mother will know her again]: Tessa is probably implying that she would pull Casilda's hair out, scratch her face to ribbons, and possibly bite off her ears and nose.

Retainers [Enter procession of retainers]: Servants employed by some person of rank.

Resign [Who resign their pet]: Relinquish.

Chapter XII

Tiddle-toddle: One who takes small, uncertain steps. One meaning of "tiddle" is small. One meaning of "toddle" is to walk, another is to "totter along" (115).

Ipso facto [he will, *ipso facto*, boil down to a single gentleman]: By the same fact, i.e., automatically. Latin for "by the very act" (66).

Tartar [To the thunder of this Tartar]: A person of bad temper, savage habits, and probably bad breath. People of this description, being unable to obtain honest employment, often end up as sarcastic theater critics. The name comes from the Mongolian and Turkish nomadic tribes of eastern Europe, more properly called Tatars.

Progenitor [your great progenitor]: Father.

Marital {MARE-it-al is correct, but mare-EYE-till sounds better as sung.} [Of marital interference]: Pertaining to marriage.

Reciprocating [A more reciprocating couple]: Working well together, cooperating beautifully, and reflecting mutual love.

Double-shotted guns: A cannon loaded with a double quantity of projectiles, which might be appropriate if the target were fairly close. Not recommended practice unless you are sure your cannon can take the extra load without flying apart and taking various valued components of your person with it.

Colours nailed unto the mast: The ship's national flag may be nailed to the mast to ensure that it will not be lowered as a sign of surrender. Of course, if the mast is shot away all bets are off. Don't try it with iron masts.

Arrear [ninety-five quarters in arrear]: Behind in his payments.

Floated at a premium: The initial sales of shares or stock in a company are said to be floated at a premium if they command more than the nominal (par value) price on the stock market.

Applied for [he was applied for over and over again]: There are two meanings here. The first is that the demand for shares of his company exceeded all expectations. The second meaning, which is brought out a few lines later, is that his creditors were also in vigorous pursuit.

Limited Liability Act: A British law intended to regulate the sale of company stocks. See the entry under "Wind him up" above. See also Chapter XIII.

Remunerative [it's most remunerative]: High-paying.

Orders [Small titles and orders]: Honors such as the Order of Thisorthat.

Recorders [For Mayors and Recorders]: In Gilbert's day a Recorder was a person whose official duty it was to register writings or transactions; he was the chief judicial officer of a city or borough (75). Today, only the second clause applies (142).

M.P.s [M.P.s baronetted, Sham Colonels gazetted]: Members of Parliament.

Baronetted: Advanced to the rank of baronet. A baronet is a hereditary title ranking above a knight and below a baron. It is the lowest hereditary title in England.

Sham Colonels: Individuals given honorary, but otherwise meaningless, titles like Kentucky Colonels.

Gazetted: Published in the *London Gazette* — an official British newspaper for announcement of government appointments, military promotions, legal notices, etc. You may be interested to learn (and then, again, you may not) that the word comes from the Italian *gazza*, or "magpie": a gossip. Another explanation is that it came from the Italian coin *gazetta* (again taking its name from the bird) and was either the sum paid for a paper or for the privilege of reading it (229).

Aldermen [And second-rate Aldermen knighted]: An alderman is a civic official, next in rank to a mayor and above an ordinary councilor (286). Here is Bierce's cynical definition: "An ingenious criminal who covers his secret thieving with a pretence of open marauding" (39).

Takings [ten per cent on the takings]: A colloquial term for the receipts (115).

Present [I present any lady]: Introduce the person into high-class social gatherings. The ultimate boost is to be presented at Court at a Drawing Room (274).

Double-barrel [Quote me as their great double-barrel]: The literal meaning of this is presumably a double-barreled gun, which we can take figuratively as anything — or anyone — of more than ordinary power or importance. Some authorities (142, 161, 286) believe it is an allusion to anyone with a hyphenated name, with its implication of uppercrusthood. In any event, the overall impression is certainly that of a person of importance.

Robinson Crusoe: The eponymous protagonist of Defoe's well-known novel about a seaman who was shipwrecked on a small island where he lived by his wits for 28 years. When finally rescued, he didn't even own an opera hat.

Jib [Would jib at their wearing apparel]: Balk.

Selection [I sit, by selection]: Chosen from among many candidates.

Bubble [Of several Companies bubble]: A slang term for a dishonest, speculative corporate formation. The best known was the infamous South Sea Bubble of 1720, which left thousands of speculators in financial ruin.

Floated [As soon as they're floated]: A new company is said to be floated when it has raised enough capital to engage in whatever enterprise it has in mind.

Bank-noted: Supplied with a promissory note on bank of issue promising to pay its face value to bearer on demand (75).

Écarté {ay-CAR-tay}: A card game for two players, using 32 cards. A popular pastime in polite society (184A).

Guineas [five guineas a night]: A monetary unit worth 21 shillings, i.e., £1.05. From 1663 to 1813 Britain issued these gold coins named after the gold's African source: Guinea. See also Chapters VI and VIII.

Preferment [To fill any place or preferment]: An appointment to a dignified official, or clerical, position of honor.

Fêting [At junket or *fêting*]: Celebrating.

Interment [sometimes attend an interment]: Burial.

State [I come here in state]: With pomp and dignity as befits a person of exalted station.

Guard of honour: Splendidly attired military men who stand at attention and add pageantry to the proceedings.

Off-hand [They are very off-hand]: Disrespectfully free and easy.

Deportment [You want deportment]: Bearing, posture, behavior, and the creation of a good general visual impression.

Soupçon {soop-SONE}: French for "suspicion" (in the sense of just a trace). In some performances the duke (not being fluent in French) pronounces it "SOUP-sahn," leading Marco and Giuseppe to ask hungrily, "soup's on?" (181).

Gavotte: An old French dance somewhat like a minuet but less stately (250). Knight (178) says it originated with the Gavots, the inhabitants of the district of Gav in the Province of Dauphiné. See also Chapter X.

Imperious [a pose imperious]: Haughty, arrogant, and dictatorial.

Deucedly … Dreadfully … Confoundedly: Asimov (11) calls attention to the cultural differences exhibited here. The duke uses "deucedly" as a euphemism for "damnably." The duchess and Casilda cannot bring themselves to use even the euphemism and must settle for "dreadfully." The ill-bred gondoliers use "confoundedly." Asimov points out that *confound* at one time took on the meaning of "send to hell."

Over head and ears: Completely (56).

Ill-starred: Born under the influence of an unlucky star.

Chapter XII

Bisected [to have been bisected]: Divided into two equal parts.

Lieges [the loyal lieges]: Those who owe allegiance. More generally, feudal vassals (feudatories).

Clarion: A shrill kind of trumpet, the kind you see page boys blowing.

Quandary [Free from this quandary]: Predicament or state of perplexity.

Premé, stalì! {PRAY-may, stah-LEE!}: These are shouts of communication between gondoliers. Their literal meanings have to do with how the oars are to be stroked. In effect they are the shouted equivalent of turn-signals on a car and indicate how the boats are to be maneuvered. For example, if a gondolier sees a gondola on a course that threatens a head-on collision with his own boat, he might shout "Premé!" which means each boat should be veered to the left and so pass one another right side to right side. Conversely, "Stalì!" means veer right and so pass left side to left side. The words have somewhat different implications in other situations, but we needn't go into them here. This information is based on writings of John Ruskin (259).

AWAY WE GO TO AN ISLAND FAIR

MY THREATENING APPEARANCE

WITH A DEMEANOR NOBLY BLAND

UTOPIA LIMITED

Crown-Princess Victoria Kaiulani of Hawaii
(1875-1899)

Although *The Gondoliers* was completed in a period of happy reconciliation, the cordial relationship was soon shattered by a bitter quarrel. It started out between Gilbert and Carte, but Sullivan was forced to take sides and chose to ally himself with Carte. The fight was sparked by a book-keeping question relating to new carpeting in the theater. Gilbert believed that Carte's allocation of the expense was unfair to both Sullivan and himself in that it reduced their rightful share of the profits. That was the start, and it led to other accusations and personal attacks. Gilbert, who always loved a battle, took the matter to court and won his case. This acutely embarrassing public brawl was extremely distasteful to Sullivan. The partnership lay shattered, and the composer turned his undivided attention to the grand opera which his Queen had suggested. *Ivanhoe* opened in Carte's new Royal English Opera House early in 1891. The opus was well-received and enjoyed a long run. Unfortunately, Carte had not commissioned a replacement, so *Ivanhoe* failed to generate a lasting demand for English opera. Ironically, although Queen Victoria had suggested a grand opera, when she wanted entertainment at Windsor Castle it was *The Gondoliers*, not *Ivanhoe*, that she specified. Sullivan now felt compelled by sheer economic necessity to rejoin Gilbert. The latter, meanwhile, had in all probability learned about Kaiulani, a thirteen year old Hawaiian princess and heiress-elect to the Hawaiian throne, who in 1889 had been shipped off to England to be educated (37). The new opera, *Utopia Limited*, with its south sea island setting (and British-educated princess) opened at the Savoy on October 7, 1893. Although widely praised by the critics, the opera enjoyed only moderate success with the public and closed after 245 performances.

Utopia Limited satirizes many conventions of the Victorian age and, as such, is rather esoteric for American audiences. Worse-yet, the wounds of the carpet quarrel were never completely healed, and the rapport between the two artists was awkward at best. The opera is rarely performed today; but given a few judicious cuts, imaginative direction, and a competent cast, *Utopia Limited* offers many delights.

CHARACTERS AND SETTING

Utopia: This was the name of Sir Thomas More's imaginary island with its ideal (in his eyes at least) social and political systems (215). The name in Greek means "no place" or "nowhere" (25) and has come to mean any ideal system governing human existence.

Limited: A limited company is equivalent to an American corporation in that the shareholders cannot lose more than their investments if the enterprise becomes bankrupt. (The word "limited" implies limited liability.) What particularly galled Gilbert was that the entrepreneurs who form a limited company are thus overly protected, being required to pay debts only to the extent of their declared capital (as brought out by Mr. Goldbury near the end of the first act). Gilbert's venom may have been inspired by the Gurneys, a wealthy family mentioned in *Trial by Jury*. In 1865, after several generations of Gurneys had grown rich in the banking business, they formed themselves into a limited-liability company, and then went into bankruptcy the following year, leaving unpaid debts of eleven million pounds sterling—something like sixty million dollars. The Gurneys themselves lost hardly a shilling. Wolfson (322) has a more intriguing target: Richard D'Oyly Carte, himself. At the time Gilbert was writing *Utopia Limited*, Carte was busily engaged in some maneuvers to sell shares in his money-guzzling Royal English Opera House. Although Gilbert and Carte had returned to some semblance of civilized relationship following the famous carpet quarrel, Gilbert still had an ax to grind—or at least that is Wolfson's thesis. A remarkable sidelight to all this occurred during the D'Oyly Carte revival of the opera in 1975. Michael Rayner, playing the role of Mr. Goldbury (the exponent of limited liability) came on stage made up and dressed to look like the *Vanity Fair* cartoon of D'Oyly Carte, complete with cigar, cane, and roll of blueprints under his arm.

Paramount [King Paramount]: Supremely important.

Chapter XIII

Tarara [Tarara (*the Public Exploder*)]: Two years before the opening of *Utopia Limited* the song *Ta-Ra-Ra-Boom-Der-Ay* become a great hit in English music halls and elsewhere (158, 161, 254, 283, 302). Tarara's name thus teems with less-than-hidden meaning. Aurora (18) tells us that the song originally appeared in the French operetta *Miss Heyett*, composed by Edmond Audran. Stone (284) adds that the music was used as the theme song for TV's Howdy Doody Show.

Vice-Chamberlain: Someone second in authority to the Lord Chamberlain, which see below.

Lord Chamberlain [Lord Dramaleigh's position]: In monarchies the Lord Chamberlain is a court official who manages the royal household and ceremonial affairs. In Gilbert's day one of the Lord Chamberlain's deputies was required to license plays and other theatrical productions. He was, in effect, a censor — and, as such, an occasional thorn in Gilbert's side. Huston (158) calls attention to the fact that since the Lord Chamberlain's duty was to shelter the stage (from anything offensive) you might say that British drama was sheltered in his lee, hence the name Dramaleigh. Egad! See also Chapters IX and XII.

Life Guards [Captain Fitzbattleaxe's regiment]: Quoting Goodman (142): "One of the two cavalry regiments of the Household Division, the other being the Blues and Royals. They haven't strictly been bodyguards since the sixteenth century, and if you asked the Queen who her military bodyguard was she would say 'The Yeomen of the Guard.' " Prestige (245) sheds additional light, explaining that the two regiments perform ceremonial duties attending the sovereign on state occasions. They also do sentry duty at Whitehall. He concludes: "Both regiments are very tough soldiers; the officers are aristocratic and wealthy, and are much more than military bodyguards." Brewer (56) says all these manly fellows have to stand at last six feet tall. Barker (25) adds that they wear a brass helmet, with long white plumes, and a red tunic over which a metal breastplate is worn when on mounted duty. See also Chapter XV.

Comptroller: An auditor in a government or other agency (in this case at the royal palace) — the hard-hearted devil who controls spending and examines all accounts.

K.C.B. [Captain Sir Edward Corcoran, K.C.B.]: Knight Commander of the Bath, one of Britain's highest honors. Can this be the erstwhile captain of *H.M.S. Pinafore*? If so, he must be Josephine's husband (formerly mistakenly called Ralph Rackstraw) and not her father (formerly mistakenly called Captain Corcoran). As Lady Blanche observes, "This sounds involved. It's not. It's right enough." See also Chapters III and IV.

Bailey Barre {Sir Bailey's family name is pronounced BAR} [Sir Bailey Barre, Q.C., M.P.]: This is Gilbert's pun on London's Central Criminal Court, usually referred to as "Old Bailey," hence "the bar of Old Bailey."

Q.C., M.P.: Queen's Counsel and Member of Parliament. The *Queen's Counsel* is a prestigious distinction conferred on eminent barristers. See also Chapter III.

County Council: Bradley (48) explains that the 1888 Local Government Act created democratically elected county councils in place of administration by justices of the peace.

Gouvernante [The Lady Sophy's office]: You guessed it: the French word for "governess."

ACT I

Lotus-eating [in lotus-eating fashion]: In Greek legends, lotus plants bore fruit which, when eaten, caused dreamy forgetfulness. You may remember that some of Ulysses's sailors succumbed to that treacherous temptation.

Poppydom [For visions come from Poppydom]: As in opium dreams.

Lyre [with lyre and lute]: An ancient stringed musical instrument somewhat like a small harp.

Lute: A musical instrument much like a mandolin, with six or more pairs of strings. It was popular in the fourteenth and fifteenth centuries. See also Chapter XI.

Lowing [The lowing herds]: Mooing.

Turtle doves: A kind of old-world pigeon, noted for soft cooing and devoted attachment to its mate The *turtle* is derived from the Latin *turtur*, which Shipley (266) says is echoic of the dove's cooing call. See also Chapters XI and XIV.

ENGLISH FASHIONS!

Girton: The women's college at Cambridge. It was founded by Emily Davies in 1869 as a college for women in Hertfordshire, but moved to Cambridge in 1873 (48). The concept of college education for women was still looked upon with misgivings at the time the opera was written.

Anglicized [to be completely Anglicized]: "Make or become English in form, pronunciation, habits, customs, or character" (290).

Coruscation [a coruscation of impromptu epigram]: That which emits vivid flashes of light.

Epigram: A witty statement, like everyday conversation in a play by Oscar Wilde.

Lalabalele, talala! (etc.): Are these supposed swear words "based on the Polynesian or Oceanic languages" as Halton (147) states? Fifteen experts doubt it (33, 35, 80, 79, 152, 172, 176, 186, 188, 190, 221, 239, 248, 305, and 308). Collectively, they have carefully searched in vain through dictionaries in the following languages or dialects: Aniwa, Anuta, Cook Island, Easter Island, Fiji, Futuna, Gilbert islands, Hawaii, Kapingamaravange, Kusaie, Maori, Marquesses, Marshall Islands (Kiribiti), Namuea, Niue, Nukoro, Rennell & Bellona, Samoa, Tahiti, Tangan, Tikopia, Tonga, Tökelau, Tuamotuan, Tuvalu, and Woleaian.

A telling clue: Wolfson (322) shows a page from Gilbert's plot-book in which the Utopian language is indicated as "gibberish."

Explosive 'cracker': "A paper cylinder which explodes when pulled asunder" (75). These are what Americans used to call party poppers (274) and the English call Christmas crackers (294). They were invented in 1847 by a confectioner named Tom Smith of Finbury Square, London (284).

Let off steam: The allusion is to reducing excess pressure in a boiler by allowing some of the steam to escape directly into the atmosphere. The expression has come to mean relieving oneself of anger or frustration by complaining to anyone who will listen. Isn't that what friends are for?

Autocrat: A ruler having absolute power over his subjects.

'Society' paper: A periodical devoted to news about the personal affairs of the upper crust.

Heliogabalian: Refers to the Roman emperor Heliogabolus (or Elagabolus). We are told (105) that he was born in A.D. 204 and was named Varius Avitus Bassianus. (Do you suppose that first name reflects on there being various possible fathers?) While a youth he was appointed high priest of the Syro-Phoenician sun god Elagabol, and thereupon assumed the name Elagabolus. Appointed emperor after a military revolt in A.D. 218, he imposed the worship of Elagabol upon his subjects. Historians believe his religious rites involved human sacrifice. He appointed obvious misfits to high office and sent more than his share of dissident generals to early graves. His reign was marked by openly held homosexual orgies. He was killed by the Praetorian Guard after only four years in office. But that was quite enough.

Chapter XIII

Profligates: People who might be described as dissolute, depraved, abandoned to vice, and shamelessly immoral. Individuals of this desription have never been known to form G&S societies.

Double-first [Double-first in the world's university]: Rees (254) explains the term in these words: "The last year of study for a Baccalaureate (the 'Honours' year) ends with an examination in which the marks are not revealed. Instead the candidates are graded into First Class, Upper Second, Lower Second, Third Class and Unclassified. A double-first would mean receiving top grades in two Honours classes. Not bad!" The OED (228) defines *double first* as "A place in the first class in each of two final examinations in different subjects." ("Subjects" here means a broad field such as theology or science.) Several authorities (116, 142, 173, 245, 257, 271) endorse the OED definition. Others (98, 314) aver that the examinations are not necessarily in two different fields, but occur in successive years—about equivalent to the junior and senior years in an American university. Everyone can agree, however, that "Double-first in the world's university" means being a world-class intellectual wizard.

Cornucopia [Cornucopia is each in his mental fertility]: Any abundant, overflowing supply. Based on classical mythology, it was "a horn containing food, drink, etc. in endless supply, said to have been a horn of the goat Amalathaea or of the goat belonging to the nymph Amalathaea, or of Achelous, who lost it when he fought in the form of a bull with Hercules" (250). Now there is a cornucopia of useless information.

SCAPHIO & PHANTIS

Lore [In every mental lore]: Knowledge or learning.

'Utility' [We're wasted on 'utility']: Playing miscellaneous minor roles in theatrical productions.

Illicities [Upon our King's illicities]: Unlawful, dishonest, or immoral acts.

Auriculars [A pound of dynamite explodes in his auriculars]: Ears.

P's and Q's [He minds his P's and Q's]: A colloquialism: "To be careful or circumspect in behavior; to be exact" (115). Nobody knows the origin of the term. Brewer (54) suggests four alternatives: (i) an admonition to children in learning the alphabet to be careful not to mix the lower-case P's and Q's, (ii) a similar admonition to printers' apprentices when handling type, (iii) a saloon keeper's accounting shorthand: *P* for pints, *Q* for quarts, and (iv) during the reign of Louis XIV dancing masters would warn their pupils to mind their *P's* (i.e., *pieds*, feet) and *Q's* (i.e., *queues*, wigs) lest the latter fall off when executing a deep bow. Atkinson (14) suggests that English lawyers are expected to appear in court properly fitted with perukes (wigs), and a century ago would also have needed quill pens to record the proceedings. If their work involved much travel, they had to take particular care that they damaged neither perukes (P) nor quills (Q), since replacements might be hard to find in the hinterlands. Had enough? Let's move on.

Requited [is your affection requited?]: Returned in like kind and equal measure.

Royal shoes: Presumably an allusion to King Paramount.

Cull [cull the roses]: Select the best and leave the rest.

Poses [our King no longer poses]: This is one of the tougher nuts to crack in the lexicographic vise. It is a word of many meanings. The one that seems best to fit the context is "to rest" (229). In short, the King is now up and about and ready to greet his subjects.

Far niente [Sing the songs of *far niente*!]: Short for *dolce far niente*, the Italian expression for "sweet idleness."

Ireland [some add—but others do not —Ireland]: This is presumably an allusion to the long-festering question of Irish independence. Huston (158) mentions that shortly before the opera was written the House of Lords defeated a bill that would have given Ireland some political autonomy.

Finished [who have been 'finished' by an English lady]: *Finish* is used in the sense of perfecting something, as in a finishing school where girls learn the social graces.

Furlongs [By furlongs far]: A furlong is one-eighth of a mile, or 220 yards. The term is archaic, but still used in horse racing (294).

Kodaks: George Eastman's earliest cameras (which he named "Kodaks") appeared in 1888 and were advertised with the slogan "You press the button, we do the rest" (89). This is why Gilbert has Nekaya and Kalyba sing, "… you only need a button press — and we do all the rest."

Ranger [Bold-faced ranger]: A rover or wanderer (228).

GO AWAY, YOUNG BACHELOR!

Settlements [Hints at settlements]: Equivalent to marriage contracts, with clauses protecting the rights of both parties. In this case the emphasis is on the wife's rights if she becomes a widow.

Dross: The formal meaning pertains to worthless matter. Stedman (273) points out,

however, that the word was often used to mean money — especially by Gilbert's characters who pretended to despise it. Belinda in *Engaged* is such a one.

Toss [they toss!]: Flip a coin.

Cogent [this cogent moral]: Powerful and convincing, like this lexicon.

Moral: The underlying meaning of a story or lesson.

Manet King: A stage direction meaning the king stays on stage.

Junius Junior: See text under "Senex Senior" below.

Senex Senior: *Senex* is Latin for "old man." Cameron (66) adds these comments: "Adding Senior is a pleonastic joke. The reference is to the pseudonymous letters to the *Times* (like the famous letters of Junius) signed with Latin designations."

Ribald ["Ribald Royalty"]: Indecent, scurrilous, vulgar, and irreverent — all rolled into one.

Mephistopheles [Mephistopheles Minor]: Faust's devil or any other fiend.

Trenchant [Biting, trenchant sarcasm]: Cutting.

Sub-acid [delicately sub-acid, are they not?]: A bit tart, but not overdone.

Tuppence ["King Tuppence, or A Good Deal Less than Half a Sovereign"]: Slang for two-pence, often used to describe something, or someone, of little significance.

Sovereign: This has a double meaning here: a king and also a gold coin worth twenty shillings or one pound sterling (229). (Over the years there were other coins with the same name, but of differing values. What they had in common was the reigning monarch's likeness on the face.)

Wilkinson [the celebrated English tenor, Mr. Wilkinson]: An assumed British-sounding name adopted by one of the natives, much

Chapter XIII

as an aspiring young British or American opera singer named Jones might call himself Broccoli Spumoni. Shepherd (263) says that in searching through Gilbert's plot books in the British Library he found that for a time Gilbert considered using a scene in which it would be revealed that Wilkinson was Paramount in disguise.

Antithetical [but consider the antithetical humour]: Diametrically opposed.

Abject [with abject submission]: Contemptible.

Farce: A light, humorous play in which the plot revolves around ridiculous situations and cardboard characters.

De trop {duh TRO} [You're decidedly *de trop*]: French for "superfluous."

Teetotum: A teetotum is a many-sided (polygonal) top with a letter or number inscribed on each side. You spin it with the fingers and the number that is on the upper face after it comes to rest dictates your next move in whatever game you are playing. A teetotum was a socially acceptable substitute for dice (251).

Quotum [Gives its quotum once a minute]: Quota, or share. In the context, Gilbert is saying that fateful things happen with considerable frequency.

I'll go bail: I'll guarantee. See also Chapters III, VIII, and IX.

Laces tightly: Pulls her tummy in with a constraining corset (hoping to transfer the displaced bulk to her bosom).

Inning [Till your inning]: Your allotted time on this earth, akin to innings in cricket or baseball.

Rates [Rates are facts and so are taxes.]: Local taxes. (In Britain, the term "tax" is reserved for levies paid to the crown.)

Soliloquizing: Talking to himself (but so the audience can overhear). A useful practice in stage productions.

Tivoli Gardens: This derives from the Renaissance garden of the Villa d'Este in the town of Tivoli, a few miles northeast of Rome. It was the name given to a famous park and amusement center in Copenhagen and subsequently adopted for similar parks elsewhere.

Exhibits [When our medical adviser exhibits rum-punch it is as a draught, not as a fomentation]: Prescribes as a remedy.

Rum-punch: Sweetened and spiced fruit drink well fortified with rum and brandy.

Draught {Rhymes with daft}: A dose of medicine.

Fomentation: A warm lotion or poultice.

Enormity [the enormity of the case]: Villainy.

Ground plans: In architectural or civil engineering designs: the layout of the floor (or floors) of a building, viewed from above.

Sectional elevations: Cutaway views showing structure in cross-section.

Capital punishments: Executions. Gilbert seems to be making a far-fetched pun by mixing *capital* (as in punishment) and *capitol* (as in a government building) (25).

Rex: Latin for "king."

Calculus [On calculus may we be fed]: The *calculus* is a branch of mathematics that approaches problems by considering the behavior of small increments of the object under study. You can think of it simply as advanced algebra. Modern major-generals are known for their facile command of the subject.

Qualmish [Though a qualmish lot]: Subject to nausea (sickness of the stomach).

Knightsbridge nursemaids — serving fairies — stars of proud Belgravian airies: Collectively, the local female domestic help with whom the royal guardsmen might naturally flirt. Knightsbridge and Belgrave Square are residential areas close to

Buckingham Palace. The Belgrave area is a particularly prestigious district, hence the "proud." *Belgravian airies* refers to the below-street-level areas surrounding the basements of the fine residences typical of the Belgrave district. The basements were used as servants' working quarters. The OED (229) gives as one definition of *area*: "a sunken court, shut off from the pavement by railings, and approached by a flight of steps, which gives access to the basement of a dwelling house." The farce *The Area Belle*, by Brough and Halliday, is set in a household kitchen opening into such a court (42). We can be sure that a good deal of unofficial socializing between the unattached nubile servants and their military admirers took place in such settings, but I wonder if the aristocratic First Life Guards were only toying with the affections of those lower class females.

Trump cards [they're all trump cards]: Winners over all.

Horse Guards: A building in Whitehall, taking its name from the regiment that was once quartered there. In Gilbert's time it was the headquarters of the London military district and the Household troops, including the Household Cavalry (see below) and the various Guards regiments. The term "Horse Guards," then, applies to the building and to the headquarters (161).

Palsied [palsied with love]: Trembling.

Ingrate [Out of my sight, ingrate!]: Ungrateful wretch.

Tête-à-tête {TET-ah-TET}: French for "head-to-head, " generally implying a confidential, perhaps romantic, conversation. See also Chapter IX.

Rival Admirers' Clauses Consolidation Act: Fitzbattleaxe's fictitious law invented to bamboozle the two Wisemen. Barker (25) comments that Gilbert is twitting Parliament's actual readiness to enact legislation governing trivial activities.

Household Cavalry: The two regiments mentioned under "Life Guards" in Characters and Setting above. (Somehow the term conjures up visions of a house full of

horse-mounted soldiers and bitter complaints from the maid.)

Tontine principle: Tonti was a seventeenth century Italian who originated a fund-raising scheme that came to be known as a "tontine." Sponsored, usually by a government, tontines borrowed capital from individuals who were paid annuities until they died. Survivors benefited from increasing income as their numbers dwindled. When the last survivor died, the entire residual capital remained with the sponsoring organization. Tontines, which reached their peak in the eighteenth century, were used in France, Britain, and the United States (105).

Machinations [Their machinations we defy]: Despicable plots.

Predilections [And all her predilections]: Tastes.

Hypothesis: A tentative proposition assumed as a basis for reasoning.

Some crumpled roseleaf light: Knight (177) quotes Thackeray as saying, "A very little domestic roseleaf crumpled puts me off my work." Fitzbattleaxe is saying perfect bliss is easily marred.

Epigrammatical: Presented in a brief and witty style, perhaps with some sarcasm.

Nominally [Nominally a despot]: In name only.

Viviparians [Ye South Pacific Island viviparians]: *Viviparous* refers to bringing forth living offspring rather than eggs. We may interpret *viviparian* as a creature so endowed. More specifically, any member of the human race will do. Gilbert was merely overreaching for a word to rhyme with *barbarians* and couldn't twist the context to fit *Rotarians*. We shouldn't try to read any deeper meaning into it.

Abstract [All, in the abstract, types]: "In theory rather than in practice" (290).

Types [types of courtly grace]: A meaning of the word that applies here is models of perfection (229).

Chapter XIII

Serried [In serried ranks assembles]: Shoulder to shoulder. If the expression sounds familiar, it should. See Chapter IX.

Ulahlica!: Hurrah! (This seems to be pure Gilbertese.)

Logician [An eminent Logician]: An expert in logic, the science of reasoning.

Philologist [A marvellous Philologist]: Someone who is an expert in the science of language and knows all the meanings of words. You, too, will be a philologist after you have studied this book.

Scout [on any subject I can scout]: Reject with scorn, flout (250).

Solicitor [Depends on whose solicitor has given me my brief]: In this context a solicitor is a lawyer who acts as a middleman between a person involved in a higher court case and the barrister who will represent him or her in court. For a more complete explanation, see the entry "Barrister" in Chapter II.

Brief: A written outline of the facts in a court case. See also Chapter II.

County Council: See under "Characters and Setting" above.

Lord High Chamberlain: See entry for "Lord Chamberlain" under "Characters and Setting" above.

Presentations [and presentations scrutinize]: This can be interpreted in two ways: (i) any public showing, or (ii) formal introductions at the royal court. Lord Dramaleigh's responsibilities (as already noted) include checking plays for moral content, but perhaps he also aspires to checking on the moral worth of individuals hoping to be presented at court.

County Rate: County tax.

Sanitate: Clean up.

And purify the Halls: Keep questionable entertainment out of the music halls.

Contango [Which teaches what Contango means and also Backwardation]: "In Stock Exchange parlance, the sum paid by the purchaser of stock to the seller, for the privilege of deferring the completion of the bargain till the next, or some future settling day" (54, 250). (The buyer is in effect betting that the market price will drop.)

Backwardation: Backwardation is the opposite of Contango. That is, it is a sum paid by the seller for the privilege of postponing completion of the transaction.

Leaven [a grand financial leaven]: One definition is: "Influence that, spreading silently and strongly, changes conditions" (290).

Ginger-pops: Ginger beer, a carbonated soft drink (257).

Floated [Successfully I've floated]: Raised capital by selling stock or by other means.

Apple-stalls [And sudden falls in apple-stalls]: Fruit stands.

Companification: A Gilbertian term meaning "to be incorporated."

R.N. [Captain Sir Edward Corcoran, R.N.]: Royal Navy.

Gauls [terrify the simple Gauls]: Frenchmen.

Saxon [And how the Saxon and the Celt]: Germanic people who invaded (and settled in) England in the fifth century.

Celt {Americans generally pronounce it SELT, but most Britishers prefer KELT. Either is acceptable}: The native people of Ireland, Scottish highlands, and Wales.

Maxim gun and Nordenfelt: Hiram Stevens Maxim and Torsten Nordenfelt (Anglicized to Thorsten Nordenfeldt) had much in common; both were immigrants living and working in England; both were prolific inventors; and both joined forces to establish the Maxim-Nordenfeldt Company in the early 1880s. Maxim, an American, invented the first fully satisfactory machine gun. It was water-cooled and employed the recoil of the barrel to eject the spent shell and reload cartridges from a belt (89). Nordenfelt, a Swede, also invented a machine gun, but of vastly different design, employing up to a dozen barrels. Nordenfelt was made a royal Chamberlain by Oscar II of Sweden in 1885. Maxim became a British citizen in 1900 and was knighted by Queen Victoria the following year (56). One of his less notable inventions was an airplane powered by twin steam engines. He never managed to make it fly, but aside from that it was an engineering triumph (89).

[**Note:** Older editions of the libretto spell the Swede's name as "Nordenfelt," while newer editions spell it "Nordenfeldt." Either is correct.]

Unbend your sails: Remove your sails from the yards. See page 49.

Lower your yards: Take down the spars that hold up the sails.

Unstep your masts: Lift your masts out of the ship altogether.

Cut your canvas short: Place minimum reliance on sails.

Float it [I'll float it as a Company Limited!]: Set it on its way.

Company Limited: (See head of chapter.)

Peers [If possible, all Peers and Baronets]: In the United Kingdom, all noblemen above the rank of baronet. See also Chapters IV, VII, XII, and XVI.

Baronets: In the United Kingdom a baronet ranks above a knight but below a baron. It is the lowest rank of nobility that is hereditary, but it does not qualify the holder for a seat in the House of Lords. (These are useful things to know if you are ever made a baronet.) See also Chapters III and X.

Panama Canal: The Panama Canal to which Mr Goldbury refers is not the one we know today. When Gilbert wrote the libretto the ill-fated canal venture started by Ferdinand de Lesseps (The Compagnie Universelle du Canal Interocéanique) had recently collapsed. The ensuing investigations were even then creating sensational international headlines as reports of incredible corruption surfaced almost daily. The now-existing Panama Canal was not seriously contemplated by the United States government until early in the 1900s (208, 282).

Twitted [with dishonesty be twitted]: Reproached.

Perdition [that signifies perdition]: Utter loss. (It can mean even worse, but I think that is all Mr. Goldbury has in mind.)

Monetary [monetary dunce]: Pertaining to money.

Winding-Up Petition: The process of stopping a company from trading by reason of its insolvency (142).

Rothschild: Prominent family of wealthy bankers. For more details see Chapter VII.

Liquidators: Those who are sent in to manage the disposal of a company's assets when it has gone bankrupt.

Joint Stock Company [The Joint Stock Company's Act of Sixty-Two]: A joint stock company is one in which the shareholders are free to sell their shares on the open market. Whaley (310) says Gilbert made a slight editorial error. ("Company's" should read "Companies." Tush!)

Act of Sixty-Two: The Parliamentary act (passed in 1862) establishing limits of liability for stockholders. Knight (177) argues that an act of 1856 was actually more instrumental in establishing such limits, to which Turnbull (294) replies that "fifty six" wouldn't rhyme with "you."

Verity [Henceforward, of a verity]: In truth.

Pink [Of sovereigns all the pink!]: Finest.

Temerity: Audacity, chutzpah.

Mercantile [this mercantile pact]: Pertaining to commerce and merchandising.

Rue [we ne'er shall rue]: Regret.

Chapter XIII

ACT II

Chromatics: Sharps and flats on the musical scale.

Shake in *vibrato*: A shake is a trill. *Vibrato* is a musical "pulsating effect caused by rapid variations of stress on the one note" (75).

Agitato [Or never attempt *agitato*]: "Agitated, hurried, restless" (102).

Palate [his sensitive palate]: The roof of the mouth.

Cadence: An ornamental musical passage (102).

Sister services: Army and Navy.

Trammels [Freed from the trammels imposed upon them]: Rigid constraints.

Prospectus: A brochure describing the attractive features of a proposed company.

Transmute [transmute by a word]: Change from one substance, nature, or form to some other.

Drawing-Room: A formal reception at Court where ladies are presented to the sovereign (75). Terry (286) states that these were afternoon affairs in Victorian times, and with this Fitzbattleaxe concurs; but the Utopians plan to hold them in the evenings because the ladies look better by candle-light. Shipley (266) says the word was derived from the old practice in which, after a formal dinner, the ladies withdrew to another room.

Court train [my Court train has just arrived]: An elongated part of a cloak or skirt trailing behind on the floor. For illustrations, see Wolfson (322). This explains why so few English ladies go to a royal reception on their bikes. Stedman (274) says that at court presentations trains were required, along with three feathers on the head.

Declamation [indulge in declamation]: Formal speech-making, in oratorical style.

Knell: Ringing of a funeral bell.

Philomel [Soft the song of Philomel]: This refers to Philomela. In Greek legend she was an Athenian princess and sister of Procne, who married Tereus. Tereus violently deflowered Philomela and cut out her tongue to prevent her from accusing him. Philomela, however, embroidered her tale on a swatch of cloth (what a collectors' item that would be) and sent it to her sister. Procne's revenge was to serve Tereus the flesh of their son, and then the sisters fled. Tereus gave chase, but the sisters were turned into birds by compassionate gods. Philomela flew away as a nightingale but, according to some versions of the tale, she never regained her tongue. That would more than explain why her song was soft. In the big transformation scene a better-organized god would have allowed her to regain her tongue and even possibly her virginity.

Lay [the notes of lover's lay]: A short poem to be sung.

Clarions [his noisy clarions bray]: Shrill trumpets.

Artless [Lovers tell their artless story]: Unaffected and sincere.

PRINCESS ZARA

Virelay [In a whispered virelay]: "An ancient form of French verse, based on two rhymes; a roundelay" (75).

Field-Marshal: The highest ranking officer in the British army. "Marshal" was presumably derived from old High German *marah*, horse + *scalh*, servant, i.e., a groom. In the old Teutonic kings' eyes the chief groom was a most important officer (266).

Utopia Limited

Statutory Cabinet Council: The OED (229) defines *cabinet council* as "that limited number of the ministers of the sovereign or head of state who are in a more confidential position and have, in effect, with the head of the state, the determination and administration of affairs." The term "statutory" implies that the head of state is required to act in concert with such a council.

Christy Minstrels: A troupe of black-faced minstrels organized by the American Christy brothers (1815-62). Singing plantation songs and cracking bad jokes, they were a popular form of entertainment in Victorian England, as well as in America (54). Bradley (48) offers further details.

Court of St. James's: St James's Palace, in London, was the site of the British royal court and where Queen Victoria held royal receptions. The term "court" has many meanings. The pertinent ones here are: (i) the residence of the sovereign, (ii) the collective body of persons forming his or her retinue, (iii) a sovereign and his or her councilors as the political rulers of a state, and (iv) a formal assembly held by a sovereign.

Court of St. James's Hall: St. James's Hall was a London music hall known then for its minstrel shows. (The Piccadilly Hotel now occupies the site.) Music halls of the time combined a restaurant/bar with a stage for entertainment (136). Goodman (140) says the hall was an extremely large edifice. It contained not only the bar/restaurant/stage but also a much larger concert auditorium in which were presented the "Monday Pops" of *Patience* and *Mikado* fame. He adds, further, that the minstrel shows featured antics and lines that were considered less than respectable. That adds light to Gilbert's irony in substituting the music hall for the palace.

Peeress [No peeress at our Drawing-Room before the Presence passes]: Female member of the nobility, either a duchess, marchioness, countess, viscountess, or baroness.

Presence: Alludes to the sovereign. In short, she'll not be introduced to the monarch. Goodman (140) mentions that Queen Victoria received débutantes in the "Presence Room" at St. James's Palace.

Willy-nilly [we've done it will-nilly]: Without conscience effort. See entry for the same term in Chapter VIII for etymology.

Belgrave Square [And all that isn't Belgrave Square is Strand and Piccadilly]: Belgrave Square was among the most prestigious residential areas of London. The Strand and Piccadilly are streets with smart shops and theaters. All fashionable areas.

Slummeries [We haven't any slummeries in England!]: Slums.

Labour question [We have solved the labour question]: Probably refers to labor-management problems. Huston (158) says that 1893, the year the opera was produced, saw the formation in England of its first labor party. Prestige (245) believes the reference is to unemployment.

Risky [Of "risky" situation]: Bordering on indecency, i.e., risqué.

Brewers and Cotton Lords: Businessmen who have grown rich in their trades (and who hope to be created peers in recognition of their public service). Bradley (48) explains that the Conservative Government had such strong links with the "drink trade," that the honors bequeathed were referred to as "the beerage." Goodman (143), on the other hand, believes it was the Whigs who were so dubbed.

Thackeray [Earl of Thackeray]: William Makepeace Thackeray (1811-63): English novelist. Like Gilbert, he was trained as a lawyer but then turned to literature. He wrote extensively for *Punch* and was the author of *Vanity Fair*. See also Chapter VI.

Dickens [Duke of Dickens]: Charles Dickens (1812-70): Probably England's best-known novelist, the author of such famous novels as *Great Expectations*, *Oliver Twist*, *A Tale of Two Cities*, and *A Christmas Carol*. Gilbert adapted *Great Expectations* for the stage, and looked upon Dickens as one of his favorite authors (240). See also Chapters VI and X.

Fildes [Lord Fildes and Viscount Millais]: Sir (Samuel) Luke Fildes, famous English

Chapter XIII

painter (1843-1927). He was knighted in 1906 — beating Gilbert by a year. He had the honor of painting the official portraits of King Edward and Queen Alexandra.

Millais {mill-A}: Sir John Everett Millais (1829-96): Another famous English painter, who (with others) founded the Pre-Raphaelite brotherhood. Baronetted in 1885, he was president of the Royal Academy at the time of his death. Goodman (140) states that Millais and Sullivan were good friends, so it is not surprising that Millais was called upon to paint the portrait of Sullivan that hangs in the National Portrait Gallery in London.

[**Note:** The next nine entries occur in the stage directions pertaining to the dignitaries who appear in the big presentation scene.]

Master of the Horse: "An official having charge of horses, hounds, etc., of a sovereign of England. He is there a member of the ministry and the third dignitary of the court" (105). In modern times the post is entirely ceremonial (142). Terry (286) says he is in charge of carriages, limousines, and mounted processions as well as the royal stables. We are unable to discover who is in charge of sweeping the street after the royal procession.

Lord Steward: The officer in charge of arranging state banquets and other important ceremonial events (154). Terry (286) adds that the appointment is only on an *ad hoc* basis.

Lord in Waiting: "A nobleman in attendance on a British monarch or the Prince of Wales" (250).

Groom in Waiting: "Any of several offices of the English royal household" (105). Terry (286) mentions that he is like a Lord in Waiting except that he is not a peer.

Field Officer in Brigade Waiting: Terry (286) defines him as the liaison officer between the household troops and the sovereign.

Gold and Silver Stick: George (123) explains that these are officers of the Court who, on major ceremonial occasions, carry distinctive gold and silver mounted batons, which are about the length of walking sticks.

Gold Stick is usually honorary Colonel of one of the two Household Cavalry Regiments, while Silver Stick is taken in turn, on a monthly basis, by the two Commanding Officers. There are certain other officers who, depending on the nature and place of the occasion, are also eligible for the honor of being a Gold Stick. Bradley (48) offers further details. (Since Gilbert has left *Stick* in the singular form, we must assume that the two Utopian positions have been combined.)

Gentlemen Ushers: These are the officials who introduce people into the presence of the sovereign (75). Terry (286) says they have varied duties at Court and in Parliament.

Pages of Honour: Boys in the service of the Royal Court. According to Terry (286) these are sons of distinguished citizens (as we might have guessed) and may be called upon to serve as train-bearers to the king as well as queen or princesses.

Ladies-in-Waiting: Ladies "in Court circles appointed to attend on a Queen or Princess" (75).

Débutantes [to embrace all the *débutantes*]: The young ladies being presented to the Court.

Undress wigs [dressed as judges in red and ermine robes and undress wigs]: These are "forensic" wigs, the short periwigs worn in British courts of law, in contradistinction to the "full-bottomed," shoulder-length numbers worn on ceremonial occasions. The judge in *Trial by Jury* is sometimes portrayed in a long wig, but that is professional license carried too far. In British law courts the barristers wear wigs with three horizontal curls running all the way round. The judges wear wigs that are similar except that they have one vertical curl just above the tail instead of the three horizontal curls (103). See two Gilbertian cartoons (129) on next page.

Blank verse: Unrhymed verse, often set down in iambic pentameter style. The libretto for *Princess Ida* is a lovely example.

Winding-up Act: The law governing procedures for going out of business as arranged by the Act of Sixty-Two (see page 189).

Temerity: Audacity.

Refractory: Disobedient.

Pas de trois {pah-d'TWAH} [With *pas de trois* we will conclude]: Dance step for three.

Bring the people about his ears: The expression "about one's ears" means causing trouble. The allusion is to a nest of hornets buzzing about one's head (54).

Put him to bed: This may be short for "Put him to bed with a pickaxe and shovel," meaning to bury him (115). Stedman (274) says "Oh go to bed" is another way of saying "Shut up!" Here the meaning is "take him away."

Drivelling [You're a drivelling barndoor owl]: Talking nonsense.

Barndoor owl: The standard references are silent on the subject of barndoor owls. The closest I have come is a reference as follows: "Barn-door fowl: a mongrel or cross-bred specimen of the common hen; a dunghill or barn-yard fowl" (70). Barker (25) suggests "a fatuous turkey." My hypothesis is that a barndoor owl is a cross-bred bird, one-third barn owl, one-third wayward hen, and one-third Gilbertian imagination.

Vapid [You're a vapid and vain old muff]: Lifeless and insipid.

Muff: Bungler.

On the *Tapis* {tah-PEE} [It's still on the *tapis*]: "On the table cloth, under discussion or consideration" (228). Notice how the meaning of the term "to table" a matter changes as it crosses the Atlantic. In England when you table a matter you bring it up for discussion. In the States when you table it you postpone discussion.

Sap [Well done, you sly old sap]: This meaning of the word is related to the military process of undermining a wall: figuratively related to "stealthy or insidious methods of attacking or destroying something" (228). Walters (301) notes that the word is used as a mild form of abuse in a friendly, jocular manner. The word is derived from the French word *sappe*, shovel (266).

Mole [cunning old mole]: The work of the military sapper involves burrowing underground much as a mole does under your lawn or garden. (The three conspirators are pleased with their undercover plan.)

Noddle [It's safe in my noddle]: A jocular expression for the head (75).

Redounds: Contributes.

Biscuits [plate of mixed biscuits]: These are what Americans call cookies. Queen Victoria's drawing rooms had been noted for their lack of victuals, but after this line appeared things at the palace improved, or so it is claimed.

Comeliness {KUM-lee-ness} [In her magnificent comeliness]: Grace, good-looks, and attractiveness.

Chapter XIII

Eleven stone two [an English girl of eleven stone two]: A stone is a unit of weight equal to 14 pounds. Eleven stone two, then would be 14x11 + 2 = 156 pounds.

"Field" tails off and the muffs diminish: The poorer riders are left strung out behind and the worst drop out altogether.

Eleven maids out — and eleven maids in — and perhaps an occasional "maiden over!": Let's poke through this thicket one step at a time. In the game of cricket there are eleven players on each team. The "eleven maids out" are the ones whose turn it is to play defensively much as one baseball team is in the field trying to keep the other from scoring. The "eleven maids in," then would be the team whose turn it is "at bat." An "over" comprises a series of six bowls (equivalent to pitches in baseball). A "maiden over" is one in which no one manages to score. Gilbert puts the two words in quotation marks to call attention to his pun.

Punts [She golfs, she punts]: Poles a boat along a river. (This often requires considerable skill and agility.)

Till all is blue: Until after dawn and the sky is blue again. See also Chapter XIV.

Drum [At ball or drum]: "An assembly of fashionable people at a private house, held in the evening; much in vogue during the latter half of the eighteenth and beginning of the nineteenth century" (228). A ball, on the other hand, would be a public gathering. Brewer (54) claims that the term "drum" comes from the resemblance of the noise to that of drumming up recruits. Tea parties became "kettle drums," and really wild affairs "drum majors." On the other hand, Bradley (48) suggests the possibility that "tea" suggests "kettle," which suggests "kettle drum," and that suggests. "drum." I confess I find neither explanation truly satisfying.

Rill [the mountain rill]: A little stream.

Maxims [These maxims you endorse]: Brief rules for behavior.

Unfurl [Your character true unfurl]: Reveal.

Fusty [All musty, fusty rules despite]: Stuffy and out of date. Derived from *fust*, meaning moldy and ill-smelling (165).

Short-petticoated: Victorian women wore full-length skirts, while little girls romped around in short skirts. That is the allusion here.

Bruited [through the city bruited]: Rumored.

Toil [caught in Scaphio's ruthless toil]: Snare.

Deigned [my sovereign has deigned]: Condescended.

Rosal [And the earth is red and rosal]: An obsolete term for "rosy" (141).

Asinorum pons {ASS-eh-NORE-um PONS} [For that *asinorum pons* I have crossed without assistance]: This translates as "bridge of asses," a Latin expression applied early in the sixteenth century to a diagram showing how to find the middle terms to arguments. The allusion seems to relate to the difficulty of getting asses to cross a bridge. The name is also given to the fifth proposition of Euclid, which sets forth that, if a triangle has two of its sides equal, the angles opposite to these sides are also equal (105). Maybe by now you are sorry you asked.

Paragons [of prudish paragons]: Models of perfection.

Tarantella [Mentioned in the stage directions]: A fast, whirling dance from southern Italy. It was originally thought to cure tarantula bites. Kravetz (182) says the concluding music of the nightmare song in *Iolanthe* is in the form of a tarantella.

Ogress [Like some remorseless ogress]: A female ogre. Derived from the man-eating giant of fairy tales, *ogre* has also come to mean "a monstrously ugly, cruel, or barbarous person" (250).

Irruption [most unmannerly irruption]: Violent invasion.

Boons: Good things given or asked for — or even both; like this lexicon. See also Chapters X, XI, and XIV.

Fico {FEE-ko} [A fico for such boons, say we!]: This is Italian for *fig* and the sentiment is much the same as "We don't care a fig!" Snapping one's fingers is an appropriate accompaniment. For the intriguing history of the word, see entry for "Fig" in Chapter XI.

Government by Party: This has been standard operating procedure in England since around 1680, in the reign of Charles II (319).

MOST SPITEFUL LITTLE APE IN CHRISTENDOM

Chapter XIV The Grand Duke

Gilbert and Sullivan both tried other partners following their work on *Utopia Limited*. None met with much success, and so they made one more combined effort: *The Grand Duke*, which opened at the Savoy on March 7, 1896, and ran for a mere 123 performances. Neither partner, it appears, had put his heart into the effort. Some lines were cut after the initial performance, but stronger measures would have been appropriate.

The Grand Duke is a much neglected opera. Its principal shortcoming is that it is too long. Its principal virtue grows out of that very shortcoming: a competent director can omit songs, chop paragraphs of dialog, and come out with a jolly evening's entertainment. Try it; you'll see.

The Grand Duke was Gilbert and Sullivan's last collaboration. In ever-failing health, Sullivan died on November 22, 1900, at the age of 58. Carte died the following April, aged 56. Gilbert lived on as a country squire and was finally knighted in 1907. He died on May 29, 1911, at the age of 74. The triumvirate left to posterity their delightfully crafted operas. Now, more than a century later, those operas are still admired and lovingly presented by hundreds of amateur performing groups all over the English-speaking world. How surprised and delighted Gilbert, Sullivan, and Carte would be if they could but know. True, Gilbert would growl about directors taking liberties with his lines; Sullivan would be distressed with some of the tempi accorded his scores; and Carte would lament his inability to collect continuing royalties. Still, on the whole, they would derive great satisfaction from the lively current Geeandessian scene.

CHARACTERS AND SETTING

Grand Duke: In 1750, the time in which the opera is set, what is now Germany was a badly divided collection of autonomous states such as Brandenburg, Saxony, and Brunswick. Each of these little states was ruled over by its own prince. (A select number of these princes were titled "Electors" because of their nominal role in selecting the Holy Roman Emperor.) There were also smaller autonomous territories known as grand duchies, ruled over by grand dukes, who were next in rank to princes. One such grand duchy that is still extant is Luxembourg, a 99-square mile area between Germany, France, and Belgium, governed as a constitutional monarchy.

Statutory Duel: A legally prescribed method for settling a grievance. In this case, a legal fiction, hence a duel that happens in theory, but has some of the effects of happening in fact (26).

Pfennig Halbpfennig [The grand duke's duchy]: Literally: penny half-penny, implying here an insignificant political entity. "Tuppeny ha'penny" is a good British slang description of anything inferior and trivial (234). Barker (26) and Bradley (48) note a historical model: Landgraf Wilhelm of Hesse Cassel, who decreed that revenue collections should avoid fractions of a pfennig and round up to the next full pfennig. This petty avarice inspired his subjects to nickname him "Halbpfennig."

Dummkopf [Ernest Dummkopf]: German for "dumb-head." More generally, "stupid."

Comedian [Ludwig (his Leading Comedian)]: One definition of *comedian* given in the OED (229) is any dramatic actor. That interpretation seems most appropriate here. The plays the troupe produces are certainly not all comedies in the usual sense, nor are the actors comedians in the usual sense.

Notary [Dr. Tannhäuser (a Notary)]: A semi-legal official authorized to record statements, certify deeds, or take affidavits. Dr. Tannhäuser, like many notaries, is also a solicitor. See also Chapter III.

Monte Carlo [The Prince of Monte Carlo]: Capital city of Monaco, the smallest sovereign principality in Europe. Its current area is 395 acres (0.61 square miles) but it was somewhat larger at the specified time of the opera, 1750. Burgess (60) notes that Monte Carlo, being but a division of Monaco, does not merit having a prince. Tush. Sullivan apparently looked upon Monte Carlo as his favorite vacation spot (324). Although he developed a reputation as a heavy loser in gambling, he denied the rumor (183).

Chapter XIV

Viscount {VIE-count} [Viscount Mentone]: A nobleman of modest rank.

Mentone {men-TONE}: A resort city in France squeezed between Monaco and the Italian border. In France it is spelled Menton, in Italy Mentone. I once witnessed a performance in which an actor, when asked who he was supposed to be, turned up the label on his costume and read out, "Viss-count Meant-one." I thought that was pretty funny, and in keeping with the part, but I doubt that many in the audience caught the joke.

Herald: A royal messenger, especially one who announces the imminent arrival of the royal personage.

Krakenfeldt [The Baroness von Krakenfeldt]: According to Norwegian legends the kraken was a giant squid-like monster, said to be a mile-and-a-half in circumference. It had a nasty reputation for pulling masts out of ships with its tentacles. It was also charged with creating giant whirlpools, drawing ships and sailors to their doom. *Kracken* is also a German colloquialism for "broken-down horses" (26), but the Norwegian interpretation seems more fitting for this particular character. *Feldt* is the German word for "field." The baroness's name therefore could be taken to mean from (or of) a field or realm of old nags — quite a charming moniker. We are left to wonder if the baroness was in any way related to the Duchess of Crackentorp, the mother in *The Daughter of the Regiment*.

Comédienne: As implied a few lines above, this is not a comic actress, just an actress.

THE BEAUTIFUL JULIA

Soubrette: An actress who plays the young and saucy roles.

Chamberlains: High officials in the ducal court.

ACT I

WON'T IT BE A PRETTY WEDDING?

Speisesaal {SHPICE-uh-tsahl}: Apparently the capital city of the Grand Duchy of Pfennig Halbpfennig. Literally: "dining hall."

Trousseau {TRUE-so}: A bride's outfit of clothes and personal effects. It is the French word for "bundle" (26).

Sposo [Am I quite the dashing *sposo*]: An Italian word for a male spouse, i.e., a bridegroom (250).

Homely [untaught and homely]: The word has several meanings, of which two are pertinent here: unattractive (surely said only in fishing for compliments), and suited to a domestic environment.

Comely {KUM-ly} [Tender, truthful, true, and comely]: Attractive in appearance. Its correct pronunciation is as shown, but I suppose Gilbert would want you to make rhyme with homely. See also Chapter III.

Rate [Should he rate you, rightly — leftly]: Berate, scold. As Samuel Johnson (165) puts it: "To chide hastily and vehemently." See also Chapter I.

Rightly — leftly: Frequently.

Solicitor [As solicitor to the conspiracy]: Legal adviser. If you want a more complete definition, see entry for "Barrister" in Chapter II.

Wedding breakfast: In Roman Catholic practice, weddings were formerly held in the morning and, being masses, no meals were eaten after the previous midnight. Consequently, the first meal after the wedding ceremony would literally break (a) fast. The celebratory meal would be of a festive nature and not just a normal breakfast.

Troilus and Cressida: Shakespeare's play about the Trojan war. Burgess (60) comments that it is seldom performed, and rightly so.

Tiled [we're all tiled, here.] (Some editions of the libretto omit this line.): It means pledged to secrecy as in a fraternal order. Brewer (54) explains the term "to tile a lodge" as follows: "In Freemasonry, is to close and guard the doors to prevent anyone uninitiated from entering." Barker (26) says that in former times Freemasons' secret meetings were guarded by a door-keeper called a "tiler." Gilbert and Sullivan, incidentally, were both Masons (142, 163, 275).

Sausage-roll: A pastry baked around a small sausage. You will, of course, recall the wise little poem: The Germans fill the body cavity with food of great specific gravity.

Bilious [But it's bilious on the whole]: Pertaining to bile: the bitter, greenish fluid secreted by the liver. Here it means anything that upsets the liver. See also Chapter VI.

Pasty: A pastry-enclosed pie baked without a dish (75). {Make it rhyme with tasty, although in other settings rhyming it with *nasty* is equally acceptable.}

Gorges [Our offended gorges rise]: Throats. (Ingesting an excess of heavy, greasy sausage rolls tends to make a conspirator throw up.)

Agamemnon [King Agamemnon, in a Louis Quatorze wig]: Agamemnon was the king who led the Greek troops in the war against Troy. He was featured in such classical plays as Aeschylus's *Agamemnon* and Euripides's *Hecuba*.

Louis Quatorze wig {lew-EE kah-TORZ}: One of those shoulder-length wigs worn by Louis XIV of France for state occasions or for having his portrait painted. We need hardly add that such wigs were rather rare in Homeric Greece, or even in Shakespearean England. Stedman (274) notes that they were worn in classic plays in the French theater. Goodman (142) says such wigs were the height of fashion at the Restoration of 1660 and for 40-50 years afterwards.

[**Note:** In some editions of the libretto the next three entries first appear early in the first act, and then again at the start of the second. In other editions they appear only in the second act.]

Citharae {SITH-are-uh} [playing on pipes, citharae, and cymbals]: Plural of *cithara*, an ancient Greek lyre (a harp-like instrument). The word is related to both *zither* and *guitar*.

Eloia! {eh-LOW-ee-uh}: This is apparently a made-up Greek-sounding word. Judging from its context it must pertain to joy.

Opoponax! {oh-POP-oh-nax}: You can interpret this as also being expressive of joy. It is actually a variant on *opopanax*, Greek for "all-healing," and the name of a plant once

Chapter XIV

believed to have that property (229). In Gilbert's day Opoponax was the trade name of a line of perfumes that were widely advertised in journals. Gilbert presumably thought it sounded right for his Greekly chorus, and we shouldn't try to read any deeper meaning into it. Cameron (66) adds that ancient Greek playwrights frequently coined words in imitation of animal calls, "like tio tio tio tinx (in *The Birds*), brekekekex (in *The Frogs*) and otototoi (nearly everywhere)."

Plump [His entire company has promised to plump for him]: To vote for but a single candidate when the ballot allows you to vote for more than one. By thus depriving the other candidates of your vote, you increase the probability that your favorite will garner the greatest total.

Tuppenny [this tuppenny state]: An Englishman's way of saying "two-penny."

Question: Should we balk at these supposedly German characters discoursing in terms of British coinage? Of course not! This is a light-hearted comic opera and the language is intended to be easily understood by a British audience. If it's accuracy you want, curl up with an encyclopedia. Let me also mention that *The Grand Duke* is saturated with anachronisms. I am not going to slow the pace by pointing them out, but you might see how many you can spot.

"All right at night": Partridge (237) says "all right on the night" (meaning opening night) is "an actors' catch phrase applied to a bad … dress rehearsal."

Square the press: Bribe some critics to write favorable reviews.

Hoydens [F claims all hoydens]: Boisterous, ill-bred, rude girls (229). The deplorable sort who prefer rock concerts to G&S productions.

Wheelers [wheelers and leaders]: Those horses in a large team that are hitched just ahead of the carriage.

Leaders: In a large team of horses, those at the front.

Fin [with a wave of his fin]: Slang for "the arm" or "the hand" (115).

Ireland [All Europe—with Ireland thrown in!]: I suppose this is a reflection on the rather bitter tensions between Ireland and England. It also reflects the typical Englishman's tendency to look upon his nation as being quite distinct from Europe. You may recall the British newspaper's headline: FOG BLANKETS CHANNEL: CONTINENT ISOLATED.

Troilus of Troy: The tragic hero of Shakespeare's play *Troilus and Cressida*, based on a narrative poem by Chaucer, which was in turn based on Homeric lore. Troilus was the son of Priam, king of Troy. His lover, Cressida, was unfaithful to him and Troilus was slain in trying to take revenge on his rival, a Greek.

Throwing it up [there's no throwing it up]: Slang for "resigning" (115).

Gerolstein {GAIR-ohl-sh'tyne} [It's a very good part in Gerolstein]: This is a sly reference to Offenbach's 1867 comic opera *The Grand Duchess of Gerolstein* (which actually opened more than a century after the specified time of *The Grand Duke*; but let it pass). Gerolstein is in fact a German health resort in the Rhineland "with a romantic ruined castle" (48).

[**Note:** Anyone playing the role of Julia should remember that all her lines are to be delivered in a strong foreign accent. As conventionally directed, the accent is German. Hyder (161) argues that a Hungarian accent would be more appealing and would accord with that of Ilka von Palmay, who created the role.]

Rancour [All rancour in my heart]: Deep malignity or spite (75).

Witch [I'd witch and woo]: Bewitch: to enchant with witchcraft (229).

Turtle [Like turtle, her first love confessing]: Turtledove. The "turtle" is derived from the Latin *turtur*, which Shipley (266) says is echoic of the dove's cooing call. See also Chapters XI and XIII.

Mock [That it was "mock," no mortal would be guessing]: This, of course, is a pun on mock turtle soup — which is made of calf's head, or other veal, and flavored to imitate real turtle soup. (Maybe you were better off not knowing.)

Jade [the forward jade]: A term of contempt for a woman (115).

Vernal [aglow with beauty vernal]: Spring-like, youthful.

Diurnal [with joy diurnal]: Daily.

Histrionic [My histrionic art]: The word has two meanings, both of which would apply: (1) pertaining to actors and acting, and (2) insincere.

Tetter: This is the name of a skin disease. Asimov (11) extends that to an itching that drives one to distraction. I think it more likely that it is just Gilbert's made-up word meaning all atwitter.

Agitato [What means this *agitato*?]: An Italian musical term for something agitated, hurried, or restless.

Eat {Rhymes with yet.} [A sausage-roll I took and eat]: He means he ate it. Stedman (274) points out that in Gilbert's day that was a common pronunciation.

Muckled [the more I muckled]: Webster (306) tells us that *muckle* is a variation of *mickle*, one meaning of which is Scottish slang for "talking with a big mouth." Another dictionary (108) defines *mucklemouthed* as "Having a large mouth."

Fell [What folly fell]: Terrible.

Muff: A bungler. See also Chapter XIII.

Candle snuff: "The charred or partly consumed portion of a candlewick" (250).

Gibbet {JIB-ett} [upon the Castle gibbet]: A frame for hanging criminals. It could be used either as a device for execution or for exhibiting those already dead. A good place to avoid in either event.

Duello: Italian for "duel."

Parliamentary draftsman: A person who devises the wording for laws (142). See also Chapter VII.

Falchions {FAWL-shuns}: A falchion is a short broad, curved sword, somewhere between a saber and a scimitar in shape. More generally: any sword. The word is derived from the Latin word for "sickle" (250).

Exigence [When exigence of rhyme compels, Orthography forgoes her spells]: Urgent need.

Orthography: The art of spelling. If you look carefully at the context again, you may smell a neat pun — which I won't spell out.

Spells: Enchantments.

Legal fiction: Something assumed under the law even though it is obviously untrue in any literal sense. See also Chapter XII.

Ipso facto [Dies, *ipso facto*, a social death]: Automatically. This is Latin for "by the act itself."

Revising Barrister: "A barrister who was appointed to revise lists of voters in parliamentary elections. While this responsibility was vested, in 1896, in specially appointed barristers, it has since been transferred to other officials" (243).

Expunges: Removes.

King's evidence [He is accepted as King's evidence]: "British Law, evidence for the crown given by an accused person against his alleged accomplices" (250). In the United States it is called state's evidence.

Chapter XIV

Miscreant: Vile and unprincipled scoundrel. The sort of blighter who would curse at his wife without first removing his hat.

Field of honour: The site where men may duel to defend their "honour."

Mould [Each is laid in churchyard mould]: Soft, rich earth, gently mellowed by all those mouldering bodies.

Suppose [Who'd suppose the method old!]: In this context the expression means "Who would consider the old method?" That is one meaning of "suppose" (250).

Rubs [Fortune's rubs]: "Rub" is a colloquialism for a difficulty or an obstacle (115). Hyder (162) reminds us of "ay, there's the rub," from Hamlet's soliloquy (Act III, Scene I).

Troth [may keep their troth]: Wedding vows.

Prig [a miserable prig]: Someone who makes a big show of virtue. As Johnson (165) defines it: "A pert, conceited, saucy, pragmatical little fellow."

Dissemble [We must dissemble]: Disguise the truth. See also Chapter IV.

Bread and cheese: The bare necessities of life (54). See also Chapter XII.

Autonomy [of monarchial autonomy]: Self-government.

Bonhomie {Anglicize to rhyme with autonomy. Sorry!} [I don't indulge in levity or compromising *bonhomie*]: French for "cheerful comradeship."

Jape [I don't see joke or jape any]: "Joke" and "jape" mean pretty much the same thing: a jest.

Tuppence-ha'penny {...-HAY-p'ny}: An Englishman's way of saying "two-and-a-half cents." It is a common expression implying disdain (234).

Snuff box: A small container for powdered tobacco. The powder, when inhaled, induces sneezing. It was often attended with elaborate ceremonial flourishes.

Wedding Breakfast Bee: A bee is a social gathering for some useful purpose. The implication here is that Rudolph's wedding breakfast will be a Dutch treat. Bring your own food and drink.

Gingerbierheim: This is simulated German for "ginger beer." Many of the famous Rhine wines come from areas with names ending in *heim*: Deidesheim, Wachenheim, Rüdesheim, and Dürkheim being four examples (226).

Currantweinmilch: Again, a simulated teutonic word for a drink made of currant wine. The "milch" is added to remind you of *Liebfraumilch*: "Milk of the Good Lady," a choice Rhenish wine. In short, *Currantweinmilch*, like *Gingerbierheim*, is a cobbled-up term intended to give artistic verisimilitude to an otherwise bald and unconvincing ale.

Mean [a mean little darling]: Of the many meanings of the word, "stingy" best describes the baroness, and also defines Rudolph's idea of a perfect mate.

Jujube {JOO-joob} [Begin with a jujube]: A lozenge made of gelatin, fruit juice, sugar, etc. (Was Gilbert trying to sneak in his lozenge plot again?) The candy (something like a jelly bean) was originally flavored with the fruit of the jujube plant, which grows around the Mediterranean (229). Barker (26) kindly informs us that the scientific name for the jujube plant is *Zizyphus jujuba*.

Charlemagne [back to the reign of Charlemagne]: Charles the Great (A.D. 742 - 814). He was king of the Franks from 768 to 814, and emperor of the Holy Roman Empire from 800 to 814.

Let [the houses wouldn't let]: Rent.

You've never been [you've never been and bought a newspaper]: Partridge (237) says that "you never did" is a Cockney catch phrase "expressive of humorous appreciation or approval or amazement." We can interpret "you've never been" in the same vein: a gentle joshing at such wild extravagance.

Penny roll [As o'er our penny roll we sing]: The smallest item of bread that can be purchased at a bakery (251). See also Chapter XV.

Two-and-six: Two shillings, six pence. A shilling was one-twentieth of a pound sterling and there were twelve pence to a shilling. That amount was worth about sixty American cents in those days.

Half-a-crown [A better man by half-a-crown]: A half crown was a British coin worth two shillings, six pence, or "two-and-six," as mentioned above.

Abear [which I can't abear]: A dialectal version of "bear" or abide.

Table beer: The cheapest kind of beer, analogous to table wine, only cheaper.

Waterbury watches: Cheap watches made in Waterbury, Connecticut. Production of these watches was started in 1879, and they soon became a byword for bottom-of-the-line timepieces (26, 103).

Malefactor: Criminal.

Trimmle and twitter [Who is all of a trimmle and twitter]: Comic dialectal phrase meaning trembling and upset.

Palate [your palate unpleasantly bitter]: The roof of the mouth. In this case the phrase probably means "a bad taste in the mouth."

Dividers [When your legs are as thin as dividers]: A device shaped like an inverted V, much like the compass you use to draw circles. Draftsmen use them to divide a space into equal segments, or to transfer a given dimension from one location to another.

Insiders [plagued with unruly insiders]: Presumably Gilbert's word for the digestive system. Walters (302) thinks it may refer to such charming creatures as tapeworms.

Gamboge {gam-BOJE}: Yellow complexion. Gamboge is a bright yellow gum-resin from a tree that grows in Southeast Asia. The word is derived from Cambodia (229).

Gill: The flesh about the cheek and jaws (75).

Swallow {Force yourself to make it rhyme with tallow.} [With a pint of warm oil in your swallow]: Slang for "gullet" or "gorge" (228).

Tin-tacks [and a pound of tin-tacks in your chest]: The OED (229) defines *tin-tack* as "A tack, or short light iron nail, coated with tin." This is probably what we call carpet tacks, although thumb tacks have also been suggested. In either event they would be downright uncomfortable in your chest.

Vapours [down in the mouth with the vapours]: An old term referring to mental depression, nervous debility, or melancholy.

Morris wall-papers: Wallpaper designed by William Morris, the Victorian artist and poet who showed that utilitarian objects could also be beautiful. Stedman (273) points out that his patterns would be particularly appropriate for beetles; they usually featured complex patterns of vines, leaves, flowers, and sometimes birds or fruit. In *Ruddigore* Morris is referred to, anachronistically, by Robin Oakapple: "From Ovid and Horace to Swinburne and Morris." He is also one of the aesthetes whose worshiping disciples were lampooned in *Patience*.

"Jim-jams": Partridge (234) cites several interpretations of *jim-jams*, including delirium tremens, the fidgets, and the creeps. But why go on? Rudolph has already described the malady to perfection.

Gruel [to give this man his gruel]: Brewer (56) says the expression means to put the man to death. In this case, we might say "a trying ordeal" (75).

Plebeian [This plebeian man of shoddy]: Pertaining to the unwashed masses. See also Chapter XII.

Shoddy: An inferior kind of woolen cloth. See also Chapter XII.

Diskiver: Comic dialectal version of "discover."

Pillory [Put him in a pillory]: One of those frames used to clamp an offender and hold him up for public ridicule and to serve, perhaps, as an inviting target for over-ripe fruit, elderly eggs, and deceased felines.

Chapter XIV

Rack [Rack him with artillery]: This can be taken to mean "punish him." If you are feeling more literal, or just a teeny weeny wee bit bloodthirsty, you can relate the word to that instrument of torture that was used to pull the victim's limbs out of their sockets. Thus, "rack him with artillery" might mean to blow him to pieces.

Doughty [two doughty heroes thunder]: Brave.

Verbum sat. {VERB-um sat}: Abbreviation for the Latin expression *verbum satis sapienti*, meaning a word to the wise is sufficient. So why did it take so many words to explain it to you?

Steps into ... shoeses: When you "step into someone's shoes" you take his place. "Shoeses" is Gilbert's way of making "shoes" even more plural.

[**Historic note:** At one time the laws of Montana held that "Anyone who slays or disables another in a duel must support the victim's family" (189).]

Malcontents [malcontents abuse you]: Those who are chronically dissatisfied, perhaps even rebellious.

Penitential fires: The punishments of hell.

Ribaldry {RIB-eldry} [the ribaldry that from you falls]: Vulgar, coarse, and mocking speech.

Wayward [wayward fate]: Unsteady and unpredictable.

Regale [Regale you, sir]: Honor or venerate as royalty. A second meaning has to do with giving pleasure, perhaps with food and drink (26).

Ascetic [I'm not an ascetic]: One who practices self-denial. In extreme cases such a person may even refrain from going to G&S shows.

Get up our hay: A variation on the old cliché: make hay while the sun shines.

"What for" [He'll give you "what for"]: I have heard the expression used as meaning a good scolding. Brewer (54), says it means to castigate thoroughly, or administer a sound thrashing.

By Jingo [by Jingo I'll do it!]: A mild oath ascribed by some to a corruption of "St Gingoulph" and by others to the Basque word for God: *Jinkao*. Asimov (11), on the other hand, states that it is a euphemism for "by Jesus." Brewer (54) says the word was used by conjurers of the seventeenth century. The important fact is that "We don't want to fight, but by Jingo if we do … " were the words of a music hall tune made popular in 1877 and still popular in the 1890s.

Tenter-hooks: Literally, these are hooks used in a device for stretching cloth. The figurative meaning is "to keep someone in suspense."

Spartan [this Spartan rule applies]: Simple, frugal, and severely disciplined.

Canons [The canons of dramatic art]: Sacred rules.

"Leading Business" [It's "leading business," pet]: In theatrical jargon: a starring role.

Jinks: Boisterous fun or merry capers.

Grig [as merry as a grig]: A "merry grig" is widely understood to mean a lively, good-humored, pleasant companion (75, 115, 234). The roots of the term are subject to some disagreement. Does *grig* mean a "cricket" or a "Greek"? (There are also a few other, less-likely candidates.) Some authorities (54, 115) give the two equal credence. Others (11, 150, 181, 302, 320) subscribe to "cricket." Other authorities favor "Greek." Applegate (8), for example, noted that in *Troilus and Cressida* Shakespeare has "Then she's a merry Greek," and "Cressid 'mongst the merry Greeks." Remember, too, that Ludwig (who uses the line) is planning to don a Greek costume from that very play — and then goes on to say in short order, "Old Athens we'll exhume!" I tend to side with "Greek" — although a chirping cricket on a hearth would suit me about as well.

Tollolish [you'll find our rule tollolish!]: The word is presumably derived from "tolerable." In his Bab Ballad "The Mystic Selvagee," Gilbert says: "Lord Nelson, too, was pretty well; that is, tol-lol-ish" (127). In the present context, we may infer that Ludwig's rule will be easygoing and permissive. Perhaps the Earl Tolloller will be brought in as a consultant.

Noblesse [Your new *noblesse*]: French for "nobility."

Dress [Must have a dress]: Costume or attire.

Athens [Old Athens we'll exhume!]: The essence of classical civilization.

Exhume: Dig out of the grave, or figuratively: revive.

ACT II

Pipes [playing on pipes]: Pandaean pipes: musical wind instruments made of hollow reeds of different lengths.

Defile [As before you we defile]: The verb "defile" has two totally different meanings: (i) to parade in single file or (ii) to desecrate. Gilbert meant the former, but some under-rehearsed performing groups may more nearly illustrate the latter.

Till all is blue: Until daylight. See also Chapter XIII.

Lesbian [Fill the bowl with Lesbian wine]: Pertaining to the Aegean island of Lesbos, now called Mytilene. Its wine enjoys a good reputation, to which Gilbert alludes in *Thespis.*

Diergeticon {Pronounce it with a hard g.} [Sing a Diergeticon]: Barker (26), Dunn (100) and Terry (286) opine that this is merely made-up Greek. Halton (147) calls it a doleful song. Cameron (66), on the other hand, says that the word is consistently misspelled in every known version of the libretto. Gilbert probably intended to say "diegerticon," which "means a rousing song or anything stimulating or exciting. In some Greek

writers it means aphrodisiac. Surely not in Gilbert." I endorse Cameron.

Hyporchematic [We've a choir hyporchematic]: A hyporchema is a song accompanied by dancing and mime; hence a choir that sings and dances (66).

Choreutae {ko-ROOT-ee} [the *choreutae* of that cultivated age]: The plural of *choreuta*, a chorus member in the Greek theater (66).

Captious [all but captious criticaster]: Ill-tempered fault-finding.

Criticaster: A really bad critic. This may be a dig at a misguided journalist who was identified only as "Our Captious Critic" and who once wrote a most disparaging column about *The Gondoliers* in particular and the Savoy operas in general. As for professional critics, Oliver Wendell Holmes had these lines: "Nature, when she invented, manufactured, and patented authors, contrived to make critics out of the chips that were left."

Choregus: The leader of the chorus in the Greek theater (66). Barker (26) says the term may imply many additional functions, including everything from finance to artistic direction.

Attic [the early Attic stage]: Pertaining to Attica, a region of south-east Greece wherein Athens is located. May be interpreted as meaning Athenian (26).

Oboloi {OH-bull-oh} [all in *oboloi* and *drachmae*]: Plural of *obol*, an Attic coin of small value.

Drachmae {DROCK-me}: Plural of *drachma*, another Attic coin, worth six oboloi. Try that on your slot machine.

Kalends {KAL-ends} [at the Kalends that are Greek!]: As far back as the emperor Augustus, the expression has been used as meaning "never" (260). The word, is a variation of *calends*, the first day of the month with the Romans, who borrowed it from the Etruscans. Calends were not used in the Greek calendar and so the expression is equivalent to "the second Monday of next

Chapter XIV

week" (115). (As Edwin so sagely observes, you don't find two Mondays together.)

Periphrastic [Periphrastic methods spurning]: Verbose. The literal meaning is "circumlocutory."

Socratic [in the period Socratic]: Pertaining to the Greek philosopher Socrates (469?-399 B.C.).

Recherché {ruh-SHARE-shay} [on a *recherché* cold ἄριστον]: French for "choice" i.e., tasty.

ἄριστον {AIR-iss-tahn or ah-RISS-tun}: This transliterates *ariston*, meaning roughly "breakfast." (66).

τρέπεσθαι πρὸς τὸν πότον {TREPP-iss-tie prahs TAHN POT-ahn}: Translates "Turn toward the drink, or to imbibe" (66). Gilbert explains it in the next line as [the way they went at] "a steady and a conscientious drink" in Attica.

Corybantian {CORE-eh-BANN-tee-en} [Corybantian maniac kick]: Refers to the Corybants, priests of the goddess Cybele, whose worship was conducted with wild orgies and frenzied dances.

Dionysiac or Bacchic: Pertaining to the alternative names for the Greek god of wine.

Dithyrambic: Refers to the dithyramb, an ancient Greek hymn sung at grape-harvesting festivals in honor of Dionysus. The inference can be made that this was no stately mass, but a wild and boisterous revel. Yesh indeed.

Mrs. Grundy: A character referred to ("What will Mrs. Grundy say?") in Thomas Morton's comedy *Speed the Plough* (1798). Her name has come to represent conventional mores (223).

Macintoshes [For they hadn't macintoshes]: Coats made of a waterproof material invented by Charles Macintosh. Oddly enough, the preferred spelling in the OED (228) is "Mackintosh." See also Chapters X and XV.

Goloshes: What Americans call galoshes (from the French *galoshe*): waterproof over-

shoes that come up over the ankles. See also Chapter I.

Played the very deuce: Played the very devil, i.e., caused great mischief.

Coan {Sounds more or less like "Cohen"} [their dress of Coan silk]: Refers to silk from the Greek island of Cos or Koa, just off the Turkish coast (103). As Ludwig leeringly points out, Coan silk was rather transparent and hardly fit for Victorian ladies' attire.

"Altogether" [something like the "altogether"]: Being in the nude. It is supposedly derived from Middle English *altogeder* (11).

Assiduously [you must assiduously watch]: Diligently.

Hardbake: Almond toffee; a kind of candy.

Hoity-toity [hoity-toity vixenish viragoes]: A colloquialism for "peremptory, waspish, and quarrelsome" (115). We might say "pretentious."

Vixenish: Like a vixen, which is a female fox. The word as used here is a colloquialism for an ill-natured, snarling female.

Viragoes {vih -RAY-goes or vih-RAH-goes}: Bad-tempered, scolding women. (The phrase "hoity-toity vixenish viragoes" forms a prolix plethora of tautologies arising from Gilbert's legal training.) See also Chapter VIII.

Untenable: Indefensible.

Ingenoo: {IN-jen-oo} Ingénue: An actress who plays the role of an artless, naive young woman.

To give the deuce her due: "Deuce" here is a euphemism for devil. "To give the devil his due" means to give a disliked person such credit as he (or, in this case, she) may merit (54).

O, jiminy: *Jiminy* is "a mild exclamation of surprise, emotion, or awe." Possibly derived from *Gemini* (250).

Miminy-piminy: Excessively affected or fastidious. The roots of the word are explained in Chapter VI.

Millstone nether: Flour is made from grain that is ground between two stones (one of which is turning). The lower one is the "millstone nether."

Leman {Rhymes with demon} [The lily-white laughing leman!]: A paramour in two syllables.

Corse [O cold unpleasant corse]: A corpse.

Avaunt!: Begone!

Chimerical {keh-MEER-eh-kell} [With fancies wild — chimerical]: The chimera was a fabulous fire-breathing monster with a lion's head, goat's body, and a dragon's tail; hence any wildly imaginative or impossible creation.

Countenance [never saw her countenance before]: Face.

Super [She's as sulky as a super]: Short for "supernumerary," a stage extra. Since many supers are thwarted would-be stars, one may expect them to be sulky. Stedman (273) notes that when Gilbert wrote reviews of plays he often made fun of supers who stood around like zombies instead of reacting to developments on stage.

Trooper [swearing like a trooper]: A cavalry soldier.

Tribulation [grief and tribulation]: Great trouble.

Hurly-burly: A colloquialism for a "commotion or uproar" (115).

Hubble-bubble: A baroque version of "hub-bub," meaning confused voice or voices (115).

À la mode [No doubt it's an expression *à la mode*]: This has nothing to do with ice cream. It is French for "style" or "manner." An expression *à la mode* is one that is new and possibly ephemeral.

Matrimonially matrimonified: Tautologically married (and perhaps one day to be divorcedly divorced).

Tol the riddle lol!: Nonsense words reflecting mock sorrow (12F).

Ebullient: Overflowing.

Accession: Promotion. See also Chapter XII.

Frump [Old frump]: A woman who is in shabby, out-of-date attire, and probably experiencing a bad hair day.

Civil death [that's only a civil death]: An imaginary death based on a legal sleight-of-hand.

Boon: Blessing. See also Chapters X and XI.

Epithalamia {EPP-eh-thal-A-me-uh} [Let festive epithalamia resound]: Plural of *epithalamium*: "A nuptial song … especially among the Greeks and Romans" (75). Bradley (48) adds that the songs were performed by young men and women outside the door of the wedding chamber. One supposes the newlyweds had the foresight to plug the key hole.

Broach [Broach the exhilarating Marsala]: Open, or tap.

Marsala: A wine from Marsala, in Sicily. Walters (301) tells us it is somewhat like Madeira wine. Our wino-readers will appreciate these details, we are sure.

Reck [you little reck]: An archaic term for "care" or "heed." (Now you know the roots of "reckless.") Gilbert is perhaps using it as short for "reckon" in the sense of understanding the value of something.

Chapter XIV

Fidgets [she fidgets me]: Read: she gets on my nerves, or she bugs me.

Plighted [every promise plighted]: A promise plighted is a promise promised or a pledge pledged. (Gilbert's legal training is showing again.) In case you want to know, the word "plight" comes from the German *Pflicht*: duty.

Repining [No good ever came of repining]: Sad reflections on the past or present. See also Chapter XI.

Viva {vee-VAH} [So *viva* Tomorrow!]: Roughly equivalent to "give three cheers."

Sepulchral [ain't his eyes sepulchral!]: Pertaining to sepulchers (graves) and by extension: deep and gloomy.

Bogy {Pronounce it with a hard g} [Haunted by a technical bogy]: A bogy is any sort of a frightening apparition. Ernest, being technically dead, is therefore a technical bogy. Rees (251) adds that Gilbert probably was punning on "technical bogy," meaning a flaw in a carelessly drafted Act of Parliament or other regulation — about equivalent to "technical booboo." After all, it was an Act of Parliament, so to speak, that declared Ernest to be dead.

Chaff [but I don't chaff bogies]: To tease or make fun of.

Dodge [the meanest dodge]: Colloquial for "a clever trick or ruse."

Cry off [But you don't mean to say that you're going to cry off!]: British slang meaning to back out of an agreement.

Lay [won't anything lay thee?]: Lay to rest, bury.

Gainsay [to deny or gainsay thee]: To contradict or dispute.

Spectre [So, spectre appalling]: Apparition or ghost.

Bogydom: State of being a ghost.

Magnum [In a magnum of merry champagne]: A two-quart bottle. (This entry and the next five are from a song by the baroness that is omitted in most versions of the libretto.)

Brindisi: A drinking song. See also Chapter III.

Bumpers [Come, bumpers — aye ever so many]: A glass filled to the brim — as in "pirate bumpers."

Pommery [Pommery, seventy-four]: An 1874 vintage champagne of particular acclaim (and another anachronism).

Panacea [old wine is a true panacea]: Cure-all, from a Greek word meaning "universal remedy" (26).

Cut-orange ball [A sandwich and cut-orange ball]: Stedman (273) recalls that Dickens refers to sliced oranges with powdered sugar in *Martin Chuzzlewit*. The implication is that the baroness's party was an austere affair.

A-poaching: [Some rascal come a-poaching]: A variant on *poaching*: to intrude on another's property, usually to take game or fish without permission.

Auric'lar [By word of mouth auric'lar]: Short for *auricular*: pertaining to the ear or hearing.

Supernumeraries: Theater extras for non-speaking roles or mob scenes.

Bated [in a whisper bated]: Abated, i.e., lessened.

Obdurate [an obdurate bootmaker]: Unyielding, pig-headed.

Train de luxe {TREN duh LOOX}: Luxurious train (French).

Job-lot [a pretty job-lot]: A "quantity of goods bought or sold together, often containing several different kinds of things usually of inferior quality" (290). Usually sold at a low price (56).

Tol-lol [I should say tol-lol, my love]: Just so-so (115).

Riviera [the Duke of Riviera]: A resort area and stretch of coast on the Mediterranean, encompassing south-eastern France and north-western Italy.

Sandwich boards: A pair of advertising posters carried front and back over the shoulders of some poor devil who is paid to parade them around town.

Numismatist: One interested in the scientific study of coins and medals (75). (The word is omitted from some editions.)

Prettily footed: Well danced.

Lead over [I'll give you a lead over]: A broad hint.

Do you take?: Short for "Do you take my meaning?" (237).

Little doddle doddle: Tiny toddler.

Rook the pigeon and the gull: Delude the suckers. Walters (301), an ornithologist of note, calls attention to the three birds involved in the expression.

***Allons, encore,* (etc.):** (French stanzas in the roulette song): Translated into English:

Let's go again,
Boys and girls —
Your gold Louis,
Your cartwheels
Ola! Ola!
Place your bets,
Come on, class,
Time passes,
Break the bank —
The play is stopped!
Black seventeen is odd and *manque*!
Ola! Ola!
Long live the bank!

Let's go again,
Boys and girls —
Your gold Louis,
Your cartwheels,
Ola! Ola!
Make your plays,
Come on, everyone,
It's spinning, it's spinning,
Time flies —

The play is stopped!
Red thirty-five is odd and *passe*!
All right, students of the class —

Let's go again,
Boys and girls —
Your gold Louis,
Your cartwheels,
Ola! Ola!
Make your plays,
Who lost before
Wins today- -
The play is stopped!
Tra, la, la! The double zero!
You lose all, my noble heroes-

Notes:

1. The term "manque" refers to the numbers below 19; "passe" refers to 19 and above (103).
2. The "Louis" referred to is presumably the gold coin issued in France during the reign of Louis XIII and subsequently to the time of Louis XVI.
3. A "cartwheel" is a more or less generic term for a large coin. It was commonly applied to the British crown, a coin worth five shillings, or a quarter of a pound sterling.
4. The translation is by Betty Benford, who cautions that she has not attempted to keep the meter — so please don't try to sing her version.
5. Since almost every living person speaks French better than I, I shall not try to tell you how to pronounce the original words in the song.

Merovingian {mer-eh-VIN-jee-en} [of the early Merovingian period]: "Of or pertaining to the Frankish dynasty established by Clovis, which reigned in Gaul from about A.D. 500 to 751" (250). This term and the next two are from lines (spoken by the Prince of Monte Carlo) that are omitted from some versions of the libretto.

Quarterns [Two half-quarterns and a make-weight]: "Quartern" is an obsolete term for a quarter of anything (228). In the context, the prince seems to be alluding to coins but is in reality speaking of the baroness, Julia, and Lisa as though they were two big loaves of bread and a bun thrown in for good measure (147, 251, 273). Rees (251)

Chapter XIV

and Stedman (273) note that one can still buy quartern loaves (four-pounders!) in England.

Make-weight: "A person or thing of insignificant value thrown in to make up a deficiency or gap" (228). Prestige (245) interprets the statement as insulting to Julia and the baroness for being over-size and to Lisa for being insignificant.

Cardiac affection: Heart disease.

Banns [The Law forbids the banns]: The banns are formal public notices of an intended marriage. The meaning here, of course, is that the wedding is to be called off. But don't be discouraged; this is a G&S opera and we know very well it will have a happy ending.

Flibberty gibberty [This flibberty gibberty kind of a liberty]: *Flibbertigibbet* is an ancient name for a fiend, dating back at least as far as 1603. Shakespeare used it in *King Lear*. It has also been used as a synonym for *Puck* (54). The OED (229) defines *flibberty gibbet* as flighty, frivolous, or senseless. This is getting close to what Gilbert must have had in mind. The term, we might add, is from a song that is left out of many editions. See Allen (3).

And so we come to the final curtain of the Savoy operas. To appease your prolonged applause and shouts of "Encore!" we obligingly append the two final chapters immediately following. Enjoy!

YOU NEVER HEARD SUCH LANGUAGE IN YOUR LIFE!

AND G MUST SHOW HERSELF IN TIGHTS

CONSPICUOUS HATS

COX and BOX

Chapter XV   Cox and Box

This mini-opera by Burnand and Sullivan is often given as a curtain raiser for Savoy operas. Based on John Maddison Morton's 1847 farce *Box and Cox*, the musical version was put together by F. C. Burnand and Arthur Sullivan during a three-week period in 1866. That was for a private gathering; but the "triumviretta" was considered such a gem that it was given a public showing at a charitable performance in the Adelphi Theatre on May 11, 1867. A week later *Cox and Box* was given a second benefit performance, at another theater, and the reviewer for *Fun* magazine was none other than W. S. Gilbert, who was not to meet Arthur Sullivan face to face for another two or three years. (His astute comment on the music was to the effect that Sullivan's notes were too good for the words.)

Cox and Box is a frothy bit of foolishness but it has its virtues, being simple to produce and full of sprightly music. Although out of place chronologically here, it seems appropriate as a brief curtain call.

My libretto is that published by Samuel French of London (undated).

CHARACTERS AND SETTING

Journeyman [A Journeyman Hatter]: The OED (228) tells us that a journeyman is a skilled craftsman who works for another. He ranks between a master and an apprentice. We might add that the term is derived from the French word *jour* for day, i.e., a journeyman is one who is paid by the day. Doesn't this exciting start make you thirst for further knowledge? Read on.

Bouncer [Sergeant Bouncer]: The name has several derogatory slang associations, including cheating, boasting, and telling fibs. The sergeant is well-named.

Dampshire [Late of the Dampshire Yeomanry]: In England, when one wishes to refer to an imaginary shire in the West Country, one may call it "Mummerset" (to rhyme with Somerset). Here Burnand is rhyming with *Hampshire*.

Yeomanry: Yeomen were small landowners. The Yeomanry was a volunteer British cavalry force made up chiefly of men of the yeo-

man class and an equal mix of presumably non-volunteer horses.

TEXT

Peremptory [the most … peremptory of hatters]: Imperious, allowing no room for debate.

Colonel Cox: Bouncer usually addresses Cox as "Colonel," but when irritated (a few lines later) he demotes him to "Captain." We may infer that Cox claims to have seen military service at one time, or perhaps this is Bouncer's standard form of flattery.

Protuberant [with a protuberant bolster]: Bulging out, like Cyrano's proboscis.

Bolster: A firm pillow, usually of cylindrical form.

Glass: Looking glass: mirror.

Cravat: Necktie.

Militia: Citizens trained for military emergencies, like the National Guard in the USA.

Hobby [Ah! now he's off on his hobby]: At this point Bouncer usually makes his broom into a hobby horse, and there you have another pun. Sorry.

Chargers: Horses trained for cavalry service.

Laurels: Crowning wreaths awarded heroes in ancient Greece and Rome. More broadly, "laurels" were honors, in this case for military valor.

Bays [and rode on our bays]: Reddish-brown horses. Since *bay* is another name for

Chapter XV

"laurel," honors are sometimes referred to as "bays." Behold, another pun!

Yeomen: See entry for "Yeomanry" above.

Van [In the rear and the van]: The vanguard or leading units of an advancing army. ("Hey, what am *I* doing here?")

Rataplan: Hyder (161) defines it thus: "This is an onomatopoetic word suggesting the beating of a drum, much used in French comic operas with a military theme, and here used mockingly by F. C. Burnand." MacPhail (194) adds that Verdi uses the word in *Forza del Destino* and Donizetti does the same in *La Fille du Régiment.* Moreover, he adds, "It's a bit ironic that if Burnand, Sullivan's first librettist, provided him with a 'Rataplan' song, so too did his final collaborator, Basil Hood: a Rataplan song in *The Emerald Isle* was one of the lyrics the composer set in his final comic opera before he died." Finally, Kravetz (182) has this simple explanation: "Rataplan" is the French equivalent of "rat-a-tat."

Emulating [instead of emulating]: Seeking to equal or excel. A secondary meaning, appropriate here, is "imitating."

Dissemble [Yes, I must dissemble]: Hide the truth. See also Chapter IV.

Sure as eggs is eggs: In those days this was a popular phrase meaning "without a doubt." It was probably a corruption of the logician's formula "x is x" (115).

Lucifers [My lucifers, candles, sugar and wood!]: Matches. Named in honor, of course, of Lucifer, the chief recalcitrant angel who was thrown out of Heaven and then reigned over the nether regions. The first mass-produced friction matches were sold under the trade name "Lucifer Sticks" (103). Hyder (161) relishes the line, "I did think my lucifers would be sacred."

Dodger [Bouncer is a dodger!]: A haggler, or one who engages in shifty maneuvers.

Cat [the cat in the Army's abolished]: Bouncer is setting up a smoke screen by switching the topic from felines to multi-

thonged whips. Captain Corcoran uses the same pun, as you may recall, in *H.M.S. Pinafore.*

Leaders [setting up long leaders for a daily paper]: Editorials.

Naps [hats with naps]: Woolly or velvety surfaces.

Effluvia [If he objects to the effluvia of tobacco]: A smoker's euphemism for the more accurate and scientific term *stench.*

Domesticate [he had better domesticate himself in some adjoining parish.]: Find lodging.

Parish: A subdivision of an English county, or an ecclesiastical district.

Evolution [there's one evolution I should much like to see you perform]: A planned military movement.

Venerable [to get rid of that venerable warrior]: Worthy of respect by virtue of advanced years.

Rasher [I've got a rasher of bacon]: A thin slice.

Penny roll: An inexpensive roll; the smallest item of bread one may buy in a bakery. See also Chapter XIV.

Purloins [he purloins my coals]: Steals.

Gridiron: A metal cooking device consisting of a frame supporting closely-spaced parallel bars, used to hold food over a fire.

Nid [Soon I'll be nodding, nodding, nid]: One dictionary (108) assures us that this means "to nod slightly," and quotes Burns as writing, "We're a' noddin, nid nid noddin."

Phiz [on showing my phiz in his shop]: Short for "physiognomy," or face.

Brighton [Visions of Brighton and back, and of Rosherville]: A well-known seaside resort in Sussex county. An English friend once told me it was a popular place for a "dirty weekend."

Rosherville: The British cultural equivalent of Coney Island, later made famous by John Wellington Wells. See Chapter III.

Squash [already the squash I feel]: The press of the crowd.

Mackintosh [put on my mackintosh I will!]: A raincoat made of two layers of cloth held together by something like rubber cement. The fabric was invented by Charles Macintosh (1766-1843), who, you may notice, spelled his name without the K in the middle. See also Chapters X and XIV.

Dejunay {day-djun-A} [Now for my breakfast, my light *dejunay*]: A corruption of *déjeuner*, the French word for "lunch." A "light *dejunay*" means breakfast.

Zounds: An archaic oath, presumably a corruption of *God's wounds*.

Tinder [lights it with a piece of tinder]: Usually scorched linen impregnated with saltpeter; used for kindling a fire from a spark.

Vociferate [I'll instantly vociferate "Police!"]: Yell.

Animosity [no violent animosity]: Strong hatred.

Antipathy [any rooted antipathy to you]: Intense dislike.

Mead [The buttercup dwells in the lowly mead]: Meadow.

Lay [to sing my lay]: A short poem intended to be sung.

Floweret [The floweret shines on the minaret fair]: A modest young flower, like Mad Margaret's poor lonely violet in that nest of weeds and nettles.

Minaret: One of those slender towers of a mosque from which the Islamic faithful are called to prayer. The word is derived from the Spanish word for "lighthouse." Use that to impress your friends.

Dahlia: You may already know that this is a flower of the aster family. Perhaps you would

also like to know that it was named for the eighteenth century Swedish botanist Anders Dahl.

Cockchafer [The cockchafer sighs in the midnight air]: A variety of beetle (of the *coleopterous* clan), well known in England.

Dicky bird: Any small bird (but none more famous than the one whose suicide is recounted by Ko-Ko).

Concertina: A small musical instrument somewhat like an accordion.

Opera hat: A man's tall silk hat, which can be collapsed. The stage directions call for Cox to play on the gridiron like a guitar, while Box uses an opera hat in imitation of a concertina.

Bradshaw [Have you read this month's Bradshaw, sir?]: This line, following a tender serenade, is a gross *non sequitur*. The literary work to which Box refers is the British railroad timetable, *Bradshaw's Railway Guide*, which was printed at monthly intervals from 1841 to 1961. My reference is a more interesting Bradshaw (50) slightly modified by (56). The turnabout here is based on the typical, stern Victorian husband who would not allow his wife to read spicy novels. Here's a wife who won't let her husband read a timetable. Sorry to beat this joke to death; let's press on.

Bathing machines: A horse-drawn wheeled vehicle used as a dressing room by modest Victorian bathers to enter the water without having to parade across the beach. For a picture see page 214.

Defunct [I've been defunct for the last three years!]: Dead or extinct.

Stop [whereby a man . . . can leave this world, and yet stop in it]: Go on living, as in a stop-over.

Doating [only one obstacle to my doating upon her]: Former spelling of *doting*, to be foolishly sentimental or sloppily affectionate.

Romance (stage direction): A sentimental and expressive musical number.

Chapter XV

Ramsgate: A holiday resort town in Kent. Stedman (273) notes that Burnand lived there after he retired.

Margate: Another holiday resort town in Kent. Those *gates* have nothing to do with hinged doors; they come from the Danish word for "road" and are an echo from the ancient days of the Scandinavian immigrations.

Life Guards: A regiment of the Household Cavalry (142). For more details see Chapter XIII.

Blues: A slang term applied to certain companies of soldiers distinguished by their blue uniforms. (142, 158).

Basin called slop: An awkward way of saying slop basin, which can be a bowl for holding the dregs from tea cups at the tea table, or a container for kitchen garbage, or (shudder!) a chamber pot! (142, 320).

Put ... back ... up: "To put one's back up" means to antagonize (274) or annoy (142). I suppose it is derived from the way a threatened cat arches its back. (The clumsy way Burnand expresses this shows why he could not compete with Gilbert as a librettist.)

Baited: Harassed or tormented.

Fraction [Between you, then, there was a fraction?]: A break, a falling-out, a domestic spat.

Action [threatened with an action]: Probably a court action for breach of promise.

Ablution [when I had finished my ablution]: Washing — usually hands and face.

Hose [my hose, my socks]: Tight-fitting breeches or pants.

Linen for nose: A clumsy way of saying "handkerchief."

Under the rose: A colloquialism for "in secret" or "in confidence" (115). Presumably derived from the Latin *sub rosa* (which has the same meaning) "from the ancient use of the rose at meetings as a symbol of the sworn confidence of the participants" (250).

Tiff [you left in a tiff?]: In a huff.

Dulcet [sort of a dulcet dirge]: Sweet-toned.

Dirge: Funeral music, from the Latin *dirige*, the first word of the prescribed service for the dead. See also Chapter XI.

Verge: The very edge (of the cliff).

Throe [in an agony throe]: Violent pang.

Chalked [where the Coast Guard's way was chalked]: Two interpretations can apply. One proposal is that the coastal patrol's path showed up white on the chalk cliffs that are characteristic of the English south coast (251). The other is that the Guard's route was shown by chalk marks on stones (142). My vote is with the first interpretation. Readers may want to know that in the days before electronic communications, Coast Guardsmen patrolled the shore on foot watching for vessels in distress.

One pound seventeen and sixpence: In the old British monetary system, this meant one pound, seventeen shillings, and six pennies. There were twenty shillings to the pound, and twelve pennies (or pence) to the shilling. In our opinion the system was invented to confuse American tourists, and we are gratified that the British gave it up. Now if they would just learn to drive on the righteous side of the road.

Barnet Races: Horse races at the Barnet fair, in the environs of London.

Half-crown: A British coin worth two shillings and six pence, or about sixty cents (American) at that time.

Toss up: Flip a coin.

Sixpence [my tossing sixpence]: A coin worth six old pennies or half a shilling. Prestige (245) proposes that a "tossing coin" is one with two heads or two tails. In the context that seems altogether likely.

Shilling: A coin worth one-twentieth of a pound sterling.

Cox and Box

Leads {leds} [I've a mind to pitch you out on the leads]: Sheet-lead roof covering.

Boulogne {boo-LONE}: A French seaport on the English Channel, popular with the British upper crust. As Rees (251) puts it, "Mrs. Wiggins was really moving above her station in Boulogne. Ramsgate and Margate were visited more commonly by the Coxes and Boxes of this world."

Colonial Office: This is the ministry that administers most of Britain's overseas empire. Box's business there is probably imaginary. Hyder (161), however, proposes that Box is planning to escape Penelope Ann by emigrating.

Cab [A cab's drawn up at the door!]: A light carriage drawn by one horse (75).

Twopenny omnibus {TUPP-enny ...}: In those days an omnibus was a horse-drawn public conveyance, seating perhaps six to eight inside and about as many on the roof. The fare was plainly marked on the outside. For an illustration see the entry for "Threepenny bus" in Chapter VI.

Brigadier [a note for Brigadier Cox!]: Shortened form of "Brigadier General," an officer in command of an army brigade. There is a hint here that, in wooing Penelope Ann, Cox may have inflated his supposed erstwhile military rank. Or is this more of Bouncer's flattery?

Apprize [I hasten to apprize you]: Inform.

Strawberry mark [Have you such a thing as a strawberry mark on your left arm?]: A soft reddish birthmark, supposed to resemble a strawberry (122). This revelation parodies the melodrama's common use of a birthmark to recognize a long-lost relation.

So much for the first encore. What to do for the second? Well, since in the normal course of human events all lists end with the letter Z, what better than *The Zoo*?

PENELOPE ANN

*TRANSLATION:
BRITANNIA RULES THE WAVES!

ÆSCULAPIUS

The first thing you should know about *The Zoo* is that the words are *not* by Gilbert; they were written by B. C. Stephenson under the pen name Bolton Rowe. The sprightly, charming music is by Sullivan. The work was first performed on June 5, 1875. (That was less then three months after the opening of *Trial by Jury*, but about eight years after *Cox and Box*.) Like *Trial by Jury*, it has no spoken lines. The work is brief and in a single act. After long years of neglect, it is now taking its place alongside *Trial by Jury* and *Cox and Box* as a popular curtain raiser for some of the less extensive Savoy operas.

The piano/vocal score for the work is available from R. Clyde, 6 Whitelands Ave, Chorleywood, Rickmansworth, Herts WD3 5RD, United Kingdom.

In his *Note on the Libretto* Terence Rees adds a few details on how one major and several minor gaps in the libretto were filled by Roderick Spencer during preparation of the published vocal score.

Present-day interest in the opera traces back to Terence Rees's initiative in acquiring the autograph score back in 1966. Here is how he describes how it all came about:

> When I was a lad, *The Zoo* like *Thespis* was very much of a mystery. It had never been published, nobody around had heard so much as a dot of the music and it received only passing mention in books dealing with the composer. And then, one day (Monday, 13th June, 1966 to be precise) the autograph full score came up for sale by auction at Sotheby's, the famous auction house in Bond Street, London. Also up for sale were the manuscripts of *Trial, Pinafore, Pirates* and many others. It was a memorable event and I was there (and where were you at the time?). Intending to bid for *The Zoo*, I had raised all the money I could, stretching my credit right, left and centre, and expecting a fine old battle. But what I never expected was that hardly anyone in the room had heard of the piece so there was consequently little bidding. In no time at all, perhaps just two or three tense, breathless minutes, the hammer fell and I became the new owner of *The Zoo*.
>
> As soon as it was all over, I paid for and collected the score, walking with it in my arms down Bond Street and along Piccadilly, past Burlington Arcade and the Royal Academy to Piccadilly Circus underground station. From there I took a train home where for the rest of that day I lay on the mat, turning the pages and wondering how I might get somebody to perform it. In the event that proved to be easier than I thought. The production at Fulham by Max Miradin was very well received, the piece caught on and has since received more performances than it ever had in Sullivan's lifetime.

CHARACTERS AND SETTING

Æsculapius {Es-cu-LAPE-i-us}: Named afer the god of medicine in classical mythology. He was the son of Apollo by Coronis (some say Larissa) and was raised by the centaur Chiron, who taught him the secrets of medicine. He became a physician to the Argonauts and later came to be looked upon as the inventor as well as the god of medicine (187).

Carboy: A large globular glass jar, usually enclosed in basket work or crate and used for transporting liquids.

Islington: A metropolitan borough of London about two miles north of St Paul's Cathedral. The site of two prisons, it does not rank high in snob appeal.

TEXT

Peg away: To plod along, to persevere.

Blanch: To turn pale.

Staves [well known English staves]: Verses or stanzas.

Chapter XVI

Forbear!: Stop! Cease! Desist! See also Chapter XI.

Apothecary: In America: a druggist; in Great Britain a dispensing chemist.

Cameleopard: Another name for a giraffe (perhaps because giraffes are shaped something like a camel and spotted something like a leopard).

Blister: A poultice used to redden or blister the skin by the application of irritant chemicals.

Scarify: {SCAR-if-eye}: To make shallow incisions in the skin for the purpose of drawing blood (254).

Draft of life: Fate (an allusion to a figurative bitter cup).

Gingerbeer: A bubbly drink made by fermenting ginger and other ingredients (75). See also Chapters I and XIV.

Mantles [the frown that mantles on your brow]: Darkens.

Horniman's tea: A widely advertised brand of tea, then popular (254). John Horniman, from the Isle of Wight, invented tea in packets back in 1826 (89).

Kidney pie: A main course still popular in England: steak and kidney pie. Contains those two kinds of meat and gravy, but no vegetables. Encased within pastry crusts (254).

Brandy: An alcoholic liquor distilled from wine. Samuel Johnson opined that claret was the liquor for boys, port for men, but brandy for heroes (45).

Minions: Low-ranking attendants. See also Chapter I, IX, and X.

Garter: Refers to the Order of the Garter, the highest order of knighthood in Great Britain. See also Chapters VII and XII.

Peer: A nobleman, and member of the House of Lords. See also Chapters IV, VII, XII, and XIII.

Sphere: Environment or place.

Hear! Hear!: English terms of endorsement and support. See also Chapters V, VII, and IX.

Change my condition: In the narrow sense he means to drop his disguise and change into attire appropriate to his noble rank.

Ducal: Pertaining to a duke, the highest order of nobility in the British peerage.

Ahem!: Rees (254) explains: "This is nothing other than an embarrassed cough. The chorus feels unable to say anything of help to Eliza. The word is quite common in Victorian plays."

Hemisphere: Read: this part of the world.

A dressing case with tops: This was a small flat container about the size of a modern brief case in which a lady would transport her articles *de toilette* when traveling. It would be a very expensive and up-market affair. There would be a hand mirror in a silver frame and various cut-glass bottles with screw tops of silver (gold of course, if you found solid silver too vulgar). It tells us nothing about her habits *en toilette* but it does tell us lots about the men she knew, and how well she knew them. Eliza was a calculating minx (254).

Tops: Screw tops for those cut glass bottles.

Diamond drops: Diamond pendants or earrings perhaps?

Covent Garden: At that time London's main wholesale flower market.

Park hack: A hack is a horse let out for hire; so a park hack is a rented horse intended for riding in a park.

Greenwich: A borough of London on the south bank of the Thames. Known to Savoyards as the site of the infamous One-Tree Hill (see page 34).

Season: Presumably refers to the period of the year when social activities in London were in full sway. That would include most of the year except the summer months.

Richmond: A municipal borough and residential suburb of Greater London, lying southwest of the center of the city. It is the site of a large deer park.

Hampton Court: The magnificent palace built a few miles up the Thames from London by Cardinal Wolsey. Completed in 1525, it was taken over by Henry VIII the following year and remained the royal residence for more than a century. The palace and formal gardens, laid out by Christopher Wren, remain popular tourist attractions today (105).

Dover: A port city in Kent on the narrowest part of the English Channel, about 75 miles from London. It is known as a favorite seaside and pleasure resort.

Parlie [Thomas Parlie]: Apparently just a made up name to rhyme with Charlie.

Progenitor: Father

City [a respectable man in the City]: Specifically, Lætitia refers to the ancient central part of London. In more general terms she means Carboy will become a successful business man.

Heartstrings: Affections or emotions. A heartstring is an imaginary tendon bracing the heart.

Grizzly [the grizzly one]: Presumably the grizzly bear.

Armadillo: A small mammal chiefly identified by its armor-like protective shell made up of articulated bony plates.

Cockatoo: A variety of parrot with a crested head.

Titivate: To tidy up. Perhaps the word should read "Titillate": to stimulate pleasurable sensations.

Hymen (By Hymen joined): The Greek god of marriage.

* * * * * *

MR GRINDER

PERORATION

Gilbert spun lines by the yard,
He found it not at all hard.
    His verses ring true
    And from our point of view
He's lots more fun than the Bard!

And Sullivan, too, had a stake
With music delightful to make.
    With simple perfection
    He enhanced the confection
And nicely frosted the cake.

D'Oyly Carte joined the good pair,
He managed the books with care.
    His accounting was right
    And accurate, quite,
(Aside from that carpet affair).

Appendix

(Isaac Asimov's special contribution in his Foreword to the first two editions of this book.)

The Gilbert and Sullivan Enthusiasts

(with apologies to W. S. Gilbert)

If you give me your attention, I will tell you
who we are.
We are G and S enthusiasts — we find
them caviar.
We know the notes of every play, excepting,
of course, *Thespis*.
For its music has been hurtled off some
undiscovered prec'pice.
But cheerfully we carol out a jolly *Trial by
Jury*
From beginning to finale when the judge
erupts in fury.
We love the patter singing — in particular,
The Sorcerer.
We yodel of John Wellington till hoarse and
growing hoarserer,
    And we'll never stop.

We'll do a bouncy hornpipe on your decks,
H.M.S. Pinafore.
If happiness is sinful, yours the music we
will sinafore.
And then as slaves of duty meet *The Pirates
of Penzance*
We will sing without regarding, now and
then, a dissonance.
But if you want some lovesick maids,
dragoons, and poets — *Patience*
(Since simple words can turn to plays with
capitalizations.)
For fairies and lord chancellors, there's
always *Iolanthe*.
The music fills us all with joy and makes us
feel romanthe,
    So we'll never stop.

In three acts and in blank verse we will greet
you, *Princess Ida*,
With cheers for Castle Adamant had you
but fortified 'er.
And then the all-time maximum, the
Japanese *Mikado*
For there, if anywhere, we'll find a tuneful
El Dorado.
Then back at once to magic spells and grim
old *Ruddigore*
Where a ghost is just as deadly as an
executioner.
In full-fledged operatic notes *The Yeomen of
the Guard*
Is where we'll sing of poor Jack Point whose
love turns out ill-starred.
    And we'll never stop.

Then everything is doubled when we sing
The Gondoliers
With babies changed in infancy (that ploy
now reappears).
And there's a pause, but they return —
Utopia Limited
Where wise men try to turn their king into a
figurehead.
So finally we end, alas, and sing of *The
Grand Duke*
And call down on the Fates an unavailing
sad rebuke.
Why couldn't G and S have written fifty
thousand more?
We'd have sung out all the notes till all our
throats were good and sore,
    And we'd never stop.
    No, we'd never stop.

Isaac Asimov

References

1. Aesopus. *The Fables of Aesop*. London: B. Quartich, 1885.
2. _____ *Aesop's Fables*. London: A. & C. Black, 1912.
3. Allen, Reginald. *The First Night Gilbert and Sullivan*. New York: The Heritage Press, 1958.
4. _____ "A Gilbert & Sullivan Collection," *Autograph Collectors' Journal*, Vol. V, No. II, Winter 1953.
5. Ambrose, Stephen E. *Undaunted Courage*. New York: Simon & Schuster, 1996.
6. *The American Heritage Dictionary of the English Language*. Boston: Houghton Mifflin Co., 1969.
7. Anon. *Glossaries*. Internet: The Gilbert & Sullivan Very Light Opera Company, 1969.
8. Applegate, George. Personal communications, 1976, 1977.
9. Applegate, Kay. *The Breakfast Book*. Santa Fe: The Lightning Tree, 1975.
10. Asimov, Isaac. Personal communication, 1976.
11. _____ *Asimov's Annotated Gilbert & Sullivan*. New York: Doubleday, 1988.
12. Aslet, Clive. *The Last Country Houses*. New Haven: Yale University Press, 1982.
13. Associated Press. "Author Peeks inside Buckingham Palace," *Ann Arbor News*, September 11, 1991.
14. Atkinson John. Personal communication, 1994.
15. Aurora, Silvio. "Modified Rapture," *Palace Peeper*, January 1992.
16. _____ "Poetic Catharsis," *Palace Peeper*, September 1995.
17. _____ Personal communication, 1992.
18. _____ Personal communication, 1998
19. _____ "Good Day, Sweet Prince: (Bab and the Bard)": GASBAG, Issue 207, Spring 1998.
20. Austen, Jane. *Pride and Prejudice*. Toronto & New York: Bantam Books, 1981.
21. Ayre, Leslie. *The Gilbert and Sullivan Companion*. New York: Dodd, Mead & Co., 1972.
22. Baily, Leslie. *The Gilbert and Sullivan Book*. London: Spring Books, 1966.
23. Bamberger, David. "Faultless Sympathy," *Palace Peeper*, February 1998.
24. Barker, John. "Glossaries," *Savoyardage*, August 1992.
25. _____ "Glossaries," *Savoyardage*, August 1993.
26. _____ "Glossaries," *Savoyardage*, July 1997.
27. _____ Personal communication, 1998.
28. Barnhart, Clarence L. *The New Century Cyclopedia of Names*. New York: Appleton-Century-Croft, 1954.
29. Bartholomew, J. G. *The Survey Atlas of England and Wales*. Edinburgh: The Edinburgh Geographical Institute, 1903.
30. Bartlett, Des & Jen. "Africa's Skeleton Coast," *National Geographic*, Vol. 181, No. 1, January 1992.
31. Basingstoke, Vladimir I. *The Bluejacket's Companion and Nautical Lore*. Aukland: Nonesuch Press, 1921.
32. Beerbohm, Max. *Rossetti and His Circle*. New Haven: Yale University Press, 1987.
33. Belcher, Patricia. Personal communication, 1998.
34. Bell, Diana. *The Complete Gilbert & Sullivan*. Secaucus, N.J.: The Wellfleet Press, 1989.
35. Bender, Byron. Personal communication, 1998.
36. Benford, Harry. "Cape Finistere," *GASBAG*, November/December, 1992.
37. _____ "Princess Kaiulani of Hawaii — A Utopian Inspiration?" *GASBAG*, March/April 1994.
38. Berlioz, Hector. *Memoirs*. New York: Dover Publications, 1966.
39. Bierce, Ambrose. *The Devil's Dictionary*. Cleveland and New York: The World Publishing Co., 1943 (originally 1911).
40. Blair, C. "The Humour of Fielding," *The Gilbert and Sullivan Journal*. London: The Gilbert & Sullivan Society, July 1926.
41. Boïalle, James (ed). *A New French and English Dictionary*. London: Cassell, 1908.
42. Booth, Michael R. (ed). *English Plays of the Nineteenth Century*, Vol. 4 "*Farces.*" Oxford: The Clarendon Press, 1973.
43. Bosdêt, Mary. Personal communications, 1992.
44. _____ "Whence Basingstoke," *GASBAG*, November/December, 1992.
45. Boswell, James. *Life of Johnson*. Oxford University Press, 1987.
46. Bradley, Ian. *The Annotated Gilbert & Sullivan 1*. Harmondsworth, Middlesex: Penguin Books Ltd., 1982.

References

47. _____ *The Annotated Gilbert & Sullivan 2*. Harmondsworth, Middlesex: Penguin Books Ltd., 1984.
48. _____ *The Complete Annotated Gilbert & Sullivan*. Oxford University Press, 1996.
49. _____ Personal communication, 1998.
50. Bradshaw, J. Stuart. Personal communication, 1976.
51. _____ Personal communications, 1978, 1989.
52. _____ Pesonal communication, 1993.
53. Breuer, Gladys. Personal communication, 1980.
54. *Brewer's Dictionary of Phrase & Fable*. New York: Harper & Row, 1970.
55. *Brewer's Dictionary of Phrase & Fable*. New York: Harper & Row, 1981.
56. *Brewer's Dictionary of Phrase & Fable*. London: Cassell & Co., 1895
57. *Brewer's Dictionary of Phrase & Fable*. New York: Harper & Row, 1978.
58. Bryson, Bill. *Made in America*. New York: Avon Books, 1996.
59. *Bulletin*, N.Y. Public Library, 1922.
60. Burgess, A.J. *The Notary and other Lawyers in Gilbert & Sullivan*. Hadleigh: Suffolk, 1997.
61. Burleigh, Diana. Personal communication, 1976.
62. Burlington, N.J. Historical Society, Delia Biddle Pugh Library, Ruth Bump, Cataloger. Personal communication, 1976.
63. Burnand, F. C. *Records and Reminiscences*. London: Methuen & Co., 1905 (originally 1903).
64. Bushland, Paul. "The Glossary," *Savoyardage*, Summer 1995.
65. Byron, George Gordon Noel. *The Complete Poetical Works of Lord Byron*. Boston and New York: Houghton Mifflin Co., 1905.
66. Cameron, H.D. Personal communications, 1976, 1977, 1989.
67. Carrol, Lewis. *Alice's Adventures in Wonderland and Through the Looking Glass*. Chicago & New York: M. A. Donahue, n.d.
68. *Cassell's Italian Dictionary*. New York: Funk & Wagnalls, 1967.
69.. Castelot, André. *Napolean* (Trans. by Guy Daniels). New York: Harper & Row, 1971.
70. *The Century Dictionary & Cyclopedia*. New York: The Century Co., 1889.
71. *Chamber's Encyclopædia*. Oxford: Pergamon Press, 1967.
72. Chambers, Kenton L. Personal communication, 1997.
73. Chekov, Anton. *Five Great Short Stories*. New York: Dover Publications, 1992.
74. Clunn, Harold P. *The Face of the Home Counties*. London: Spring Books, 1958.
75. *Collins English Dictionary*. London: William Collins Sons & Co., 1972.
76. Colson, Warren. Personal communication, 1977.
77. *The Columbia Encyclopedia*. New York: Columbia University Press, 1950.
78. *Concise Dictionary of American Biography*. New York: Scribner's, 1964.
79. Cookson, David. Personal communication, 1998.
80. Craven, David. Personal communication, 1998.
81. Creasy, E.S. *The Fifteen Decisive Battles of the World, from Marathon to Waterloo*. London: Macmillan, 1851.
82. Cunliffe, Richard John. *A New Shakespearean Dictionary*. London: Blackie and Son, 1910.
83. Dahms, William. Personal communication, 1996.
84. *Dance Encyclopedia* (Chujoy & Manchester, ed). New York: Simon & Schuster, 1967.
85. Dann, John C. (ed). *The Nagle Journal*. New York: Weidenfeld & Nicholson, 1988.
86. Darlington, W.A. *The World of Gilbert and Sullivan*. New York: Crowell, 1950.
87. Delany, Ruth. *Ireland's Inland Waterways*. Belfast: Appleton Press, nd.
88. De Lorme, Eleanor. Personal communication, 1998.
89. Desmond, Kevin. *A Timetable of Inventions and Discoveries*. New York: M. Evans & Company, Inc., 1986.
90. Dickens, Charles. *Sketches by Boz*. London: Oxford University Press, 1957.
91. *Dictionary of American Biography*. New York: Charles Scribner's Sons, 1929 (Supplement One, 1944).
92. *Dictionary of the Italian and English Languages*. Florence: G.C. Sansoni, 1972.
93. *The Dictionary of National Biography*. London: Oxford University Press, 1921.

94. Dixon, Geoffrey. Personal Communication, 1998.

95. Dixon, William Hepworth. *The Match Industry*. London: Sir Isaac Pitman & Sons Ltd, n.d.

96. Doyle, Arthur Conan. *The Illustrated Sherlock Holmes Treasury*. New York: Avenel Books, 1976.

97. D'Oyly Carte Opera Company. *Playbill (for The Mikado)*. New York, 1976.

98. _____ *Playbill* (for *H.M.S. Pinafore*). New York, 1976.

99. Duffey, D. Personal communication, 1998.

100. Dunn, George E. A. *Gilbert & Sullivan Dictionary*. New York: DaCapo Press, 1971.

101. Ellmann, Richard. *Oscar Wilde*. New York: Alfred A. Knopf, 1988.

102. Elson, Louis C. *Pocket Music Dictionary*. Bryn Mawr, Pennsylvania: Oliver Ditson Co., 1909.

103. *The Encyclopædia Britannica*. 11th ed. Cambridge, England: University Press, 1910.

104. *The Encyclopædia Britannica*. 14th ed. Chicago: William Benton, 1973.

105. *The Encyclopedia Americana*. New York: Americana Corp., 1952.

106. *The Encyclopedia Americana*. New York: Americana Corp., 1976.

107. *The Encyclopedia Americana*. Danbury CT: Grolier, Inc., 1989.

108. *The English Dialect Dictionary*. London: Henry Frowde, 1898.

109. Epton, Nina. *Josephine: The Empress and her Children*. London: Weidenfeld & Nicolson, 1975.

110. Erickson, C.T., ed. *The Anglo-Norman Text of* "Le Lai du Cor." Oxford: Basil Blackwell, 1973.

111. Evans, Aidan. Personal communication, 1976.

112. _____ Personal communication, 1981.

113. Evans, Bergen. *Dictionary of Quotations*. New York: Delacorte Press, 1968.

114. Falconer, William. *An Universal Dictionary of the Marine*. London: T. Cadell, 1780. Reprint. Devon: Newton Abbot, 1970.

115. Farmer, J. S., and Henley, W. E. *A Dictionary of Slang*. Ware, Hertfordshire: Woodsworth Editions Ltd., 1987 (originally 1890).

116. Fava, Jean and Fava, Ronald. Personal communications, 1990.

117. Feldman, Alex. "Glossary," *Savoyardage*, July 1984.

118. Feldman, Alex and Barker, John. "Glossary for *Patience*," *Savoyardage*, July 1991.

119. Fido, Martin. *Oscar Wilde*. New York: The Viking Press, 1973.

120. Forty, Sandra. *The Pre-Raphaelites*. New York: Barnes & Noble, 1997.

121. Fry, Plantagenet Somerset. *The Kings and Queens of England and Scotland*. New York: Grove Weidenfeld, 1990.

122. *Funk and Wagnalls New Standard Dictionary of the English Language*. New York: Funk and Wagnalls Co., 1947.

123. George, J.C.G. Personal communications, 1976, 1977.

124. Gibbon, Edward *The Decline and Fall of the Roman Empire*. New York: Washington Square Press, 1962.

125. Gibson, Edmund A. *Basic Seamanship and Navigation*. New York: McGraw-Hill Book Co., Inc., 1951.

126. Gilbert, W.S. *The Bab Ballads: With Which are Included Songs of a Savoyard*. London: Macmillan & Co., 1927.

127. _____ *The Bab Ballads*. James Ellis. (ed). Cambridge, Mass.: Harvard University Press, Belknap Press, 1970.

128. _____ *The Complete Plays of Gilbert and Sullivan*. New York: W. W. Norton & Co., 1976.

129. _____ *The Savoy Operas*. London: Macmillan & Co., 1959.

130. _____ *Songs of a Savoyard*. London: G. Routledge & Sons, 1890.

131. _____ *The Savoy Operas*. London: Oxford University Press, 1962, 1963.

132. _____ *The Pinafore Picture Book*. New York: The Macmillan Company, 1908.

133. _____ *The Story of the Mikado*. London: Daniel O'Connor, 1921.

134. Gilbert, W. S., and Sullivan, Arthur. *Songs of Two Savoyards*. London: George Routledge and Sons, Ltd., n.d.

135. Gillette, Mitchell Scott. Personal communication, 1998.

136. Girouard, Mark. *Victorian Pubs*. New Haven: Yale University Press, 1984.

137 Goldberg, David. "A Cloth Untrue," *GASBAG*, Vol. 20, No. 4, March/April 1989.

138. _____ "U800 or Armor News," *GASBAG*, October/November/December 1990.

139. Goldberg, Isaac. *The Story of Gilbert*

References

and Sullivan. New York: Crown Publishers, 1935.

140. Goodman, Andrew. *Gilbert & Sullivan's London*. Tunbridge Wells: Spellmount, Ltd., 1988.

141. _____ *Gilbert & Sullivan at Law*. London: Associated University Press, 1983.

142. _____ Personal communication, 1989.

143. _____ Personal communication, 1998.

144. Grand Pierre, C. *Dictionary of Sea Terms*. Valley Cottage, N.Y.: private publication, 1928.

145. Green, Martyn. *Martyn Green's Treasury of Gilbert & Sullivan*. New York: Simon & Schuster, 1961.

146. Grossmith, George. *A Society Clown*. Bristol: J. W. Arrowsmith, 1888.

147. Halton, Frederick J. *The Gilbert & Sullivan Operas, A Concordance*. New York: Bass Publishers, 1935.

148. *A Handy Dictionary of the English Language*. New York: American Book Co., ca. 1900.

149. Hardwick, Michael. *The Osprey Guide to Gilbert & Sullivan*. London: Osprey Publishing Ltd., 1972.

150. Hargrave, Basil. *Origins and Meanings of Popular Phrases and Names*. London: T. Werner Laurie, Ltd., 1932.

151. Hazon, Mario, ed. *Garzanti Comprehensive Italian-English English-Italian Dictionary*. New York: McGraw-Hill, 1961.

152. Heath, Jeffrey. Personal communication, 1998.

153. Hershey, Robert D., Jr. "Queen's Banker Stays Selective," *New York Times*, August 7, 1978.

154. Hibbert, Christopher. *The Court of St. James's*. New York: William Morrow & Co., 1980.

155. Hilton, George W. *Nellie Farren*. Saffron Walden: Sir Arthur Sullivan Society, 1997.

156. Hoare, Alfred. *An Italian Dictionary*. Cambridge: University Press, 1925.

157. Hudson, Derek. Notes in *The Savoy Operas*. London: Oxford University Press, 1962, 1963.

158. Huston, John. Personal communication, 1989.

159. Hutchinson, Ann. *Fanny Elssler's Cachucha*. New York: Theatre Arts Books, 1981.

160. Hyder, William. Personal communication, 1977.

161. _____ Personal communications, 1989, 1990.

162. _____ Personal communication, 1998.

163. Jacobs, Arthur. *Arthur Sullivan: A Victorian Musician*. Oxford: Oxford University Press, 1984.

164. _____ Personal communication, 1980.

165. Johnson, Samuel. *A Dictionary of the English Language*: Reprinted by Barnes & Noble, 1994.

166. Joseph, Tony. Personal communication, 1979.

167. _____ Personal communication, 1990.

168. Kane, Sara. Personal communication, 1976.

169. Kanthor, Hal. "The Dark Side of Baby Farming," *GASBAG*, November/December 1991 and January/February 1992.

170. Karr, Phyllis. Personal communication, 1976.

171. _____ Personal communication, 1989.

172. Kelly, Raymond. Personal communication, 1998.

173. Kenny, Nigel. Personal communication, 1990.

174. Kesilman, Sylvan. Personal communication, 1989.

175. Kline, Peter G. *Gilbert & Sullivan Production*. New York: Richards Rosen Press, 1972.

176. _____ Personal communication, 1989.

177. Knight, Daniel, and Knight, Marsha. "Glossaries" (Program notes for The Savoy Company). Philadelphia, 1978-89.

178. "Glossaries," (Program notes for the Savoy Company). Philadelphia , 1990 - 1998.

179. _____ Personal communication, 1976.

180. Kotzebue, August Fredrich Ferdinand von. *The Stranger*. London: R. Pitkeathley, 1799.

181. Kravetz, Daniel. Personal communication, 1989.

182. _____ Personal communications, 1998.

183. Lawrence, Arthur. *Sir Arthur Sullivan: Life Story, Letters and Reminiscences*. London: James Bowden, 1899.

184. Ledbbetter, Steven (ed). *Trial by Jury*, Vol. 1 of *Gilbert & Sullivan: The Operas*. New York: Broude Brothers, 1994.

185. Lederer, Richard. *Anguished English*. New York: Bantam, Doubleday Dell, 1987.

References

186. Lee, Ernest. Personal communication, 1998.
187. Lempriere, John. *Classical Dictionary of Proper Names Mentioned in Ancient Authors*. rev. ed. London: Routledge & K. Paul, 1949.
188. Leonardi, Gene. Personal communication, 1998.
189. Lindsell-Roberts, Sheryl. *Loony Law & Silly Statutes*. New York: Sterling Publishing, 1994.
190. Linnekin, Jocelyn. Personal communication, 1998.
191. Lyell, Thomas R. G. *Slang, Phrase and Idiom in Colloquial English and Their Use*. Tokyo: Hokuseido Press, 1931.
192. Macaulay, Thomas Babington (Lord). *The History of England*. Vol. I. Philadelphia: The University Library Association, 1910.
193. Macgeorge, Ethel. *The Life and Reminiscences of Jessie Bond*. London: John Lane the Bodley Head, Ltd., 1930.
194. MacPhail, Ralph, Jr. Personal communications, 1987, 1989.
195. _____ "Finger Stalls," [letter], *The Gilbert & Sullivan Journal*, London, Autumn 1980.
196. _____ Personal communications, 1998.
197. Malm, William. Lecture at University of Michigan. April 15, 1989.
198. Manheim, Leonard F. Personal communication, 1977.
199. Marius, Richard. *Thomas Moore, a Biography*. New York, Alfred A. Knopf, 1984.
200. Marryat, Captain. *Peter Simple*. London & Glasgow: University Press, 1929.
201. Massie, Robert K. *Dreadnaught*. New York: Random House, 1991.
202. _____ *Peter the Great*. New York: Alfred A. Knopf, 1980.
203. Maurois, André. *Disraeli*. New York: Modern Library, 1928.
204. May, Thomas Erskine. *A Treatise on the Law, Privileges, Proceedings and Usage of Parliament*. London: William Clowes and Sons, Ltd., 1893.
205. _____ *A Treatise on the Law, Privileges, Proceedings and Usage of Parliament*. London: William Clowes and Sons, Ltd., 1906.
206. McCann, William. Personal communication, 1998.
207. McClure, Derrick. Personal communication, 1998.
208. McCullough, David. *The Path Between the Seas*. New York: Simon & Schuster, 1977.
209. McElroy, George. Personal communications, 1976, 1977, 1978, 1981.
210. _____ "Professionalism at the Savoy," *GASBAG*, Vol. XXI, No. 2, Nov./Dec. 1989.
211. McShane, Paul. Personal communication, 1998.
212. Melville, Herman. *Billy Budd*. New York: NAL Penguin, 1979.
213. Merivale, Herman Charles. *Bar, Stage and Platform: Autobiographic Memories*. London: Chatto and Windus, 1902.
214. Mitchell, Ronald E. *Opera Dead or Alive*. Madison: University of Wisconsin Press, 1970.
215. More, Thomas. *Utopia*. (Translated by Ogden, H. V. S.). New York: Appleton-Century-Croft, Inc., 1949.
216. Morningstar, Gershom Clark. Personal communication, 1976.
217. Morris, William, and Morris, Mary. *Harper Dictionary of Contemporary Usage*. New York: Harper & Row, 1975.
218. Mossiker, Frances. *Napolean and Josephine: The Biography of a Marriage*. New York: Simon & Schuster, 1964.
219. Muir, Frank. *The Oxford Book of Humorous Prose*. New York: Oxford University Press, 1990.
220. Munich, Adrienne. *Queen Victoria's Secrets*. New York: Columbia University Press, 1996.
221. Neale, Judith. Personal communication, 1998.
222. *The New American Webster Handy College Dictionary*. Springfield, Mass.: New American Library, 1961.
223. *The New Century Cyclopedia of Names*. New York: Appleton-Century-Crofts, 1954.
224. *The New Encyclopædia Britannica*. 15th ed. Chicago: Helen Hemingway Benton, 1975.
225. *The New Encyclopædia Britannica (Micropedia)*. Chicago: University of Chicago, 1987.
226. Nowacki, Horst. Personal communication, 1976.
227. Ossa, Eugene. Personal communication, 1998.

References

228. *The Oxford English Dictionary.* Oxford: Clarendon Press, 1933.

229. *The Oxford English Dictionary: Compact Edition.* New York: Oxford University Press, 1971.

230. Paget, Julian. *The Yeomen of the Guard.* Poole, Dorset: Blandford Press, 1984.

231. Papa, Christopher M. "A Scientist Replies," *Palace Peeper,* January 1996.

232. _____ Personal communication, 1998.

233. Partridge, Eric. *A Dictionary of Slang and Unconventional English.* 4th rev. ed. London: Routledge & Kegan Paul, 1956.

234. _____ *A Dictionary of Slang and Unconventional English.* 7th rev. ed. London: The Macmillan Co., 1970.

235. _____ *A Dictionary of the Underworld.* 3rd ed. London: Routledge & Kegan Paul, 1968.

236. _____ *The Routledge Dictionary of Historical Slang.* London: Routledge & Kegan Paul, 1973.

237. _____ *A Dictionary of Catch Phrases.* New York: Stein and Day, 1977.

238. Paulshock, Bernadine Z. "Letters to the Editor, " *Smithsonian,* April 1990.

239. Peacock, Karen. Personal communication, 1998.

240. Pearson, Hesketh. *Gilbert: His Life and Strife.* London: Methuen and Co., 1957.

241. Pooley, Beverley. Personal communication, 1977.

242. _____ Personal communications. 1989, 1990.

243. Prestige, Colin. Personal communications, 1976, 1977.

244. _____ Personal communications, 1978 and 1984.

245. _____ Personal communications, 1990.

246. *Punch.* November 1, 1884.

247. Raedler, Dorothy. Personal communication, 1976.

248. Rames, Richard. Personal communication, 1998.

249. Randall, David A. "The Gondoliers and Princess Ida," *W. S. Gilbert, A Century of Scholarship and Commentary.* New York: N. Y. University Press, 1970.

250. *The Random House Dictionary.* New York: Random House, 1966.

251. Rees, Terence. Personal communications, 1976, 1977.

252. _____ Thespis: *A Gilbert & Sullivan Enigma.* London: Dillon's University Bookshop, 1964.

253. _____ *Theatre Lighting in the Age of Gas.* London: The Society for Theatre Research, 1978.

254. _____ Personal communications, 1981, 1989, 1990.

255. Ridley, James. *The Tales of the Genii: or the Delightful Lessons of Horam, the Son of Asmar* "faithfully translated from the Persian manuscript, etc. by Sir James Morell (pseud.)" London: J. Wilkie, 1766.

256. Robinson, Arthur. "A Greek Remark," *Precious Nonsense,* May 1995.

257. Round-table discussion with Patricia Cope, Lorraine Daniels, Alistair Donkin, David Mackie, Kenneth Sandford, and Geoffrey Shovelton. Ann Arbor, March 1990.

258. Rowell, George. *Queen Victoria Goes to the Theatre.* London: Paul Elek, 1978.

259. Ruskin, John. Appendix to "The Stones of Venice," Reproduced in Pergolis, Ricardo, *The Boats of Venice.* Venice: L'Alto Riva, 1981.

260. SavoyNet: The Gilbert & Sullivan Internet Bulletin Board.

261. Scott, Sir Walter. *Marmion: And Other Poems.* Boston and New York: Houghton Mifflin Co., 1923.

262. _____ *Peveril of the Peak.* Boston and New York: Houghton Mifflin Co., 1923.

263. Shepherd, Marc. Personal communications, 1989.

264. _____Personal communications, 1998.

265. Shereff, Jesse. Personal communication, 1977.

266. Shipley, Joseph T. *Dictionary of Word Origins.* New York: Philosophical Library, 1945.

267. Shovelton, Geoffrey. Personal communication, 1984.

268. Sims, Sir Alfred. Personal communication, 1976.

269. Smith, Geoffrey. *The Savoy Operas.* London: Robert Hale Ltd., 1983.

270. Sperling, Susan Kelz. *Tenderfeet and Ladyfingers.* New York: The Viking Press, 1981.

271. Stasheff, Edward. Personal communication, 1990.

272. Stedman, Jane W. "The Genesis of 'Patience.'" *Modern Philology,* Vol. 66 (1968).

273. _____ Personal communications, 1976, 1977.

274. _____ Personal communication, 1989.

275. _____ *W.S. Gilbert: A Classic Victorian and His Theatre*. New York: Oxford University Press, 1996.

276. _____ Personal communication, 1993.

277. _____ *Gilbert Before Sullivan*. Chicago: The University of Chicago Press, 1967.

278. Stell, John. Personal communication, 1976.

279. Stephenson, B. C. [Bolton Rowe], and Sullivan, Arthur. *The Zoo*. London: 25 Nightingale Square, n.d.

280. _____ *The Zoo, Vocal score*. Chorleywood, Herts , R. Clyde, 1991.

281. Stephenson, Thomas. "Remarkable People in History," *The Gilbert and Sullivan Journal*. London: The Gilbert & Sullivan Society, July 1926.

282. Sternenberg, Philip. Personal communication, 1998.

283. Stone, David. Personal communications, 1989.

284. _____ Personal communication, 1998.

285. Terry, Madge; Johnson, Reavely; and Davis, D. Graham. "An Operatic Glossary." *The Gilbert and Sullivan Journal*. London: The Gilbert & Sullivan Society, 1935-1937 and 1948-1949.

286. Terry, Madge. *An Operatic Glossary,*. rev. ed. London: The Gilbert and Sullivan Society, 1975.

287. Thackeray, William Makepeace. *Vanity Fair*. New York: W.W. Norton, 1994.

288. Thomas, Joseph. *Universal Pronouncing Dictionary of Biography and Mythology*. New York: AMS Press, 1972.

289. Thompson, Constance. Personal communication, 1977.

290. *Thorndike-Barnhart Comprehensive Desk Dictionary*. Garden City: Doubleday and Co., 1954.

291. Tillett, Selwyn. Personal communication, 1997.

292. Trevelyan, George Otto. *The Life and Letters of Lord Macaulay*. London: Longmans, Green, and Co., 1878.

293. Trollope, Anthony. *The Small House at Allington*. London: Penguin Books, 1964.

294. Turnbull, Stephen. Personal communication, 1998.

295. Venman, William. Personal communication, 1989.

296. Vizetelly, Francis H.; and De Bekker, Leander J. *A Desk Book of Idioms and Idiomatic Phrases*. New York: Funk & Wagnalls Co., 1926.

297. Von Eckhardt, Wolf; Gilman, Sander L.; and Chamberlain, J. Edward. *Oscar Wilde's London*. Garden City, N. Y.: Doubleday, 1987.

298. Wallworth, Bernadette. "*Iolanthe* Glossary," *Katisha Scream*, 1988 No.1.

299. Walmisley, Guy H., and Walmisley, Claude A. *Tit-Willow*. London: privately printed, n.d.

300. Walsh, Philip. Personal communication, 1998.

301. Walters, Michael. Personal communications, 1976, 1977.

302. _____ Personal communication, 1989.

303. _____ "Origin of Ko-Ko's Name," *Palace Peeper*, June 1992.

304. Ware, Em. Personal communication, 1998.

305. Weaver, Daniel. Personal communication, 1998.

306. *Webster's New International Dictionary of the English Language*. 2nd ed. Springfield, Mass.: G. & C. Merriam Co., 1959.

307. *Webster's Third New International Dictionary of the English Language*, unabridged. Springfield, Mass.: G. & C. Merriam Co., 1963.

308. Wenzel, Duane. Personal communication, 1998.

309. Wernick, Robert. "Bewigged, bothered and beleagured, the barristers of London carry on," *Smithsonian*, June 1991.

310. Whaley, Douglas. Personal communication, 1997.

311. Whipple, A. B. C. *Fighting Sail*. Alexandria, Virginia: Time-Life Books, 1978.

312. *Who Was Who in America*, 1607-1896. Chicago: Marquis Who's Who, 1967.

313. Wilde, Oscar. *The Importance of Being Earnest*, New York: Dover, 1990

314. Wilkes, James O. Personal communication, 1990.

315. Wilkes, Jocelyn. Personal communication, 1979.

316. Williams, Frank F. "Heigh-ho," *The Gilbert & Sullivan Journal*. Vol 10, No. 11. London: The Gilbert & Sullivan Society, autumn 1976.

References

317. Williams, George. Personal communication, ca. 1979.

318. Williamson, Audrey. *Gilbert & Sullivan Opera*. London: Marion Boyars, Ltd., 1982.

319. Wilson, Derek. *The Tower of London*. London: Constable/Dorset, 1989.

320. Wilson, Fredric Woodbridge. Personal communication, 1989.

321. Wilson, Geoffrey. "Teeming with Hidden Meaning," *The Savoyard*, D'Oyly Carte Opera Co., September, 1978.

322. Wolfson, John. *Final Curtain*. London: Chappell & Co., 1976.

323. Wright, Elinor. Personal communication, 1998.

324. Young, Percy. *Sir Arthur Sullivan*. London: J. M. Dent & Sons, 1971.

325. _____ *The Flotation of* H.M.S. Pinafore *1878*, The University of Birmingham Institute for Advanced Study in the Humanities, 1998.

326. Zavon, Peter. Personal communication, 1976.

INDEX

INDEX

INDEX

INDEX

INDEX

INDEX

INDEX

CARBOY & LAETITIA

ENGLISH FASHIONS!

THE HEADSMAN